The Dynamics of Japanese Organizations

This volume provides an overview of approaches to dynamic processes of organizing currently dominating academic discussion in Japan. Looking at the extent to which Japanese firms master the increasing complexity of the business environment by stimulating processes of organizing, the book first discusses the foundations for a philosophy of organizational dynamics. Particular management tools appropriate to stimulating dynamic processes of organizing are then examined. The book closes with a discussion stressing the importance of the linkage between industrial organizations and their emerging environments.

The contributors offer a critical approach to the dominating management paradigms of the Western mould. Their discussion of key problems and their suggestions for sharpening strategies and improving organizational performance will be thought-provoking and of key interest for all those studying Japanese management and organizational behaviour.

Frank-Jürgen Richter holds a management position with Robert Bosch Ltd in Stuttgart, Germany. He has been a research fellow at the University of Tsukuba, Tokyo and has taken part in international comparisons covering inter-firm networks.

Routledge Advances in Asia-Pacific Business

This series focuses on styles of business and management in the Asia-Pacific. It draws together the latest research into the key business topics such as finance, management, investment, joint ventures, strategy, business policy and marketing, as well as exploring current themes like change, transformation, economic growth, corruption, ethics and competition. It covers:

- manufacturing industries
- service sectors
- small and medium-sized companies
- large companies and transnationals
- specific country studies
- broader regional analyses

It assesses the growth and success of business enterprise in the region.

1 **Employment Relations in the Growing Asian Economies**
Edited by Anil Verma, Thomas A. Kochan and Russell D. Lansbury

2 **The Dynamics of Japanese Organizations**
Edited by Frank-Jürgen Richter

3 **Business Relationships in East Asia**
The European Experience
Edited by Roger Strange and Jim Slater

The Dynamics of Japanese Organizations

Edited by Frank-Jürgen Richter

London and New York

First published 1996
by Routledge
11 New Fetter Lane, London EC4P 4EE

Simultaneously published in the USA and Canada
by Routledge
29 West 35th Street, New York, NY 10001

Typeset in Times by Keystroke, Jacaranda Lodge, Wolverhampton

Printed and bound in Great Britain by TJ Press Ltd, Padstow, Cornwall

British Library Cataloguing in Publication Data
A catalogue record for this book is available from the British Library

Library of Congress Cataloguing in Publication Data
The dynamics of Japanese organizations / edited by Frank-Jürgen Richter.
p. cm. — (Routledge international studies in Asian-Pacific business ; v. 1)
Includes bibliographical references and index.
1. Industrial management—Japan. 2. Organizational behavior—Japan. I. Richter, Frank-Jürgen. II. Series.
HD70.J3D96 1996
658′. 00952—dc20 95-34232
CIP

ISBN 0–415–13191–X

Contents

Figures

Tables

Contributors

Charles Adamson was born in Rhode Island, USA, in 1940. He received a BA from Goddard College, Vermont, USA, with a triple major in Electrical Engineering, Computer Applications and Japanese studies in 1973. He received a Doctorate in Education from Columbia Pacific University, California in 1988. After eight years of studying information with the US Army Intelligence Command and a year as Administrative Assistant at the Systems Science Center, Busch Center, University of Pennsylvania, he was Chief Researcher at the Kawai Institute of Suggestive Accelerative Learning, Trident College, Nagoya, Japan for 15 years. He became Professor of English at the Shizuoka Rikoka University in 1991.

Born in 1960, **Vera Calenbuhr** grew up and was educated in Cologne, Germany. She graduated from the University of Cologne in Chemistry (specialization: physical chemistry) and received her PhD from the Free University of Brussels on theoretical models of the self-organization of social insect behaviour using chemical communication. Post-doctoral work includes models on the immune network (Ecole Polytechnique, Paris and Free University of Brussels) and modelling in chemical engineering (IST, Joint Research Centre of the European Communities, Ispra, Italy). Currently she is Professor at the IMISE, University of Leipzig, Germany. Her articles on self-organization and networks appeared in the *Journal of Theoretical Biology*.

Nobuyuki Chikudate is an Assistant Professor at the School of Business Administration, Asia University, Tokyo. He was born in 1963 and received his PhD from State University of New York at Buffalo, in Organizational Communication. He completed his post-doctoral fellowship at the School of Hygiene and Public Health at the Johns Hopkins University, USA. His specialities include information management, communication, corporate culture, research methods, and theories of organizations. One of his recent publications is: Cross-cultural analyses of cognitive systems in organizations: a comparison between Japanese and American organizations (*Management International Review*, 2, 1991).

Haruo Hata was born in Tokyo in 1923. He graduated from the School of Technology, Tokyo Imperial University in 1946, and received a Doctorate in Engineering in 1961. After working for Sumitomo Electric Industries for 33 years, he joined the School of Business Administration, Kyushu Sangyo University, Fukuoka City, as Professor of Production System Engineering in 1979 and became Professor of Industrial Engineering at the School of Business Administration, Asahi University, Gifu Prefecture, in 1986. He was Dean of the School from 1989 to 1993. His most recent work is: *Johogakku josetsu* – Introduction to Informatics (Tokyo: Chuo Bijutsu Kenkyujo, 1992).

Keiko Ishihara is a lecturer at Hiroshima Chuo Women's College. Her current research interests are in a neural network model of human visual information processing.

Shigekazu Ishihara is a lecturer in the Department of Management Information of Onomichi Junior College. His current research interests are in cognitive and social psychology, neural networks, and Kansei engineering.

Kenshu Kikuzawa is Associate Professor of Administrive Science at the National Defense Academy, Japan. He graduated at Keio University, Tokyo, and received his PhD in Business and Commerce in 1986. Currently he is a visiting researcher at the Stern School of Business at New York University. His research interests include philosophy of science, economics of organizations, and the theoretical reconstruction of German classical managerial economics. His publications include 'Rolle und Status des Rationalitätsprinzips in Poppers kritischem Rationalismus' (*Keio Business Review*, vol. 27, 1990 with K. Sakakibara) and *Interaction between Market and Finance – German Classical Managerial Economics and Theory of General Equilibrium* (Tokyo: Chikura Shobo, 1990).

Tetsunari Koizumi received an undergraduate degree in Economics from the Hitotsubashi University, Tokyo, in 1963 and an MA in Economics from the University of Hawaii in 1966. He holds a PhD in Economics from Brown University and is currently Professor of Economics at the Ohio State University (Columbus, Ohio, USA). His fields of interest are Systems Theory, History of Thought, Philosophy of Science as well as Comparative Management. His most recent publications include *Advances in Education and Human Development* (Windsor: International Institute for Advanced Studies in Systems Research and Cybernetics, 1990, edited with George E. Lasker) and *Interdependence and Change in the Global System* (Lanham, MD: University Press of America, 1993).

Born in 1929, **Magoroh Maruyama** studied at the Universities of California (Berkeley), Munich, Heidelberg, Copenhagen and Lund. He taught at the Universities of California (Berkeley), Stanford, Illinois, Montpellier, Uppsala and Singapore and is currently a Professor at the School of International Politics, Economics and Business of the Aoyama Gakuin University in Tokyo. His mindscape theory is a programme that has spanned several decades. His work comprises 130 publications including 'The Second Cybernetics' (*American Scientist*, 51, 1963), which initiated research on mechanisms of self-organization. Beside his academic positions he has been consultant to Volvo, NASA, Federal Motors of Indonesia, US Department of Commerce, MITI of Japan, etc.

Mitsuo Nagamachi has been a Professor of the Faculty of Engineering at Hiroshima University, since 1978. He obtained his PhD degree in Psychology from Hiroshima University in 1963. His current research interests are ergonomics, Kansei engineering, organization management, human-centred CIM and intelligent interfaces.

Ikujiro Nonaka is Professor of Management at the Institute of Business Research of Hitotsubashi University in Tokyo. He is also research group director of the National Institute of Science & Technology Policy (NISTEP). He received MBA and PhD degrees from the University of California (Berkeley), and won the Nikkei Award in Economics and Business in 1974 for his book, *Organization and Market: A Contingency Theory*. Professor Nonaka has published widely on organizations, strategy, and marketing. His research, consultancy and educational activities have involved him in more than 300 corporations and fifty government agencies in Japan and elsewhere.

Tsuyoshi Numagami is an Associate Professor of the Institute of Business Research at Hitotsubashi University, Tokyo. He received his MS from the Graduate School of Commerce, Hitotsubashi University in 1985. His recent publications include 'Dynamic Interaction between Strategy and Technology' (*Strategic Management Journal*, 1992, vol. 13) (co-authored with Hiroyuki Itami).

Toshizumi Ohta is a Professor of the Graduate School of Information Systems at University of Electro-Communications, Tokyo. He is also a lecturer of the Tokyo Institute of Technology. He received his M Eng and Dr Eng degrees from the Tokyo Institute of Technology. His recent publications include 'Implementation of Decision Support Systems: An Empirical Study of Japanese Production and Control Systems' (co-authored with Takehiko Matsuda and Toshiyuki Sueyoshi, in Yuki Ijiri (ed.) *Creative and Innovative Approaches to the Science of Management*, Quorum Books, 1993).

Alfredo Pinochet is a Japanese government sponsored graduate student of Systems Engineering at Hiroshima University. During the period 1985–7, he worked for the Pontificia Universidad Catolica de Chile as lecturer. His current research interests are human-centred CIM, Human–Computer Interaction and expert systems.

Frank-Jürgen Richter holds a position with Robert Bosch Ltd, Stuttgart (Germany). He was educated in business administration and mechanical engineering in Germany, France and Mexico. He received his doctoral degree from the University of Stuttgart, Germany and has been a research fellow at the University of Tsukuba, Tokyo. Under ERASMUS and DAAD (German Academic Exchange Service) grants he has taken part in international comparisions covering inter-firm networks. He is particularly interested in the theory of self-organization and its application to management. His articles have appeared in such journals as the *Long Range Planning* and *Human Systems Management.*

Haruo Takagi received his bachelor's (1973) and master's (1975) degrees in Administration Engineering from Keio University, Japan, and his DBA from Harvard University. He is an Associate Professor at the Graduate School of Business Administration at Keio University. His current research interests are in organizational behaviour and information technologies, leadership in networks, organizational communications and organizational innovation. His publications include *The Flaw in Japanese Management* (Ann Arbor: UMI Research Press, 1985) and 'Keeping Managers off the Shelf' (*Harvard Business Review*, July–August 1986). He has published several contributions to Japanese management journals such as *Journal of the Japan Society for Management Information* and *Keio Business Forum.*

Kenji Tanaka received his BSc in mathematics from Kyoto University, Japan in 1981 and his MSc and DrSc degrees in systems sciences from Tokyo Institute of Technology, Japan in 1983 and 1988, respectively. He is currently Assistant Professor at Ibaraki University, Japan. From 1993 to 1994, he was a visiting scholar at the Department of Systems Sciences of the State University of New York at Binghamton. His research interests include decision making under uncertainty, maintenance management systems, and decentralized autonomous systems. He received the Plant Maintenance Excellent Paper Award in 1993.

Yoshiya Teramoto is Professor of Management and Organizational Behaviour at the Graduate School of Management, Tsukuba University in Tokyo. Born in 1942, he graduated from Waseda University and worked 5 years for Fujitsu before he entered an academic career. Since 1972, he has held several university or research institute positions in Japan as well as in England. He also works on programmes for clients including NTT and Toshiba. His research focuses on innovation and internalization within industrial networks. Currently he is directing comparative studies of decision-making processes within large Japanese companies. His most recent books include *Network Power* (Tokyo: NTT Press, 1990) and *Power Middle* (Tokyo: Kodansha, 1993).

Milan Zeleny holds a DiplIng from the Prague School of Economics and MS and PhD degrees from the University of Rochester. He is currently Professor of Management Systems at Fordham University in New York City. He has served on editorial boards of such journals as *Human Systems Management* and *Journal of International Strategic Management*. Zeleny has published over 280 papers and articles, ranging from operations research, cybernetics and general systems, to economics, history of science, total quality management, and simulation models of autopoiesis and artificial life. Zeleny's writings have appeared in Japanese, Chinese, French, Italian, Hungarian, Slovak, Czech, Russian and Polish. He has also published over 300 short stories, literary essays and political reviews in Czech, Slovak and English.

Introduction and background

During the last few years Japanese management has increasingly attracted attention, not only due to the rapid expansion of the Japanese economy and the consistent redefinition of the familiar economic world order, but also because Japanese management is apparently opposite to Western ways of thinking. For decades Western scholars and management practicians relied on management approaches which were based on stability and relative rigidity against changes in the industrial environment. Contingency theory, transaction cost and population ecology approaches are examples from this tradition of Western thinking. What all three approaches have in common is that organizational self-renewal is widely neglected. Grown structures confirm the further course of organizational development and sudden organizational reversals are the exception rather than the rule. Up till now this management paradigm has described Western corporations rather well as, due to to their success hitherto, they have not had to care about organizational renewal.

As to Japanese firms the situation is quite different: during the last few decades they have developed a high degree of organizational flexibility and pragmatism traditionally unknown in the West which allowed them to react swiftly on market demands and to conquer key positions in the world markets. This development has not been flanked by an adequate academic support because management sciences have traditionally been influenced by Western models and original approaches have hardly been available. During the last few years however, an increasing number of independent schools of thinking have been formed. They intended to reflect the development of the management practice of Japanese firms by deriving models of organizational theory. Although the available approaches are not implicitly congruent, they all revolve around dynamic processes of organizing. In contrast to Western models which focus on preserving existing structures or adapting them to the corporate environment, the Japanese models assert that although change is an irreversible process, organizational self-renewing is possible. An organization is seen as a system that both reduces and amplifies variety.

This book intends to provide an overview on such approaches of dynamic processes of organizing, which currently dominate academic discussion in Japan. The authors contributing to this book have been given as much creative leeway as posssible in order to guarantee the heterogeneous character of the approaches. Hence, each approach is unique, although all have a common thread in so far as they criticize the dominating management paradigm of the Western mould.

The papers of Part I develop the foundations for a philosophy of organizational dynamics. It is astonishing that the approaches are partly based on a Western body of thought. Since the time of the Greek philosopher Heraclitus, it was known that all being is subject to a continuous flow of becoming and passing. This thought, although well known, has seldom been anchored in organizational models of corporate management. The four chapters of Part I of this book find the way back to this body of thought and enrich it with specific Japanese elements of thinking.

Numagami, Ohta and Nonaka describe a model which they call 'self-renewing organization'. This model asserts that although the designer is an insider and change is an irreversible process, organizational self-renewal is possible. The key difference between this model and mainstream organizational models is that it views the organizational process as not only one of information processing, but as one of information creation. The self-renewing model offers insights into organization structure and the relation between organization and environment that differ from those offered by other models. It also provides a powerful framework which explains the self-renewal process in large organizations.

Hata and Adamson consider some of the basic aspects of 'Informatics', a new science dealing with the study of information as meaning, which draws on both natural and social science. The approach holds that information is integrally related to life and is concerned with the meaning of information rather than merely with its carrier. The approach is a newly supplemented form of both cybernetics and the principle of self-organization which serves as a basic tool for corporate management.

Maruyama's agenda is to understand some of the very different 'mindscapes' that form organizational activities. He suggests that frictions in multicultural management are often a result of cultural differences that involve not only differences in behavioural patterns but also differences in epistemological differences. Cultural differences evolve from the way an epistemological type becomes dominant and suppresses or transforms other types. A key to success in multicultural management is to discover and to use non-dominant epistemological types as bridges between cultures.

Calenbuhr discusses some self-organization processes in biological networks that lead to intelligent behaviour. Moreover, given that many biological systems can display intelligent behaviour without the need for centralized control mechanisms, it is tempting to learn from biological design in order to implement certain of these structures in human made contexts. Once these structures are implemented, one should expect similar types of behaviour as in the original context. Calenbuhr suggests the implementation of such structures in enterprises at the level of the interaction schemes of the people working there. To this end she discusses several mechanisms of self-organization in the context of human behaviour.

Part II goes into concrete issues of organizational behaviour and the management of the firm. Dynamic processes of organizing are used as concrete tools in order to realize an effective corporate management.

Koizumi thinks about Japanese management as a set of cybernetic principles of managing human systems. He investigates in the first place what is meant by Japanese management before he turns to examine the sense in which it can be judged as containing universally applicable principles of human systems management. It is argued that Japanese management is based on the idea of positive feedback rather than negative feedback in motivating individuals. The organization is a system whose operations are defined by a nexus of mutual obligations among its members. Koizumi then examines whether or not Japanese management is exportable to Western countries.

Takagi reports the results of a series of observation studies carried out on group decision-making meetings. The purpose of the studies is to acquire knowledge of the structures and processes of meetings, which is in turn used to raise the intellectual productivity of the meetings and also for designing computerized group decision support systems for this end. After a historical overview of organizational behaviour research on the meeting process and its control, the self-organization perspective of social systems is introduced as a new theoretical framework to conduct the observation studies. Results of the studies show that knowledge is available for increasing the intellectual productivity of meetings.

Kikuzawa considers the question of organizational evolutionism.

Normally, a historically newer organizational form is often regarded as logically better. However, if the development of organizational form is reconstructed rationally based on Popper's methodology of science, the change to a newer matrix form or 'Bunsha' form is degenerating rather than progressive. Thus, a historically newer form is not necessarily better from a logical point of view. To prove this, Kikuzawa first explains Popper's scheme of the growth of knowledge. Second, on the basis of his scheme, he reconstructs progressive and degenerative problem shifts of organizations. Finally, he shows some examples of its application in some Japanese companies.

In Chapter 8 Ishihara, Ishihara, Nagamachi and Pinochet describe the self-organizational process of Quality Control circles and the influence different styles of leadership have on it. Different kinds of information created by the members of Quality Control circles compete with and complement each other so that the collective information leads to change. The authors perform a computer simulation of Quality Control circles and introduce a neural network based simulator of self-organizational behaviour in order to show personal traits such as personality, problem solving ability and influence on other members. The computerized model is a powerful tool for probing into dynamic processes of organizing.

Part III, 'Symbiotic interaction with the environment', stresses the importance of the dynamic linkage between industrial organizations and their emerging environments. The four chapters investigate this aspect of organizational dynamics from different viewpoints.

Richter and Teramoto discuss Hannan and Freeman's population ecology approach as an example of recent research in the field of organizational evolution and of organization–environment interaction. Hannan and Freeman assume that the business environment is the critical factor for an organization's evolution. Economic reality shows however, that organizations evolve along with other organizations and that the environment is no longer a limiting factor. The study proposes a revised model of evolution and leads to a perception of co-evolution which encompasses the dynamics of an organization's integration into the industrial network.

Zeleny explores the radical and challenging idea of the context-dependent nature of trade-offs among economic and business variables. Because trade-offs are created by context, they can also be changed or removed through the change in context: through its redesign or reengineering – trade-offs are not necessary. Lean manufacturing activities of Japanese companies have apparently eliminated the trade-offs among productivity, investment, and variety. Zeleny presents practical and theoretical arguments for suggested trade-offs elimination, shows how profitability and productivity can be improved through optimal system design, and provides a simple numerical example demonstrating a basic trade-offs-free process and its competitive benefits.

The purpose of Chikudate's chapter is to propose the application of information technologies to corporate communication research. On-line database systems are chosen from various kinds of newly developed information technologies. The application of on-line database systems to corporate communication research is derived from transactive strategy, autogenetic model of organizations, functional approach to public relations and two-way symmetrical model of public relations. These emphasize the monitoring capabilities of external environments. The study proposes the possibility of designing customized trend reports for each corporation and of battling a crisis by using on-line database systems.

Tanaka discusses an 'autonomous' anticipative management system that can itself improve its internal model. Such a self-improvement mechanism would be effective in unpredictable environment changes. Because it is 'decision making about decision making', it is performed by metamanagement. The autonomous anticipative management system is shown here to evolve through repeated alternation of a stationary anticipative process and an autonomous self-improvement process. An application to maintenance management is illustrated, and it is further pointed out that, under certain circumstances, a total management system can constitute an autonomous decentralized management system.

The chapters in this volume are a glimpse of models which try to describe dynamic processes of organizing within industrial organizations. As the organizations are in the midst of change, the models too are subject to changes and developments. Hence, there is the hope that the academic discussion around dynamic processes of organizing will furthermore be based on fruitful grounds. It is further desirable that Western organizational science will also be increasingly influenced by the Japanese trend.

Frank-Jürgen Richter

Part I

Philosophy of organizational dynamism

1 Self-renewal of corporate organizations

Equilibrium, self-sustaining, and self-renewing models

Tsuyoshi Numagami, Toshizumi Ohta and Ikujiro Nonaka

Can an organization renew itself? Two models that characterize much of organization theory today offer contradictory answers to this question. Equilibrium models hold that the organization designer is able to redesign the organization to adapt to environmental change. As long as top management is competent, an organization is capable of adaptive restructuring. In contrast, self-sustaining models hold that an individual organization reproduces itself through iterative interaction with the environment and maintains its structure in a constant state, independent of change in the environment. While evolution through single-loop learning is possible, 'revolution' that changes the organization's basic form is not. Change occurs on the level of society as a whole, rather than within individual organizations, when organizations with new characteristics are founded and those with older forms do not survive.

While these models provide valuable insight into organizations, they do not explain the phenomenon of self-renewal that is observed in many organizations, especially larger ones. The objective of this article is to compare the underlying logic and assumptions of the equilibrium and self-sustaining models, discuss the implications of these models regarding self-renewal, and propose a new model of the 'self-renewing organization'.

EQUILIBRIUM MODELS

Much of organization theory can be characterized by equilibrium models. Examples include contingency theory and the transaction cost approach. Contingency theory addresses the equilibrium of environmental and organizational diversity (Thompson 1967, Lawrence and Lorsch 1967, Nonaka 1972, Galbraith 1973, Kagono 1980). Transaction cost economics views organizations as systems of economic transactions and explains actual organization forms and their relationships as efforts to reduce transaction costs (Williamson 1975, Williamson 1985, Ouchi 1980).

According to equilibrium models, the source of organizational change is the environment. The environment has a distinct boundary with the organization, and it is the organization's leader who recognizes and promotes internal change based on the concept of congruence. Equilibrium models imply the congruence assumption: that performance will improve as congruence between environment and strategy is approached. A potential level of performance can be achieved only if all variables are in accordance. The organization's leader sponsors change with the objective of achieving a state of congruence and realizing this potential performance.

The congruence assumption in itself does not imply that self-renewal is possible. As will be seen later, self-sustaining models, which also make this assumption, assert that an organization cannot change its structure. Equilibrium models assume that an organization is capable of changing its structure to reach a state of equibrium as long as two conditions are satisfied: divergence from a state of congruence is recognizable; and change toward a state of congruence can be executed. Signals that indicate divergence in various equibrium models include transaction costs, uncertainty (gap between information-processing load and information-processing capability) and variety.

Equilibrium models satisfy the condition of recognizability by making the implicit assumption that members of the organization, at least top management, are able to observe the organization objectively and evaluate these signals from an external perspective. We call this the externality assumption. To satisfy the condition of executability, a model must assume that organizational change is reversible: that each increment of organizational change can be reversed in time, and after a change, an organization can revert to its original form. We call this the reversibility of change assumption.

Recognizability of congruence: the transaction cost model

The transaction cost approach, which can be characterized as an equilibrium model, illustrates the assumption of externality of the organization's designer. According to this approach, an organization is said to have reached a state of congruence when transaction costs (or if the discussion is limited to within an organization, control loss) are minimized. According to Williamson (1975, 1985), the divisional system (M-form) is the best fit when the rationality of organization members is bounded, there is a tendency towards opportunistic behaviour, and the scale of the organization increases.

When an organization is small, cognitive limits of top management are not problematic and opportunistic behaviour can be controlled through internal monitoring devices and incentive mechanisms. Centralized information-processing technology is effective and a functional U-form organization is appropriate. When scale increases, however, top management faces an increased information processing load. Because cognitive limits exist, the number of organization layers will increase. Opportunities for members to manipulate information for their own interests increase, thereby increasing the probability of opportunistic behaviour. An organization form that economizes on the cognitive limits of top management as well as controlling opportunistic behaviour is required. The M-form, to the extent that it satisfies these two conditions, is superior to the U-form. The M-form organization first classifies decisions into day-to-day decisions and long-term strategic decisions and then allocates them to separate organizational units. Self-sufficient operating divisions make the day-to-day decisions, while headquarters, supported by elite staff, is responsible for the long-term decisions, thus avoiding the problem of cognitive limits of top management.

According to the logic of the transaction cost approach, if opportunism, bounded rationality or scale decreases, the U-form will again be more appropriate. The organization designer must constantly be aware of the level of opportunism and other conditions and the extent of control loss in order to ensure that the organization is always in the form that is most congruent with the environment. This assumption that members are fully cognizant of their organization and the environment is similar to that made by other equilibrium models. Equilibrium models establish an objective reality in which no substantial difference exists between the knowledge of insiders and outsiders. For example, control loss that can be recognized by outsiders such as consultants and researchers, but not by top management, does not exist unless one side or the other has intentionally (strategically) falsified information.

In equilibrium models, organization members communicate information premised on fact and need to rely only on their own judgement. They are able to step outside of the organization at any time in order to evaluate the organization and environment from an external, objective perspective. Congruence is achieved through rational analysis and design by top management and strategic staff. They are heroes who grasp the relationship of organization and environment, envisage the type of organization that is most appropriate, and effect change. If other members act along the lines foreseen by top management (it is not necessary for them to follow orders exactly) and act more rapidly than environmental change, the organization will be able to achieve a state of congruence with the environment. The significance of the ability of members to take an external perspective is that an organization designer can, at least in principle, specify all variables relevant to design, making the organization a logically closed system. Whether the design is appropriate or not depends solely on the skill of the designer.

If an insider is unable to evaluate the environment from an external perspective, there is no guarantee that a state of congruence will be achieved, although it is possible to improve the fit between organization and environment through trial and error. If for each incremental change an organization takes towards congruence the environment returns a positive signal, while for each step away from congruence the signal is negative, each step is reversible and the rate of feedback is faster than that of environmental change, then it is possible for the organization to improve its own performance gradually. It is impossible, however, to evaluate whether the organization has found the optimal solution, or has merely reached a local maximum. If a costless simulation or organizational change were feasible, it would be possible to search for another maximum through simulation. Even in this case, however, whether or not the best solution could be found depends on the simulation, and there is no guarantee that the best solution could ever be found.

Executability of change

The second assumption generally made by equilibrium models to allow for organizational change is reversibility. Change must be reversible if an organization is to maintain a state of congruence in an uncertain environment. For example, according to the transaction cost approach, the U-, M-, and H-forms can be selected freely according to firm size, level of opportunism, and level of bounded rationality. The transaction cost approach implicitly assumes that if an organization changes, it is always able to revert to its original form at a later date. If the scale of an M-form organization decreases, or homogeneity of its product or utilizable economies of scale increased through technological innovation, the U-form organization, which reduced the cost of headquarter staff, would again become the most appropriate form and the organization would revert to it.

SELF-SUSTAINING MODELS

Self-sustaining models hold that even if performance is determined by fit between environment and organizational characteristics, an organization is not necessarily able to achieve this state of congruence. If the divergence from the congruent situation is not recognizable and/or if change towards the congruent situation is not executable, inertia will result and the organization will be unable to adapt to the environment as flexibly as hypothesized by equilibrium models. Such situations are not at all unusual and stem from the fact that the organization is a social rather that physical phenomenon. If an organization was like a machine and, once designed, costlessly maintained the same state until its design was changed, structural inertia might not be a problem. However, when an organization is more than a mere tool through which to achieve an objective and is the objective in itself, and/or institutionalization has been effected intentionally to facilitate the reproduction of organization structure, structural inertia will result. As soon as values and institutionalization are introduced into a model, the assumptions of externality of the designer and reversibility of change hold no more, rendering self-renewal impossible.

The assumption of externality of the designer can be made only if the information communicated by members is premised on fact and context-free transmission of those factual premises is possible. This can only occur when a one-to-one correspondence exists between a specific signal and its meaning. Because transmission of information in a social system is not only transmission of syntactic signals but is also transmission of semantic information, communication between members is only possible if they share a value system through which to encode meaning into specific signals. If members share a value system, they are unable to step freely outside the organization to observe it objectively. Their definition of 'external perspective' will be coloured by the organization's value system (Nonaka and Amikura 1987).

The assumption of reversibility of organizational change can be made only if (1) the organization is nothing more than an artificial tool for the achievement of specific objectives, and (2) members make conscious calculations at high speed and low cost and can change their behaviour at a speed which corresponds to environmental change. Condition (1) does not hold when a shared value system and/or institutionalization are brought into consideration. Condition (2) is not realistic when costs of maintaining an organization and achieving the reliability and accountability necessary for survival are considered.

Shared values in self-sustaining models

Institutional theory and the organization as paradigm perspective consider an organization as more than a task-structured tool for achieving an objective (Selznick 1957, Brown 1978, Sheldon 1980, Pfeffer 1981, Kagono 1982, Scott 1987). Members are not merely processors of syntactic information but are human beings linked by meaning and values. Shared values facilitate communication and encourage integration, bringing forth from members a greater amount of energy than that determined by economic calculations alone. Therefore, shared values play an essential role in organization analysis as well as management practice. Unless the formal structure of an organization is considered as a symbol of its value system, the organization cannot be understood completely. Performance of organizations similar in structure and facing the same environment differs depending on the nature of their value systems and the level to which they are shared (Kagono 1988). Additionally, because organizations with shared values are able to achieve higher levels of performance, the more adverse the environment, the more essential shared values are to survival (Deal and Kennedy 1982, Ouchi 1981, Peters and Waterman 1982, Pascale and Athos 1982).

Shared values are double-edged swords for organizations. While they give an organization stability, they also cause insensitivity towards environmental change. They make it impossible for an organization to realize its divergence from the state of congruence, rendering change impossible. Shared values make an organization susceptible to inertia and self-renewal impossible for two reasons. First, the assumption of externality of members does not hold. Because an organization sees the environment through its shared values, it ignores environmental signals that cannot be described through the symbols of its value system. Moreover, since top management and elite staff are also organization members who share these values, their own cognition is affected by them. Second, the assumption of reversibility of organizational change does not hold in organizations with shared values. A change in value systems is by definition a change in world view. Once a value system changes, it is nearly impossible to see the world again as before.

We call models such as the above self-sustaining models because they hold that an organization maintains its structure in a constant state, independent of environmental change. This does not mean that self-sustaining models represent closed systems. The organization perceives the results of its activities through its value system, and ignores information that cannot be described through its value system, even if it directly impacts performance. Through this process, an organization's values constantly reproduce their own legitimacy and are reinforced. An organization, while remaining open, maintains a constant state through interactions with the environment.

The population ecology model as a self-sustaining model

The theoretical structure of the ecology model developed by Hannan and Freeman (1977, 1984) resembles that of a self-sustaining model in that an organization maintains a constant state through self-reproduction, resulting in inertia. Hannan and Freeman hold that for an organization in modern society to enhance its ability to survive, it must increase its reliability and accountability. To increase reliability and accountability, it must be highly capable of self-reproduction. An organization is more desirable than an ad hoc group due to its superiority in reliability and accountability. In modern society, a low variance of outcomes – reliability – is more important than the efficacy of the outcome. While an organization is not necessarily required to report accurately the purposes for which it mobilizes resources, it must establish that it has followed specific rules and procedures for allocation of these resources.

To increase reliability, an organization must reproduce constantly, maintaining the same structure in the present as it has in the past. To increase accountability, it must remember specific rules and procedures so that it can employ the same ones at all times. It is conceptually possible for an organization to reproduce its structure through repeated negotiations and conscious decision making. In reality, however, organizations tend to reproduce their structure through institutionalization and routines. Institutionalization reduces the cost of group behaviour by giving the organization characteristics that members take for granted. At the same time, it obstructs conscious change and inertia results. An organization is always 'remembering' by reproducing a specific set of routines through iterative interaction with the environment. Routines which are not used for a long period are forgotten and consequently, an organization holds a small repertoire of routines that are relatively easy to reproduce. Selection pressure favours organizations that have a high ability to reproduce, and organizations that have a high ability to reproduce have a high degree of structural inertia. Hannan and Freeman assert that in modern society only organizations with a high degree of inertia will survive, and due to this inertia, organizations will not be able to adapt to large-scale environmental change. Change in organization form will be seen on the level of society as a whole, and will be driven by selection rather than adaptation.

The assumptions of organizational externality and reversibility of organizational change do not hold in self-sustaining models. Consequently, organizations described by self-sustaining models possess a strong inertia; even if they are capable of single-loop learning (Argyris and Schön 1978), they cannot change form. This contrasts with equilibrium models which hold that, for example, an organization designer is able to select the M-form over the U-form and restructure the organization if scale increases. According to self-sustaining models, only inflexible organizations survive, regardless of whether they are M-form or U-form. The environment selects the form that is most congruent with the environment. Even if the environment faced by a U-form organization becomes an environment more appropriate for an M-form organization, an organization will not be able to adapt.

EVALUATION OF THE TWO MODELS

Although both equilibrium and self-sustaining models imply the congruence hypothesis and consider the environment to be the source of change, their implications for organizational self-renewal are contradictory. These models take different positions on recognizability and executability of change. These differences are determined by the fact that self-sustaining models emphasize a distinction between insider and outsider while equilibrium models do not, and equilibrium models view change of an organization as a reversible process while self-sustaining models do not.

These models hold divergent views on recognizability of change and distinction between insider and outsider because their treatment of meaningful information differs. Equilibrium models do not incorporate meaningful information explicitly and assume that the information processed by members has meaning that can be established objectively. In contrast, self-sustaining models either consider the indeterminancy of meaning communicated between members and make shared values a key concept, or emphasize the necessity of organizational reproduction and see institutionalization as a means of facilitating it. Equilibrium models cannot be criticized on the grounds that they do not incorporate meaningful information. This sort of model is a simplification of human behaviour and is appropriate as a parsimonious modelling strategy as far as it is supported by empirical research (Armour and Teece 1978, Palmer *et al.* 1987). Equilibrium models can be criticized on other points such as lack of internal consistency. For example, they assume cognitive limits on one hand, while on the other hand assuming top management who possesses complete knowledge of the environment and organization and members who are able to calculate expected loss and expected gain through opportunistic behaviour faster than environmental change.

A more significant criticism of equilibrium models is in their assumption of reversibility of organizational change. Consider the choice between U- and M-forms. If, as hypothesized by equilibrium models, change is reversible, organizations reverting from M- to U-form should be observed with change in economic conditions or increase in economies of scale due to advances in technology or information processing. Organizations should be observed to move from a diversification strategy to a single-unit strategy. Empirical research in a number of countries, however, indicates that change to the M-form tends to be irreversible (Rumelt 1974, Channon 1973, Dyas and Thanheiser 1976). It can be argued, of course, that the environment is increasing in complexity. But to make this assertion, it is necessary to explain why the environment is becoming irreversibly complex, and to prove that the environment is increasing in complexity more rapidly than advances in information processing technology which economize on the bounded rationality of decision makers.

Self-sustaining models hold that organizational change is irreversible for individual organizations, although it is reversible through the process of selection on the level of society as a whole. This point is consistent with empirical research. The move from U- to M-form organizations hypothesized by this model, however, is not supported empirically (Fligstein 1985, Palmer *et al.* 1987, Oliver 1988). For example, Fligstein's research suggests that the individual selection model is not appropriate, at least for large organizations. According to Fligstein, the M-form innovation tends to arise when the organization pursues a diversification strategy, a competitor changes to an M-form organization, or top management is from sales or finance. Oliver, after indicating that his research does not support the individual selection model, asserts that there is no unique congruence relationship between the organization and environment, and an organization has room for strategic choice. In light of this research, it can be said that, for large-scale organizations at least, organizations are in fact effecting adaptive self-renewal, although this change is not necessarily a reversible process. In other words, organizations exist which do not simply change their condition but develop through a process of cumulative change (Nonaka 1985).

A MODEL OF THE SELF-RENEWING ORGANIZATION

Equilibrium models explain adaptive self-renewal but not the irreversibility of organizational change. Self-sustaining models explain the irreversibility of change but not adaptive self-renewal. Yet empirical research suggests the existence of both. Although organizations rarely revert to their original structure once change is made, adaptive self-renewal can be observed, especially in large organizations. Attempts at a theory that explains both phenomena have been offered occasionally in recent years (Weick 1979, Nonaka 1985, Nonaka 1988, Nonaka 1989, Takeuchi and Nonaka 1986, Kagono 1988, Ohta 1988, Sakakibara *et al.* 1989, Numagami 1989). These argue that organizations not only process information but also create it, that organizations that maximize information processing do not necessarily maximize information creation, and that an organization is able to reorganize its structure based on information that it has created. Information creation is not merely one aspect of information processing, but is an activity of its own. Phenomena interpreted as pathological by much organization theory are seen as necessary for survival. For example, disequilibrium between organization and environment and the resulting disorder is not a problem to be avoided, but a necessary condition.

Below, we integrate this separately developed research and propose a model which emphasizes creation of meaningful information by organization members. By self-renewing organization we mean an organization that orders its activities through meaningful information which it creates itself in a cumulative fashion. We will compare three aspects of this model with the other two models: assumptions concerning information, the relationship between organization and environment, and structure.

Information creation as an amplification of equivocality

The theory of information creation assumes that every piece of information has syntactic and semantic aspects. The former aspect concerns the quantity of information while the latter relates to its quality. The nature of the syntactic aspect of information is illustrated in the Shannonian analysis of physical information measured in bits in which no attention is given to meaning (Shannon and Weaver 1949). An example of syntactic information is a telephone bill, the calculation of which is based not on the content of the conversation, but on its length and distance. An organization that is a system for processing syntactic information should be designed to reduce redundancy and process information speedily and effectively.

The semantic aspect of information is its meaning. In this sense, the creation of information is actually the creation of information with new meaning. Examples of semantic information in corporate organizations are unique concepts for new products or new businesses. The meaning of information is necessarily context-specific and can be generated through new combinations of concepts. New meaning is often born of intuition and speculation, dialogues and reflective thinking. Continual creation of information in an organization requires flexible associations and networks of concepts. To create information rather than simply process it, an organization needs redundancy and instability (also known as fluctuation, noise and chaos).

Equilibrium models describe a system that processes only syntactic information. In contrast, self-sustaining models consider an organization to be a value-laden system and consequently incorporate meaning, although they emphasize sharing of established meaning rather than creation of new information. Both models view the reduction of equivocality of information as an important objective. The self-renewing model describes an organization that creates new information through synthesis of meaningful information and both reduces and amplifies equivocality. The exchange of both syntactic and semantic aspects of meaningful information is an essential element of a social organization; however, it does not necessarily reduce equivocality.

Consider the communication of an order from superior to subordinate. Equivocality will be reduced only if the information received from the superior implies the set of alternatives for action faced by the subordinate. In this case, only top management creates information and lower levels merely replace the syntactic aspect of the information with another signal. Such a case is unusual in an actual organization. The communication process between superior and subordinate in a social system is not a process by which the subordinate merely selects a specific element from a set of alternatives established by his or her superior. Transmission of information in a social system is not only transmission of its syntactic aspect but is also a process in which the receiver combines information received from the sender with information he or she already possesses and creates a new set of alternatives that are not necessarily logically implied in the information received.

For example, if the superior orders the subordinate to investigate entry into the information processing industry, the subordinate can construct an unlimited set of choices concerning everything from the definition of the industry to the timing and method of entry. Even if the superior specifies that the industry should be entered within two years, there are unlimited possibilities in other dimensions. It is impossible for the set of alternatives created by the subordinate to include only what the superior originally intended. The information possessed by the subordinate and used to create a new set of alternatives includes tacit as well as articulable knowledge (Polanyi 1958) that the superior cannot fully anticipate and control. Information transmission in a social organization is a process in which various types of meaningful information are linked and new meaningful information unintentionally created (Miyadai 1986). Differences between individual organizations result from differences in the method of linkage and in potential of information created.

The self-renewing model holds that even if shared values or institutionalization is present, information linkage in an organization remains a process that both reduces and amplifies equivocality. Institutionalization gives the organization characteristics that members take for granted and facilitates transmission of meaningful information. Taken-for-granted characteristics have a stabilizing effect on the organization, but do not decrease flexibility by reducing the number of alternatives that memebrs can create. Institutionalized systems have an exemption function (Gehlen 1975). Self-sustaining models hold that institutionalization results in inertia as it causes assumptions shared by members to go unquestioned. We argue that the effect of institutionalization is just the opposite. Without institutionalization, each member of a group must constantly try to anticipate the behaviour of the others, and freedom of action is restricted. Institutionalization offers behaviour patterns that members can anticipate; as a result, each member is able to choose his or her behaviour more freely than in a pre-institutionalized setting.

Variations of behaviour are unlimited, even in a specific institutionalized system. Consider language as a social system. Language is highly institutionalized, in the sense that no one ever thinks deeply about the original meaning of the language that they use. Nonetheless, when a person becomes skilled enough in language that he or she can use it unconsciously, he or she becomes able to generate diverse ideas and create new expressions. It is conceivable that humans use language to create an environment; therefore, their imagination is constrained by their language. An organization is able to choose from a variety of actions only when it has developed a highly institutionalized symbolic system. It may be that an organization creates an environment within the limits of its symbolic system and adapts to that environment. If an organization adapts to an environment that it has created itself, then its survival is not determined by environmental selection but by the richness of its creation.

Another reason that institutionalization does not necessarily reduce flexibility is that a system often is equipped with a structure that allows it to reproduce or change itself. There are social systems that have institutionalized self-reflection functions. For example, the legal system includes processes through which to change the legal system. Law is revised based on law. Although the organization design determines the roles of strategic staff and organization designers, the function of these individuals is to redesign the organization of which they are a part; therefore, the assumption of externality does not hold and a logically closed system cannot be designed (Gödel 1962), and the details of the plan for change are always indeterminate ex ante. For this reason, a self-designing organization includes a noise-generating apparatus (Miyadai 1986).

The self-renewing model explains the irreversibility of the M-form as a function of its superior information-creating qualities rather than inertia. If there were a simple trade-off relationship between the U-, H- and M-forms, an organization would be able to move back and forth between these forms freely. If the relationship between the three forms could be simplified by categorizing the U-form as the most centralized, the H-form the least, and the M-form somewhere in between, or the M-form could be described as maximizing centralization and decentralization simultaneously, but at higher cost than the other forms, this simple trade-off relationship might hold true. The self-renewing model argues that these three organizational forms are not appropriate adaptations to different levels of conditions such as scale, environmental complexity, and opportunism. The M-form is superior to the other two under any condition because it is the more advanced form. The M-form differs from the U-form and H-form in that it separates issues of long-term and short-term adaptation. It is equipped with an organizational design subsystem that creates new meaning and incorporates it into the organization. By this separation of long- and short-term tasks, the M-form organization creates long- and short-term environments. In this way, the M-form organization can create new opportunities, and more opportunities mean a richer environment.

Organization and environment as a cooperative system

According to equilibrium models, the organization determines the behaviour of its members and the environment determines the most adaptive organization structure. Each time the environment changes, the designer redesigns the organization. According to the self-sustaining models, organization structure creates incentives and determines the behaviour of members; those incentives and behaviour than sustain and strengthen the organization structure. Organizations with a stable structure are selected by the environment. Although one views organizational form as chosen by the designer and the other views it as selected by the environment, both models assume an environment clearly bounded from the organization and posit that the environment determines the characteristics of a viable organization. The self-renewing model argues that the environment and organization do not have a distinct boundary. The environment is not an external given that impacts the organization but cannot be affected in turn. Rather, the environment and organization are a cooperative system that creates information through iterative interaction.

Consider the environment to be the market. If it is the market that determines the most viable characteristics of an organization, the market should know the exact output that it desires at all times. The organization whose output is closest to this output will be most viable. In this relationship, only the environment creates information. Any information created by the organization beyond that necessary to achieve what the market desires is simply excess, and with excess, cost and performance suffer.

Markets which inform the organization of desired output do exist. In such environments, both efficiency and reliability are important. Research on the longitudinal change of organizational output (Abernathy 1978, Abernathy *et al.* 1983, Clark 1985, Rosenbloom and Cusumano 1987), however, indicates that in most cases organization and market learn from each other and do not know the desired output ex ante. Even after the market and organization agree on a definition of output and even after the market has matured, the market and organization will enter a new learning phase with the introduction of new technology or entrance of new competitors. The market and organization mutually create meaningful information and continuously construct new definitions of appropriate output through iterative interaction. Novelty, diversity, and surprise (any difference that makes a difference (Bateson 1979)) are more important to the creation of information than efficiency or reliability. The organization–market relationship is not one in which information is created by the market, but rather a cooperative process. Novel, diverse, and unexpected output activates the market's information creation process, and information created in this way can be utilized by the organization at a later date.

In the self-renewing model, the organization also determines the size of the utilizable opportunities in the environment. The environment is not an uncontrollable external factor. This differs from theories that hold that an organization is able to choose strategically the portion of the environment to which to adapt (Child 1972). Strategic choice theory holds that an organization is able, for example, to select market segments with either high or low price elasticity. Because an organization is able to select its own market segment strategically, the characteristics of viable organizations can differ even in the same market. The environment does not determine the characteristics of a viable organization, but neither does the organization affect the environment.

The self-renewing model, in contrast, posits a relationship of mutual influence between organization and environment. According to this model, the basic competitive strategies of cost leadership and differentiation have very different implications for the creation of information. A strategy that pursues economies of scale and learning effects is an effort to control change and diversity in the market as well as reduce costs through standardization of products. This strategy does not only mitigate changes in the market temporarily. Such control of environmental fluctuation prevents information creation by the market and hinders the creation of opportunities that can be utilized by the organization at a later date. While cost leadership strategy increases market size and number of information-creating subjects (customers), it causes information-creation to stagnate, and it is inevitable that the market will mature and become saturated. Strategies of differentiation and innovation have the opposite effect, creating new information and introducing it into the market. This new information 'surprises' the market and activates its information-creating activities. Market diversity (the number of segments and the difference in their sizes) is a result of interaction between organizations employing a cost leadership strategy, those employing a differentation strategy, and customer's information-creating activities. The diversity of the organization is not unilaterally determined by the market.

Requisite variety and organization structure

In their treatments of organization structure, both equilibrium and self-sustaining models presuppose cognitive limits. Organizations attempt to circumvent these limits by solving problems through a quasi-decomposable system. Complex problems are not solved all at once, but are first separated into parts which require minimal co-ordination. Problem solving is most efficient when the organization structure forms a hierarchy isomorphic with the structure of the problem. Identical to this logic is the argument that the diversity in the structure of an organization should match that of the environment. According to the principle of requisite variety, an organization can maximize efficiency by creating within itself the same degree of diversity as the diversity it must process. While the equilibrium and self-sustaining models differ on whether or not an organization can actually construct requisite variety, they agree that, *ceteris paribus*, requisite variety renders an organization more viable.

The self-renewing model also assumes cognitive limits. It holds that hierarchy is necessary and does not deny the necessity of requisite variety. This model, however, treats an organization not only as a cooperative system for solving complex problems but as a system that creates information to enrich its environment and faces the divergent requirements of reducing as well as amplifying variety.

Hierarchy is an efficient structure for processing information required for problem solving. Consider a case in which a complex problem is not returned into a quasi-decomposable system, but is decomposed randomly. The amount of coordination necessary to solve this problem will be by definition greater than that required by a quasi-decomposable system. Even if the problem is solved, efficiency is low. Despite higher levels of efficiency, hierarchy also creates some undesirable consequences. Because it reduces the frequency of interaction between members, it obstructs the creation of information.

The self-renewing model emphasizes the creation of new meaningful information through the synthesis of heterogeneous meaningful information. The environment is not an external element clearly bounded with the organization but, together with the organization, comprises an information-creating system. Therefore, not only members but also individuals outside the organization have their own unique information and contribute to the linkage of meaningful information. This information includes unarticulable tacit knowledge or articulable but perishable on-the-spot information that can only be communicated through the system at a high cost (Hayek 1945). New information is created through the synthesis of unique information possessed by individuals. Given that not only the organization but each individual possesses a memory, and the contents of each individual memory change quite rapidly, an organization that can link as many diverse individuals as possible simultaneously will be able to create more information. A heterarchical system with channels between each member that enables the member who creates the richest information to take the lead in the current situation is a superior system from the perspective of creation of meaningful information.

Here, the organization faces a dilemma. To create information most effectively, it must construct as many linkages as possible between individual members and between organization and environment. A hierarchy, on the other hand, processes information most efficiently. Moreover, as the number of members increases, direct linkage between each member will overload the cognitive abilities of each individual. A realistic response to this dilemma is a structure that enables an organization to move between heterarchy and hierarchy with maximum speed. The self-renewing model creates such a structure through the principle of requisite accessibility. While not all organization members are linked directly, information held by each member and organizational subunit can be accessed through the shortest possible route whenever and wherever necessary. Two conditions are needed for requisite accessibility: each individual must possess an address, so that all members know where the information exists, and there can be no linkages that overload the cognitive abilities of an individual. Addresses enable all members to know who possesses what type of information, without having to know the actual details of the information. 'Know where' is more important than 'know-how'. An organization must publicly announce to the environment its unique capabilities and its mission. An organization chart serves not to indicate the chain of command as much as to categorize the organization's accumulated information and assign addresses to this information to facilitate access by all members.

One method of linkage between members is the Boolean hypercube. This can be thought of as a type of cube of various dimensions, constructed as follows (see Figure 1.1). A straight line is a 1-cube, or a cube in a one-dimensional space. Two 1-cubes linked together end-to-end form a 2-cube, or a rectangle. Repetition of this operation forms an n-cube with 2^n corners. The Boolean hypercube fulfils the principle of requisite accessibility. Consider each member of a self-renewing system as located at one corner. The maximum distance

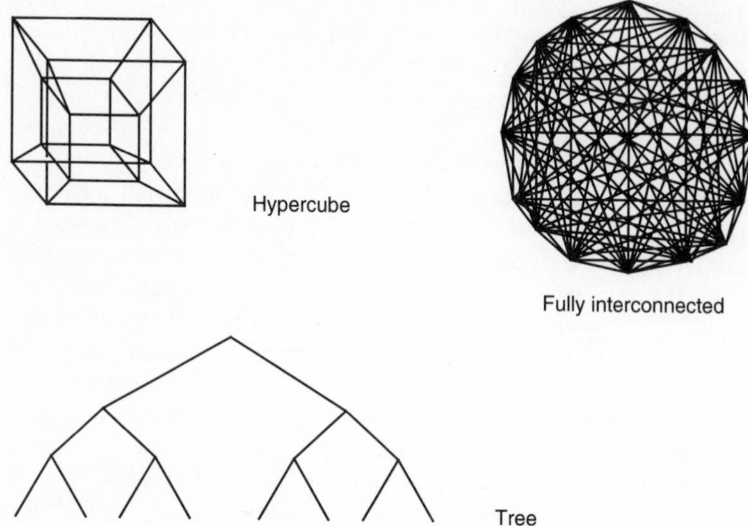

Figure 1.1 Hypercube in contrast to tree and interconnected circle

from one member to another is never more than *n* channels. Because each corner member has his own address, even if one channel is busy, a subsitute route can be found that follows access but does not exceed the maximum number of *n* channels (the number of dimensions). By repositioning the corner members, it is possible to shorten the channel length even further.

The Boolean hypercube is more efficient than the total linkage, but is redundant when compared to hierarchy. Assume for simplicity that there are eight members. Because eight is 2^3, a Boolean 3-cube is formed with each corner member having three channels. Because each channel is shared by two members, a total of 12 channels ($[3 \times 8]/2$) is necessary. If all members were linked ($[n \times (n-1)]/2$) 28 channels would be necessary; for a group of 8 in a hierarchy, only seven channels (8–1) are necessary because top management members need not report to a superior. When viewed from the perspective of equilibrium models, the number of channels in the Boolean hypercube is clearly excessive. But compared to total linkage, the Boolean hypercube retains redundancy of potential command, while increasing efficiency. We believe that this type of structure satisfies the contrary conditions of information creation and information processing and provides the medium through which an organization can renew its structure. Of course, we are not saying that all of a large-scale organization should adopt a Boolean hypercube structure. Rather, this structure is advantageous for organizations or parts of organizations that rely on effective production of information. As a structure-generating structure (Sahal 1982) that allows effective creation of ad hoc structures in order to solve various problems, the Boolean hypercube is a promising conceptual model.

CONCLUSION

Can an organization renew itself? We begun our discussion with a comparative investigation of two models that offer contrasting answers to this question. Equilibrium models assume externality and reversibility of change and argue that an organization's designer can effect change in structure. Self-sustaining models do not make these assumptions and deny that self-change is possible. Both models provide a useful perspective for the analysis of organizations and have encouraged the development of excellent conceptual and empirical research.

However, the equilibrium model's assumption that a social organization can be designed in the same way as an engineering system is nothing more than a theoretical construct. The assumptions of externality and reversibility of organizational change transform social organizations into something else. Due to its interdisciplinary nature, organization theory has frequently used methodology that invokes metaphors from diverse disciplines. In this sense, the methodology of equilibrium models is quite useful in its simplicity. The problem is that the methodology cannot expose its own shortcomings (Morgan 1983).

A creative discourse with other models is necessary in order to illuminate the limits of the equilibrium system methodology. In fact, reflective discourse between equilibrium and self-sustaining models is beneficial in clarifying the strengths and weaknesses of both theories. Because they deny the assumptions of externality and reversibility of change, self-sustaining models can add insight into organizational phenomena that are difficult to handle in equilibrium models (Carroll 1988). The superior intellectual contribution of self-sustaining models on this point cannot be denied.

A weakness of self-sustaining models is that they give no suggestion of possibility of self-renewal in large organizations. Why is it that certain organizations are capable of self-renewing while others are not? The objective of our research was to develop some suggestions

Table 1.1 Comparison of equilibrium, self-sustaining and self-renewing models

	Equilibrium	*Self-sustaining*	*Self-renewing*
Information and knowledge	Only information expressed in bits processed	Established meanings shared to stabilize a value-laden knowledge structure	New information created through interaction of syntactic and semantic information
	Equivocality of information reduced	Equivocality of information reduced	Knowledge restructured through dynamic transformation of tacit to articulate knowledge
			Equivocality of information *increased* as well as reduced
Organization and environment	Clear boundary	Clear boundary	No clear boundary
	Environment determines organization's characteristics; designer chooses form	Environment selects viable organization	Environment and organization a cooperative system that creates information through iterative interaction
Structural characteristics	A hierarchy	A hierarchy	A hypercube
	Problems solved through quasi-decomposable system	Problems solved through shared paradigms that constantly reproduce their own legitimacy	Problems both solved and *created*
			Principle of requisite accessibility

on this point. The difference between organizations capable of self-renewal and those that are not is not complete coincidence or selection pressure from the environment, but is due to the organization's information-creating potential. An organization not only processes information but also constantly creates new meaningful information. The self-renewing process is the reorganization of structure using this new information (Table 1.1). The true nature of organizational change can be perceived completely only through an understanding of the process by which information is created through interaction between organization members and outside systems.

This perspective, which views an organization as capable of restructuring itself based on information created through its environmental subsystem, provides a powerful framework through which to explain innovation and the process of self-renewal that can be observed in large organizations.

REFERENCES

Abernathy, W.J. (1978) *The Productivity Dilemma: Roadblock to Innovation in the Automobile Industry*, Baltimore, MD: The Johns Hopkins University Press.

Abernathy, W.J., Clark, K.B. and Kantrow, A. (1983) *Industrial Renaissance*, New York: Basic Books.

Argyris, Ch. and Schön, D.A. (1978) *Organizational Learning*, Reading, MA: Addison-Wesley.

Armour, H.O. and Teece, D.J. (1987) 'Organization Structure and Economic Performance: A Test of the Multidivisional Hypothesis', *Bell Journal of Economics*, 9, pp. 106–22.

Bateson, G. (1979) *Mind and Nature*, New York: Routledge and Kegan Paul.

Brown, R.H. (1978) 'Bureaucracy as Praxis: Toward a Political Phenomenology of Formal Organizations', *Administrative Science Quarterly*, 23, pp. 365–82.

Carroll, G.R. (ed.) (1988) *Ecological Models of Organizations*, Cambridge, MA: Ballinger .

Channon, D.F. (1973) *The Strategy and Structure of British Enterprise*, New York: Macmillan.

Child, J. (1972) 'Organizational Structure, Environment and Performance: The Role of Strategic Choice', *Sociology*, 6, pp. 1–22.

Clark, K.B. (1985) 'The Interaction of Design Hierarchies and Market Concepts in Technological Evolution', *Research Policy*, 14, pp. 235–51.

Deal, T. and Kennedy, A.A. (1982) *Corporate Cultures*, Reading, MA: Addison-Wesley.

Dyas, G.P and Thanheiser, H.T. (1976) *The Emerging European Enterprise: Strategy and Structure in French and German Industry*, New York: Macmillan.

Fligstein, N. (1985) 'The Spread of the Multidivisional Form among Large Firms, 1919–1979', *American Sociological Review*, 50, pp. 377–91.

Galbraith, J.R. (1973) *Designing Complex Organizations*, Reading, MA: Addison-Wesley.

Gehlen, A. (1975) *Urmensch und Spätkultur: Philosophische Ergebnisse und Aussagen*, Stuttgart: Aula-Verlag.

Gödel, K. (1962) *On Formally Undecidable Propositions*, New York: Basic Books.

Hannan, M.T. and Freeman, J. (1977) 'The Population Ecology of Organizations', *American Journal of Sociology*, 82, pp. 929–66.

—— (1984) 'Structural Inertia and Organizational Change', *American Sociological Review*, 49, pp. 149–64.

Hayek, F.A. (1945) 'The Use of Knowledge in Society', *The American Economic Review*, 35, pp. 519–30.

Kagono, T. (1980) *Keiei Soshiki no Kankyo Tekio* (Environmental Adaption of Business Organizations), Tokyo: Hakuto Shobo.

—— (1982) 'Paradigm Kyoyu to Soshiki Bunka' (Sharad Paradigm and Organizational Culture), *Soshiki Kagaku*, 16(1), pp. 66–80.

—— (1988) *Soshiki Ninshikiron Josetsu* (Steps to the Theory of Organizational Cognitive Maps), Tokyo: Chikura-Shoba. (In Japanese.)

Lawrence, P.R. and Lorsch, J.W. (1967) *Organization and Environment: Managing Differentiation and Integration*, Graduate School of Business Administration, Harvard University, Cambridge, MA.

Miyadai, Sh. (1986) 'Shakai System no Saihen ni Mukatte' (Toward a Reconstruction of Social System Theory), *Sociologos*, 10, pp. 96–119.

Morgan, G. (ed.) (1983) *Beyond Method: Strategies for Social Research*, Beverly Hills, CA: Sage Publications.

Nonaka, I. (1972) *Organization and Market: Exploratory Study of Centralization versus Decentralization*, unpublished PhD, dissertation, Graduate School of Business Administration, University of California at Berkeley.

—— (1985) *Kigyo Shinkaron: Joho Sozo no Management* (Evolutionary Theory of the Firm: Management of Information Creation), Tokyo: Nipponkeizai Shinbunsha.

—— (1988) 'Creating Organizational Order out of Chaos: Self-Renewal in Japanese Firms', *California Management Review*, 30, pp. 57–73.

—— (1989) 'Joho to Chishiki Sozo no Soshikiron' (An Organizational Theory of Information and Knowledge Creation), *Soshiki Kagaku*, 22(4), pp. 1–14.

Nonaka, I. and Amikura, H. (1987) 'Kigyo no Chiteki Kozo Kaikaku: Chi no Kumikai no Management' (Restructuring Organizational Knowledge), *Business Review*, 35(2), pp. 1–12.

Numagami, T. (1989) 'Sijo to Soshiki to Koso: Concept Driven Model ni Mukatte' (A Concept-Driven Model of Innovation), *Soshiki Kagaku*, 23(1), pp. 59–69.

Ohta, T. (1988) 'Jiko-Seiseiteki Rensa Model to Soshiki Chino' (Autopoietic System and Organizational Intelligence), *Operations Research*, 33(3), pp. 144–8.

Oliver, Ch. (1988) 'The Collective Strategy Framework: An Application to Competing Predictions of Isomorphism', *Administrative Science Quarterly*, 33, pp. 543–61.

Ouchi, W. G. (1980) 'Markets, Bureaucracies, and Clans', *Administrative Science Quarterly*, 25, pp. 129–41.

—— (1981) *Theory Z*, Reading, MA: Addison-Wesley.
Palmer, D., Friedland, R., Devereaux, J. and Powers, M.E. (1987) 'The Economics and Politics of Structure: The Multidivisional Form and the Large U.S. Corporation', *Administrative Science Quarterly*, 32, pp. 25–48.
Pascale, R.T. and Athos, A.G. (1982) *The Art of Japanese Management*, New York: Simon & Schuster.
Peters, T.J. and Waterman, R.H. (1982) *In Search of Excellence*, New York: Harper & Row.
Pfeffer, J. (1981) 'Management as Symbolic Action: The Creation and Maintenance of Organizational Paradigms', in L.L. Cummings and B. Staw (eds) *Research in Organizational Behavior*, 3, pp. 1–52, Greenwich, CT: JAI Press.
Polanyi, M. (1958) *Personal Knowledge: Towards a Post-Critical Philosophy*, Chicago, IL: University of Chicago Press.
Rosenbloom, R.S. and Cusumano, M.A. (1987) 'Technological Pioneering and Competitive Advantage: The Birth of the VCR Industry', *California Management Review*, 24, pp. 51–76.
Rumelt, R.P (1974) *Strategy, Structure and Economic Performance*, Division of Research, Harvard Business School, Cambridge, MA.
Sahal, D. (1982) 'Structure and Self-Organization', *Behavioral Science*, 27, pp. 249–58.
Sakakibara, K., Ohtaki, S. and Numagami, T. (1989) *Jigyo Souzo no Dynamics* (Dynamic Theory of New Business Venture), Tokyo: Hakuto-shobo.
Scott, W.R. (1987) 'The Adolescence of Institutional Theory', *Administrative Science*, 32, pp. 493–511.
Selznick, Ph. (1957) *Leadership in Administration: A Sociological Interpretation*, New York: Harper & Row.
Shannon, C.E. and Weaver, W. (1949) *The Mathematical Theory of Communication*, Urbana, IL: University of Illinois Press.
Sheldon, A. (1980) 'Organizational Paradigm: A Theory of Organizational Change', *Organizational Dynamics*, 8(3), pp. 61–80.
Takeuchi, H. and Nonaka, I. (1986) 'The New Product Development Game', *Harvard Business Review*, January–February, pp. 137–46.
Thompson, J.D. (1967) *Organization in Action*, New York: McGraw-Hill.
Weick, K.E. (1979) *The Social Psychology of Organizing* (2nd edn), New York: Random House.
Williamson, O.E. (1975) *Markets and Hierarchies: Analysis and Antitrust Implications*, New York: Free Press.
—— (1985) *The Economic Institutions of Capitalism*, New York: Free Press.

2 Self-organization in Informatics

Haruo Hata and Charles Adamson

PREFACE

The effects of recent fundamental developments in communications and computer systems are beginning to be felt throughout the advanced societies of the world. In response, college-level educational programmes are beginning to change and the study of information is becoming popular in many different disciplines: Information Engineering at schools of technology, Information Science in the Natural Sciences, and Informatics in Business Administration and Economics. This is causing some confusion, because the faculties for these programmes are being assembled from many different fields and do not agree on exactly what constitutes this new field of study. Even in Information Engineering, which has the longest history, there seems to be a substantial amount of disagreement about the proper content for the curriculum.

The Informatics curriculum in Business Administration and Economics is usually considered to be part of Social Science, but the curriculum is generally developed in parallel with those of Information Engineering or Information Science.

The Informatics curriculum at Asahi University, where one of the authors (Hata) teaches, is an example of this sort of programme. The School of Business Administration was established in 1985 and the facilities include a large number of computers for use in teaching. Hata was Dean of the School from 1989 to 1993, in spite of having an academic and industrial background in engineering. In 1991 a new department of Information Management was established and Hata began work on developing a general theory of Informatics which would cover the areas of interest to not only Natural Science, but also to the Humanities and Social Science. The result of this work was the publication in 1992 of the book *Introduction to Informatics* (Hata 1992).

As this study progressed, it soon became apparent that there are two different interpretations of 'information'. Information Engineering is mainly interested in the carrier of the information. Business Information, on the other hand, stresses the meaning of the information. This new study of the meaning of information, Informatics, is based on the thesis that Information is a consequence of life and employs the fundamental principles of Cybernetics and Self-Organization.

Previous work by natural scientists has discovered much about the carriers of information, but because life has been deleted from the equations, natural science is not able to effectively address the meaning of information. This would seem to be a natural area for study by the humanities and social sciences, but the investigation has barely begun because information is not a major interest of researchers.

Traditional science based on European ideas appears to be nearing the end of its mission. In recent years new natural sciences, new humanities, and new social sciences have been invading each other's territories and competing with each other to stake out areas of study. This chapter continues this trend by presenting initial thoughts on parts of a new general theory of Informatics which lays claim to territories previously in the realm of social science, natural science, and the humanities.

THE NEWLY DEVELOPING STUDY OF INFORMATION

Umesao's paper on 'The Information Industries'

One of the pioneers in the study of information is Tadao Umesao, who published 'Joho Sangyo Ron' (The Information Industries) in 1963, more or less simultaneously with the surprisingly robust development of the commercial broadcasting companies in Japan (Umesao 1963). Umesao suggested that industries which systematically supply information should be called 'information industries', a term which includes all businesses engaged in mass communication.

Information industries do not belong to traditional industries

Umesao pointed out that the products sold by the information industries are a series of symbols, and that they cannot be measured by the tools used to measure the output of other industries. The commodities sold by a newspaper company are not so much the physical newspaper, but the news that is printed in them. Commercial broadcasting companies are said to sell 'time', but this is not correct: what is sold is the information that fills that time. Umesao pointed out that broadcasting companies are founded on the realization that they can sell a range of time filled with information.

This selling of information, not space or time which is only the container for the information, is quite different from what happens in other industries, since information cannot be measured by the usual standards, even those used in Information Science where information is measured in bits. It is nonsensical, for example, to say that the information contained in a TV drama is some specific number of bits. Umesao concluded that there are no accurate measures of the information by the information industries.

Information as meaning has the special characteristic that vendors can put a price on it only before revealing it to the customer. Thus, people normally buy the products of the information industries before they know their contents. We do not find such strange commodities anywhere else, and Umesao said that, because of this, it was unreasonable not to differentiate between traditional commodities and this strange new variety.

Umesao considered these new non-traditional industries to be 'virtual' industries, pointing out that they represent the coming of a new age. The history of mankind may now be said to have three stages: the age of agriculture, the age of industry, and the age of virtual industries.

These phased enlargements of the functions of man's organic organizations parallel the development of mankind's self-realization. The age of agriculture corresponds to the repletion of man's eating function, that is, the function of the endoderm organs, in which the digestive organs are dominant. The age of industry is characterized by the production of a wide variety of goods and forms of energy which expand on and replace physical labour by humans. This represents the functional enlargement of the mesoderm organs, of which the muscles are most dominant.

This leads Umesao to believe that the modern development of information industries can be thought of as the dawn of the coming age of the ectoderm industry.

A new offering principle

Modern economics must be considered as part of the mesoderm age. Economists have clearly built their pricing mechanism theories on the basis of commodities produced by the manufacturing industries. What price mechanism, however, can we find for the products of the virtual industries, such things as fees for copyrights, patents, manuscripts, lectures, and musical performances, for example? What is the price of information in general? According to Umesao, this information cannot be measured, so there can be no marginal utilities placed on them, but they do differ from each other in principle.

During the mesoderm age, information had little effect on the total economy, but today we find some virtual industry products are occupying important parts of our lives. This leads Umesao to believe that the age of industry may pass in somewhat less that two hundred years. If virtual industry does become dominant, these ectoderm industries will become the core of economics and price mechanisms will follow those of the ectoderm industry's products.

Umesau claims that the price mechanism for ectoderm industrial products should be related to the mechanism determining the appropriate value of offerings to religionists, a value that can be determined by the status of the payer as well as the payee and that bears no relation to the information or labour of the religionists. Actually the fees for lectures, performances, and manuscripts are being paid under almost the same principle. Status, in the sense of recognition of one's social or public personality, has become a valuable commodity and no new pricing mechanism can be developed without considering its economic effects.

These preliminary ideas of Umesau have taken about a quarter of a century to be utilized in the construction of the 'high-tech' information systems by entrepreneurs and engineers. Intellectuals, however, are mainly interested in historical materialism and have not been able to incorporate his ideas.

A claim that the study of information belongs to social sciences

The study of information started with the study of information in libraries and was carried on mainly by natural scientists and only later were claims raised that it should belong to social science. Machalup and Mansfield (1983) pointed out that modern society has had to struggle with the great gaps that have arisen between and within the rapidly emerging new natural sciences as well as social sciences and technologies. He also claimed that modern societies are too complicated to be analysed by the methods used by natural scientists, so he believed that Information should be studied by social scientists. While admitting that Informatics contains some areas that are properly in the realm of natural science, he pointed out that it is silly to use physical measures like 'bit' in cases of human beliefs, creeds, likings, and values. However, he could not propose adequate social measures.

Does the study of information belong to natural science?

In the following paragraphs we will briefly consider the positions of three Japanese researchers on the above question.

Yoro's Brainism (Yoro 1989)

The present age is essentially the age of the brain. Since the brain is the organ for handling information and society is now becoming information oriented, we can say that society has, in an interesting sense, become a 'brain'. It can also be said that cities are the products of the brain. This is also true of tradition, culture, social systems, and languages.

Using this as a starting point, Yoro defines Brainism as a basis for the study of human activities in relation to the characteristics of the organs making up the brain. Previously the study of the brain was under a kind of taboo, but in order to understand the true nature of humans, the taboo must be broken and Brainism or something like it will be necessary.

In some aspects Brainism seems to be a natural science, but in other respects it is not. Therefore, Brainism's position on the above question is unclear at this time.

Sakai's information science (Sakai 1988)

The fundamental theories of information science are relatively less developed than those of the rapidly developing information engineering, but they are now under development. Sakai points out that information science clarifies three theoretical aspects of information:

1 Object, subject, and environment affect each other. In other words information is thought to be context-dependent. This means that information science is basically different from modern natural science and more like social science. This also means that many of the approaches and tools of natural science are not applicable to information science whose approaches and tools remain under development.
2 Modelling theories, beginning with the black box theories, must be developed. This is a most fundamental issue in the underdeveloped field of information theories. This also applies to social science in general.

3 Issues about openness and closedness of information, and related problems, which have been newly raised by developments in social and natural sciences, will be important problems for information science.

From the above, it can be seen that information science positions itself as being different from natural science.

Shimizu's new approach to life sciences (Shimizu 1989)

Shimizu is working on the development of a new natural science of life. According to this work, living systems dispatch information constantly, and since modern natural sciences have not previously dealt with living systems, current natural scientists are less familiar with the concept of information than with other physical quantities. Information quantities relate to the concept of value, which has been difficult for natural science to deal with. So, Shimizu believes that natural science, which has been developed without consideration of the world of values and beauty, will begin to build links to social science and the humanities, which have dealt with values and beauty, through the study of information. Shimizu's idea will be more fully discussed later in this paper.

Informatics includes parts of both natural science and social science

The authors believe that Informatics must occupy itself with an area that includes portions of both natural science and social science as well as other fields of study such as the humanities. Dealing with information as meaning is a new field and as such it needs specialized methods. Some of these methods will be drawn from natural science and some will come from social science. Additionally, completely new methods and tools will be developed as our understanding of information as meaning increases.

INFORMATION IS A CONSEQUENCE OF LIFE

Descartes' *cogito ergo sum*

Umesao's definition of information

In 1988 Umesao published another paper (Umesao 1988) *Joho no Bunmeigaku* (The Science of Information Cultures) in which he modified his previous definition of the meaning of information. The following paragraphs summarize the main points of this new work.

In the past information has been defined in pragmatic terms of the profits that it could bring to the holder. However, it is a mistake to think that all information has such a pragmatic meaning. Actually most of the information in circulation brings no profit to anyone and is thus meaningless in the traditional sense. This 'meaningless' information does perform an important function in relation to the stimulation that it provides while passing through the sense organs and the cranial nerves. This is similar to the function of non-nutritious fibrous foods which, although meaningless in the sense of nutrition, promote good health by helping to activate the digestive organs. It is apparent in light of this that in order to truly understand information, we must consider both 'meaningful' and 'meaningless' information.

Next Umesao says that we must distinguish between information and communication. Information is not necessarily something that is sent from a sender to a receiver. Information can exist independently of the sender and receiver. In fact, we should think of the world itself as information.

The essence of information is the perception of the external world by the sense organs and the subsequent deciphering of the output of the sensory organs by the cranial nerves. Umesao believes that, if there is activity of the sensory organs and cranial nerves, there is life and accompanying that life is information. Even if we ignore the philosophical implications, this biological aspect is clearly reflected in Descartes' statement *cogito ergo sum* (I think therefore I am.)

Brainism's interpretation of consciousness

According to Yoro, the brain is an organ for knowing and this knowing exists only in the brain. When we feel an itch on our back, the brain knows nothing of the back. The brain has only a map of the back. What we know is not the back itself, but only the brain's map, a model or representation of the back. Alfred Korzybski (1980) made the same point when he said, 'The map is not the territory.' Yoro goes on to say that language is the reason we think we know the back, and that language itself is a product of the brain.

Yoro also says that, when Descartes wrote *cogito ergo sum*, he meant that for the consciousness there exists only what occurs in the brain.

The evolutionary role of the animal brain, according to Yoro, is to receive external stimuli and to make the body move appropriately. To do this, the brain must work with two types of knowledge: about the external world and about the body, a division that may be considered the origin of the materialism and spiritualism duality.

Knowledge of the body is nearly complete when the brain has made up its map of the body. However, in at least the case of human beings, this knowledge also must contain information about the conscious since the brain is part of the body.

Yoro cites a law of nerve cell growth, 'the nerve cell that does not control its periphery dies'. He says that normally this implies that growth of the evolutionary brain will be accompanied by a corresponding growth of the sensory nerves. This has not yet happened for human beings; instead humans have developed consciousness. Individual nerve cells interconnect with as many other nerve cells as possible and each attempts to increase the size of its own territory, while mutually supporting the other nerve cells. If consciousness is considered in light of this, its biological function would appear to be the maintenance of the nerve cells themselves, and the exernal world including other people has little meaning.

The psyche as a subject of study

Sayeki prepared three answers to the question 'What is Cognitive Science?' In this section we will summarize his first answer which was published as 'Cognitive Science is the Science of Psyche' (Sayeki 1983).

Ever since Descartes delineated the psyche–physis dualism, psychologists have considered the body and its movement to be independent of the psyche. The investigative methodologies employed in physics, which have been regarded as the mainstream of modern science, began to be applied to the study of the response mechanisms of the body and behaviour of all animals, including humans, was modelled as the formation of specific reactions to external stimulation. This resulted in the conditioned reflex theory of the 1920s and the behavioural psychology of the 1930s. However, Gestalt psychologists pointed out that there are many aspects of the behaviour of higher animals and humans that are difficult to explain as a result of simple stimulus/response mechanisms.

Cognitive psychology was developed in the 1950s and within it Chomsky's work showed that human language cannot be described as the limited automation of a stimulus/response system. He demonstrated through mathematical linguistic methods that mind must be working in the process of language information processing (Chomsky 1957).

In the 1960s the study of language and memory progressed further and Chomsky developed a generative and transformational theory of language which described the human intellectual activities of realizing, generating, and using language as the result of the application of a generalized set of rules. This theory contradicted the then mainstream behavioural psychology, and it gradually increased in influence as it was further developed. Linguistic psychologists began to adopt this theory into their psychological hypotheses and to release studies on the relation between human cognitive activities and language. This resulted in the Cognitive Psychology of Ulric Neisser (Neisser 1967).

Studies of memory progressed rapidly during the 1960s, and psychologists became interested in the study of knowledge. In the 1970s the results of these memory studies were integrated with the results of artificial intelligence studies and became Cognitive Science, the study of the generation, use, and understanding of knowledge.

The psyche, which had been forgotten by science since Descartes, was highlighted and once again became a proper subject for scientific study.

The psyche–physis problem

The origin of the psyche

Yoro feels that the philosophical psyche–physis problem arises from the human feeling that the psyche is sacred and mysterious in a religious sense, a feeling which causes many people to believe that the psyche could not have emerged from the gross material of the brain (Yoro 1989). He says that, while it may seem strange to many, Brainism's explanation of how the psyche emerges from the mass of material we call the brain gives an adequate explanation of the origin of the psyche. However, before discussing Brainism's answer, we should consider Kurimoto's explanation.

Kurimoto's solution to the psyche–physis problem

In trying to answer the question of the origin of the psyche, Hiromatsu (1982) organized the various theories into three classes with a total of eight categories. Of these, he concluded that existing conditions could be explained by either materialism, accepting only the existence of the physis, or the Two Aspects theory, the psyche and the physis combining into a single entity.

Kurimoto criticized this interpretation, saying that the former was unacceptable due to its reductionism and the latter would only be acceptable if the mechanism for bringing the psyche and physis together were explained (Kurimoto 1980). He felt that the answer lay in the theory of hierarchical levels and the theory of tacit knowing developed by Polanyi (1969).

Kurimoto seems to understand tacit knowledge to be the result of the integration of the active participation of the personality of the knower and the condition of knowing. It includes the integrated personal acts of both understanding the object as well as separating the object from the background. It is not, however, a replacement for potential sensory perception by the physis, although that is a part of tacit knowing too. The goal of these integrated personal acts is to know the personal ontological situation within the universe, which implies an enlargement of the personal physis as a physiological but not a physical process.

For Kurimoto, the fundamental position of language within all this is to assist in the reading of meaning from an object, to describe objects for the self and others, and to read meaning from the language of such descriptions. For example, if we look at the scenery in a country we have not previously visited, the following could occur: (1) through the use of language we understand more than we could with purely sensory data; (2) we can than describe the scenery in a letter; and finally (3) someone can read the letter and make meaning from it. In each case a meaning is built, a kind of fiction which does not consist of the scenery itself. In this paper we refer to this as a map or a model. Each of these (1, 2, and 3) is an example of tacit knowledge and Polanyi called these three cases the triad of tacit knowing (Polanyi 1969).

According to Kurimoto (1980), Polanyi defined the psyche as the mechanism of the physis, but the psyche disappears if we focus only on this mechanism. Therefore, we must work with two kinds of awareness, focal and secondary. With the former we lose sight of the psyche in the mechanisms of the physis, but with the latter we find that the psyche is rooted in the physis but independent of it. In other words, the psyche depends on the mechanism of the physis, but is not determined by it.

Tacit knowing can, in Kurimoto's understanding, be realized by personal commitment through the act of using a language or through goal oriented activities. Existence is ultimately the reflection of the ego on the internal map of the world. Being can only exist in thinking, or rather thinking itself is being. All personal understanding is tacit recognition through tacit knowing, the only process through which a person can acquire a meaning for the self and become a person. The world itself emerges through this process and resembles the person who is seeing it. This means that asking which takes precedence the world or the person is a meaningless question since they must co-exist. The world was not pre-existing and later joined by the perceiver, rather they emerge and vanish together.

Brainism and the psyche–physis problem

We can now return to Brainism's answer to the question of the origin of the psyche.

The problem of the relation of the brain to the mind, or the psyche–physis problem, could be a result of the relation between structure and function. For instance, the heart is basic to the circulatory system: the circulation of the blood stops when the heart stops. However, disassembling the heart and circulatory system would not result in finding circulation, because the heart is material and circulation is function.

The brain is surely material and the mind is a function of the brain. So we should not expect to find the functional mind as part of the material of the brain, in the same way that circulation is not found in the material of the heart.

Brainism proposes that people distinguish between the brain as material and the mind as function because human brains are structured to think this way. That is, distinguishing between structure and function is a characteristic of the human brain.

Thinking that the mind is not a function of the brain seems to be caused by treating the mind as exceptional because it has a peculiar characteristic, consciousness, which cannot be found in other organs. Descartes might have started his study from this point of view and Yoro thinks that many other philosophers have forgotten the fact they are thinking with their brain.

Brainism does not deal with the brain as the cause of the mind, rather it deals with the correspondence between the structure of the brain and the functions of the mind. So Brainism is, at its basic stage, morphology.

Brainism does not treat the world as a product of the brain: it treats consciousness as the product of the brain.

Probably the most familiar, and important, example of the

psyche–physis problem is the corpse, an object which has caused people to believe in a simple severence of the mind and body. Biologists think it is the severence of structure and function. It has long been held that structure and function separate in the object itself, but Brainism holds that they separate in the brain.

The genesis of language

There are three representational modes which are in common use as carriers of information: visual, auditory, and tactile which is also called kinesthetic (Dilts *et al.* 1980). The visual representational mode conveys large amounts of information as data and its interrelations in the form of a picture, but it tells little or nothing of the flow of the time element. The auditory representational mode provides information in a single line on a time axis and this timeflow is immanent to the understanding process. The kinesthetic representational mode normally carries somatic and emotional information and will not concern us here.

Brainism suggests that the brain's sense of time is closely related to the structure–function phenomenon. Our sense of time is quantumized in structure but in function it flows. One reason for the coexistence of these two different senses in the human brain might be that they are the result of the separation of the visual and auditory senses within the brain. Since structure and function are obviously not merely two different aspects of a single unit, this internal division of time must be due to circumstances within the brain. It may be that there is no simple way for the brain to combine the time-independent information from the visual mode with the time-independent data from the auditory mode.

Brainism's position is that conscious thinking may be the brain's way of unifying the information from the visual and auditory channels. We normally assume that this unification is natural, but the existence of the psyche–physis problem, structure and function, and particles and waves in light should make us question the validity of this assumption. There may be no external necessity for combining the information from light and sound, which have quite different physical natures. Natures that are so different that eyes and ears evolved independently. This leaves the proposition that the combination is the result of circumstances within the brain and that this has facilitated the development of human languages.

Yoro concludes from this line of reasoning that the combination of these two fundamentally different kinds of sensory information is nearly synonymous with the genesis of language which functions as the vehicle for unifying the time-dependent and the time-independent information processed in the brain.

Life and information

According to Shimizu, living systems are constantly generating information (Shimizu 1989). He says that life was previously thought to be specific to the individual, but the invention of the microscope allowed the discovery that individuals are made up of cells, each of which has an independent life of its own. Recently we have been forced to think of life in terms of systems that are higher than the individual: the ecosystem, society, and civilization, for example. Additionally many individuals, enterprises, societies, and nations are being forced to address the difficult question of what life is. Their answers are becoming an important factor in human activities.

What is life? Shimizu basically approaches the question from the standpoint of natural science. He believes that the totality of the nature of existence is far beyond the capacity of natural science to understand, but feels there are many aspects of the problem that only natural science, with its assumption that living systems are composed of material, can solve.

Shimizu says that the question of why a particular consciousness is living in the universe at a specific time can never be solved by natural science. Also the question of whether a world unanalysable by natural science exists is neither verifiable nor deniable by natural science. The difficult question of what constitutes life is also not solvable by scientific thinking (atomism) alone. In light of these beliefs, Shimizu thinks that solving the problem of the nature of living, including mankind and civilization, will require a revolution in science, the establishment of a new life science with new options and new methods.

There are two states for a body, living and dead. Shimizu claims that the essential difference betwen the two is represented in the global characteristic of the molecular assembly of the body, in a manner similar to the three states of gas, liquid, and solid. His reasons for this are that:

1 Large numbers of individual elements in the form of atoms and molecules are assembled to construct the body.
2 The characteristics of the assembly cannot be determined from the sum of the characteristics of the individual molecules. Because

of the large numbers of molecules involved, the way they are assembled has a strong effect, and non-linear factors become dominant.

These assemblies are characterized by the phenomenon of phase transition, where each phase has a distinguishable global state, such as appears in the gaseous, liquid, and solid states of water. Phase transition is defined by Shimizu as the change from one global state to another, with the changes occurring all at once and discontinuously. Thus the change of a living body into a dead body can be interpreted as a phase transition.

The reason phase transitions occur discontinuously is that interactions between elements induce a dynamic cooperation between the individual elements, a kind of self-organization.

ASPECTS OF INFORMATION AS A PHENOMENON

Cybernetics

The cybernetics of Wiener

The first emergence of information in science came with Wiener's cybernetics (Wiener 1948), which was the result of the collaboration of Wiener, a mathematician, and Rosenblueth, a physician, with additional input from others including Shannon, who is famous for defining the bit as a measure of information. To explain cybernetics, Wiener used the metaphor of steering a ship by using changes in wind and sea conditions to determine the corrections needed to remain on a given course.

The principal concept in cybernetics is feedback, a concept from Control Engineering where a control centre controls by using information about the current state of affairs. Feedback in cybernetics is restraining and negative, working against deviation from a given objective.

Sakai (1988) points out that information science is difficult to study because subject, object, and environment affect each other (see p. 36). However the authors believe that at least in mathematical models cybernetics has almost solved this problem. To understand this let us return to Wiener's metaphor of steering a ship. The steerer is the subject, the ship is the object, and the wind and sea conditions are the environment. The object is affected by both the actions of the subject and the environment. Therefore, if a specific action is repeated by the subject, it may result in a different effect on the object, because the object is also affected by the environment. Therefore, in order to control the object, the subject must constantly consider the results of previous actions as a way of estimating the effect of the environment. That is, the subject utilizes feedback of information, and this process has been satisfactorily modelled by mathematicians.

The second cybernetics of Maruyama

Maruyama's position is that, while the negative feedback of cybernetics explained much, positive feedback is effective in explaining previously difficult to understand phenomena, such as social and living beings (Maruyama 1963). He said that cybernetics was deviation counteracting and positive feedback was deviation amplifying. To distinguish the two, he termed the former first cybernetics and the latter second cybernetics.

Maruyama pointed out that second cybernetics could solve many previously difficult problems that seemed to violate both the law of causality and the second law of thermodynamics.

Maruyama uses the growth of a city in an agricultural plain as an example of this sort of problem. At first all areas on the plain are equally suitable for agriculture, so the initial farmer selects the site for his farm by chance. This becomes the initial kick. Other farmers then come and start farms nearby. Eventually one of the farmers opens a tool shop, which becomes a meeting place for the farmers. Later a restaurant is built, then other stores and gradually a village develops. More farmers then come because of the services offered in the village, and they generate an increase in agricultural activity which necessitates the development of industry, and the village gradually becomes a city.

This well-known process contains some theoretically interesting implications for Maruyama. First the initial location was chosen randomly. Any one location was as good as another, but once a site was chosen, the plain that was orginally homogeneous became heterogeneous. Historians studying the development of the city would find no geographical reasons for this specific place to have been selected in preference to other places. Maruyama says the cause does not lie in the initial conditions or in some kick start. The cause lies in deviation amplifying, mutual and positive feedback. This process of deviation amplification and mutual causality is morpho-generative.

This finding that deviation amplifying, not the initial conditions, generated the resulting city with its complex structure causes Maruyama to modify the law of causation: the same initial conditions can result in different results. Also the gradually progressing increase in heterogeneity as the city replaced the plain represents a decrease in entropy, a violation of the second law of thermodynamics, and a change in the direction of lower probability which is against the law of causation.

New supplements for cybernetics

From a mathematical point of view, a problem with the positive feedback model is that its solution shows only the transition between stable states without specifying the states themselves. One solution to this problem is the concept of the positive and negative feedback network which was introduced by Maruyama. Such a network is characterized by its various mutual-cause loops, where each loop contains elements with positive and negative feedback so that the loop is either deviation amplifying or deviation counteracting. However, this is still insufficient for solving all the relevant problems of Informatics. Therefore, the authors, based primarily on the work of Hata, feel that cybernetics needs to be supplemented even further. The proposed supplements are discussed in the next section. We should also mention at this point that a fuller exposition of Informatics, something which is beyond the scope of this chapter, draws on Maruyama's later work. This extensive work includes his formulation of the concept of various epistemological types underlying different causal models, and his studies of the meaning of the contents of communication in terms of such considerations as relevance, criticality, context, situation, intention, manipulation, deception, insinuation, and epistemological framework (Maruyama 1991, see also Morin 1992).

Information changes discontinuously

The snowman model

First, we will consider Shimizu's discussion of what we shall call the snowman model. A snowman is relatively stable in its normal orientation where its centre of gravity remains in the vertical space between the original fulcrum and the fulcrum after the force is applied. Within a wide range of forces, this condition will pertain and the snowman will return to or near its initial position following the removal of the external force, a situation described by first cybernetics. However, if we invert the snowman, even a small force will move its centre of gravity outside this area and the snowman becomes unstable and will fall in the direction of even a small applied force. This situation is described by second cybernetics. It also shows Marauyama's initial kick effect. Shimizu says that in the first case, randomly applied forces generate a symmetrically directed state, but in the second case a randomly applied force results in the selection of some definite transition and the establishment of a new global condition.

Modelling of unstable states

The normal position of the snowman discussed above can be modelled by a stable thermo-dynamic state (called a steady state in physics) and the inverted position by an unstable state.

We will now reconsider the snowman model in terms of phase transitions of these thermo-dynamic states. As discussed above, because of the interactions between elements, phase transitions occur discontinuously and abruptly. An additional characteristic of phase transition is order. What changes is not the characteristics of the individual elements but the degree of order in the assembly of the elements. For example, the strength of a magnet is indicated by the degree of order in the assembly of magnetized atoms.

Thermodynamics shows that a high level of order occurs at low temperatures, particularly near absolute zero. This is exemplified by the orderly structure of crystals at very low temperatures.

Now let us consider Maruyama's example of a city growing on the plain. At first the plain was homogeneous, so its entropy was nearly infinite and the degree of order was low. The farmer could choose any place to start a farm, but once the place was chosen (the initial kick), the city grew up and the plain became heterogeneous, entropy decreased, and the degree of order increased.

It is clear that the plain example is quite different from the case of the crystal whose temperature is near absolute zero. As Maruyama pointed out, the second law of thermodynamics is not effective in the city example. Shimizu believes that the process is induced because the system is in a thermo-dynamically unbalanced state.

Generally speaking such a system demands the inflow of free energy, or material supplying energy, and an outflow of entropy (heat) or decomposed material. In this example the inflow comes from people who enter the village and work. The outflow comes from the trash and garbage they discard.

Such an open system, to use the same term as Shimizu used, is connected to two different thermal sources (a source of energy and an absorbent for entropy) and, since neither source is in equilibrium with the system, the system remains unstable, remembering that our term stable is called constant by physicists.

Self-organization (self-formation of dynamic order)

We will use another example of an open system, convection in a liquid, to investigate self-organization. First we construct the system by placing a liquid in a vessel, and then applying heat from the bottom and allowing heat to escape from the top. Now consider what happens. The molecules in contact with the bottom experience a rise in temperature, causing movement which tends to lower the density. This movement is the rapid, random movement of individual molecules and has an average velocity of zero. On the other hand, the liquid contacting the top of the vessel experiences a decrease in temperature, a decrease in random movement of the individual molecules, and a rise in density. Energy transfer now equalizes the density throughout the vessel. This is due to the law of increasing entropy and the energy is conducted through the mechanism of molecular collisions. This is heat conduction.

Heat, or the random movement of individual molecules, with an average velocity of zero, can spread faster than a collective movement of the molecules, so at first the process takes place without collective movement, because the energy is transferred before the molecules can move collectively.

If we increase the temperature gap between the top and bottom, the energy transmitted by heat conduction can no longer meet the demands of the energy gap because of the limited capacity of heat conduction. Now, because of this insufficiency, the density increases substantially at the top and decreases at the bottom. The viscosity of the liquid causes this state to continue for a while, but when the temperature reaches a threshold value, we observe a phase transition to a new steady state, just as we did in the snowman example. In this new state, called convection, the mechanism for energy transfer has the additional factor of particle flow (systematic collective molecular motion) rather than only the previous heat flow (random molecular motion). This new state dominates because it is more efficient. It results in a decrease in entropy if we consider only the open system within the vessel.

When a system is in a steady state, it may undergo some changes causing entropy to increase, but it will never change so that entropy decreases. Additionally, when the system is below the threshold temperature any collective particle motion is suppressed by the system's entropy. Once the threshold motion is passed, however, the mechanical forces induced by the top heavy distribution of liquid density become superior, causing entropy to decrease and instability to increase.

Shimizu calls the phenomenon of change to a new global order with an accompanying decrease in entropy, self-formation of dynamic order, or self-organization, and distinguishes it from the static order of a crystal (Shimizu 1989). Thus the self-organization problem in the cybernetic positive feedback model can be eliminated by adding the concepts of phase transition and self-organization.

Dynamic cooperation and the holonic loop

In exploring the concept of self-organization of dynamic order as a characterisitic of life, Shimizu develops the idea of dynamic cooperation and the holonic loop (Shimizu 1989). We will explore these through his example of the laser, an instrument which uses chemical processes to produce light that is more highly ordered than light from normal sources.

In relation to the emission of light, there are two molecular states that are of interest, ground and excited. When ground state molecules absorb energy, they become excited, emit light, and return to the ground state. There are two ways that light emission from the molecule can take place, naturally or induced by light from the outside in which case the generated light has the same frequency as the inducing light.

In normal situations, molecules are mostly in the ground state with only a few molecules in the excited state. However, by using the energy from chemical processes, the energy level of the molecules can be pumped up, so that excited molecules vastly outnumber the stable molecules. These excited molecules are heavy in the same sense that the inverted snowman was, so when some event triggers light emission from one molecule, this light in turn induces light emission from the other unstable molecules. Since this is excited emission, the light will all be of the same frequency and phase. In a real sense we can say that the molecules cooperate to emit the phased light. Shimizu defines this as 'dynamic cooperation'.

There are two logical levels involved in the generation of light in a chemical laser. The first is the micro-level where the energy absorption occurs. As we have seen, these reactions produce the phased light, the strength of which depends on the rate of these absorptions (the number of molecules emitting light per unit of time) which must be above a certain lower limit. Together these micro-level reactions determine the macro-level characteristics of the laser system, which is the second level. However, the intensity of the phased light at the macro-level controls the micro-level absorptions since the rate depends upon the intensity of the laser light. In other words, there is an interactive feedback loop between the micro-level (absorption) and the macro-level (the whole system including the absorptions) by means of a self-catalytic reaction triggered by the phased light quanta.

Shimizu thinks that the most important feedback loop in living beings is between the macro- and micro-levels, and this loop is called the 'holonic loop'.

Systems containing information

The general characteristics of information

Natural Science is based on observable measures, but if information obtained by such measures does not prove to be effective, it is not recognized as 'information'. Information can be defined only together with a system which can generate effective results from the given information. Therefore, in order to consider information, we must first consider systems in which information appears.

Information must generate some observable effect (some kind of choice among apparently random events or the emergence of order), so a system in which information appears must have two or more realizable macro-states (states distinguishable to external observation), the distribution of which cannot be predicted prior to receiving the information.

In such a system, there must be a kind of self-formation of dynamic order, a self-organization.

Muscular contracting motions

The thermo-dynamic mechanism of the motion of muscular contraction is a good example for understanding the importance of self-formation of dynamic order, or self-organization, in a living body. Shimizu has explored this mechanism and the following discussion is based on his work.

The muscles are made up of fibres and their contraction, which begins after reception of an electro-chemical signal from the brain, is generated by a relative sliding motion of the fibres which, according to the generally accepted position, is caused by a systematic motion of molecules where each molecule moves independently. Shimizu claims that the molecules must cooperate to make the dynamic order, saying that this is an example of the previously mentioned 'dynamic cooperation'. The standard position says that the motion of living beings can be reduced to the motion of an element. Shimizu's position is that the motion of a living being should be thought of as one of the global characteristics of the system. The difference between these two positions is truly enormous.

Shimizu has demonstrated the existence of dynamic cooperation and a holonic loop between the individual molecular motion (micro-) and the sliding motion of the fibres (macro-) in the case of muscular movement.

The motion of muscular fibres is similar in mechanism to the chemical laser, except that in the laser the change is triggered by a random event and the induced phase is randomly determined, whereas for muscle the change is triggered by the information in the electro-chemical stimulus and the direction of change is definitively determined by the structure of the muscular fibres.

Field information

In a holonic loop, information is transmitted from the micro- to the macro-levels by molecular motion and from the macro- to the micro-levels by field information, which is based on how each molecule determines its own motion. In muscle there are two kinds of structure: the first is static and encoded with the rules for producing the field information; the second is the dynamic pattern of motion by the group of molecules, which changes as the field information varies with the contracting speed. The existence of the dynamic structures means that the molecules originally have various degrees of inner freedom and that one of them is chosen by the field information according to the speed of contraction. Thus, the field information can selectively generate one of the various potential orders with which the system can self-organize.

Kankeishi (self-organizing unit)

Shimizu proposes modelling the above situation with a generative unit processor that produces the mutual relationships. He calls this the *kankeishi*. We might call it the self-organizing unit, but in this chapter will use the Japanese term. The *kankeishi* must have various degrees of inner freedom which can be selected by the mutual relationship. According to Shimizu, researchers tell us that most of the solid structure of the molecular assembly of the muscles has rules, written into the static network structure, for producing field information. These rules describe the dynamic connection between molecules in relation to the whole motion speed.

Shimizu says that studies of the neuron in nervous systems have shown that the neuron can change according to its state. It is, then, one of these changes that is selected by the cooperative process described above. As the neurons change, the whole character of the network changes as in the phase transitions discussed above. This means that the static structure of the network functions transitionally between the dynamic states. An example is the walking pattern of four-footed animals, like the horse or the cat, which changes autonomously from 'walk' to 'trot' to 'gallop' as the animal's speed increases.

Shimizu defines the *kankeishi* as a unit processor having a multi-valued, cooperative and competitive character. The *kankeishi* is itself a mini-system and may generate information. An assembly of *kankeishi* can produce a system that produces not only multi-valued tactics, but also multi-valued strategies and objectives. An example of this is the brain.

SELF-ORGANIZATION BETWEEN THE WHOLE (COMPREHENSIVE ENTITY) AND THE PARTS (SUBORDINATE ELEMENTS)

In terms of information, the questions of how the whole can be made from the parts, how parts are made from the whole, and what is the reaction between these two kinds of information can be approached in two different ways: social science and natural science. These two approaches are discussed below.

The social science approach by Kurimoto

The theory of hierarchical levels

Below we discuss an example offered by Kurimoto (1980) in order to explore the idea of hierarchical levels.

When we look at the stones and flowers on the hill near the Parthenon in Athens, the stones and flowers are not 'Greek'. We can, however, while looking at these objects change our focus, altering the level of abstraction of our thought, and look at things that are 'Greek'. What we have done is to use our attention and our inner integrative ability to build a meaning, a fiction, wherein the observed particulars have no such meaning in and of themselves.

In this case the object that we want to sense, to focus on, is 'Greek', which we can call the comprehensive entity and the stones and flowers near the Parthenon can be called the particulars in the comprehensive entity. The particulars are observed directly and for a distinct period of time, but we cannot directly observe 'Greek'. Here 'Greek' functions like a grammar in that it is a controlling principle for the parts, and of course we can never observe a grammar directly. We can only observe its manifestation through its particulars. To summarize, the way to know a comprehensive entity is to look at the definite particulars first, and then to change the focus to a higher level of abstraction.

Our knowing of a comprehensive entity always consists of moving the focus from the particulars at a low level to the comprehensive entity as a principle at a higher level. Kurimoto calls this the 'from-to relation', in which the source and the destination are lower and higher levels within a hierarchy of levels. Actually, any level within the hierarchy may present a comprehensive entity, e.g., we may take the stones and flowers above to be the comprehensive entity, then the particulars might be the molecules making up the stones and flowers.

Aspects of meaning

Generally speaking, we can extract meaning from the world in two different ways. We use one of these ways when we recognize a face. First we look at the specific features of the face and then focus on the face as a whole. We move from particulars to the comprehensive entity which all lie within the same logical space. The second way occurs when we use a probe or tool to investigate something which cannot be directly accessed by the senses. Here the particulars are inferred from the reactions of the probe or tool, so the particulars and the comprehensive entity lie in different logical spaces. This second way of extracting meaning is also commonly employed in the learning of skills.

Both of these types of meaning arise from tacit knowing. The second type, however, clearly shows that personal inner processes participate in the personal formation of information. These non-conscious processes, which are mobilized every time we give meaning to something, extend down to the lowest reaches of the hierarchy of logical levels contained in the body. At this level we find DNA, which through evolution has developed an almost limitless capacity for storing information. The existence of the second type also suggests that humans have the ability to probe inside themselves to understand these processes.

Aspects of tacit knowing

For Kurimoto, tacit knowing is the building of meaning by looking at the particulars and then refocusing to construct a comprehensive entity. It consists of four phases: functional, phenomenal, semantic, and ontological. The functional phase consists of observing the particulars and metaphorically turning towards the comprehensive entity. The phenomenal phase is a static phase where the particulars are seen as subsidiary parts of a whole. In the semantic phase the particulars are semantically positioned within the whole. Finally in the ontological phase the comprehensive entity is seen as existing independently. These phases can be thought of as phase transitions within the act of tacit knowing.

Imagination and intuition

Kurimoto understood Polanyi to say that the processes and mechanisms of the physis are located directly under the psyche, but that the physical organs and organ systems are never directly controlled by the psyche. The psyche can be thought of as the meaning of the physis. We commonly think that we actualize the making of meaning directly through the body as when sensing the world with our hands or feet, but this is not correct. The mechanisms of the physis are located between the body and psyche.

Polanyi thought that all behaviour of the body was the result of arousal of internal systems by prior functioning of the imagination or intuition. This arousal allows the lower level particulars, which are not pre-arranged in relation to the upper level, to restructure themselves as subsidiaries to the comprehensive entity.

When we are aware of the physical movement of the body, we often focus on the movement as the object of our senses. Sometimes, however, we focus on the result of the movement (a hammered nail, for instance) rather than the movement itself. In this case the movement will be a logical level lower than the whole and will become one of the particulars.

The natural science approach by Shimizu

The brain has active parts

Shimizu studied the processes of sight and took the position that cognition is the interpretation of signals from the external world by the brain. This assumes that the brain contains autonomous and active parts as opposed to the traditional view that it is static. Shimizu called the parts the 'ego' or 'symbolic field of the brain' and the autonomous functions 'symbolic dynamics' (Shimizu 1989).

The symbolic field generates, integrates, and stores symbolic elements which have elementary meanings. These symbols are encoded and stored as various inner dynamics (rhythmical activity) of nerve *kankeishi* groups in the field. The activated inner state is determined by the self-organized dynamic connections in the network of the *kankeishi* assembly.

The inner states of the *kankeishi* dynamically encode various meanings. The dynamic connections between *kankeishi* determine the activated inner state dynamic order within the whole *kankeishi* assembly.

In other words, the meaning held in the individual *kankeishi* is determined by the self-organization of the dynamic order in the whole assembly of *kankeishi* and there is a mutual interdependence between the whole and the parts, just as there is an interdependence between the meaning as a whole and its parts.

Symbolic space in the brain

The symbols of high grade meaning are generated as self-organized dynamic orders among the *kankeishi*. The symbolic dynamics take place in the symbolic space within the brain. This metaphoric space manipulates meaning as opposed to the information space which handles the sensory output representing the external world.

The dynamic connections between *kankeishi* within the assembly and the rules for selecting the meaning (inner) state of the *kankeishi* corresponding to a grammer, defined in a broad sense. Symbolic dynamics are influenced by the output form of the signals from the outside, emotions, and past memories as well as the complex, inherited construction of the brain. Long-term memory consists of these symbols.

Signals from the external world are dissolved into raw elemental information having no meaning. This information is sent to the sense field of the brain, the sight sense field, for example, where a network of neuron *kankeishi* makes the raw information mutually interrelated and changes it into some number of basically settled (characteristic) signals. Then these signals are given a meaning and integrated with symbolic elements to make the whole meaning. If such meaning-giving fails, a new symbol may be generated.

Kankeishi perpetually generate information

Field information flows in a top-down direction from environment to system to *kankeishi*, passing the states of the environment and system to the elemental *kankeishi*. Information generated by the *kankeishi* flows in the opposite direction, passing information from the individual *kankeishi* states to the system and to the environment. The result is information flow within a loop. This locates the influence of the *kankeishi* in not only the system but also the environment.

Shimizu thinks that it is important to create a new science dealing with the relation between environment, system, and elements in relation to environmental complexity. Such a system would decipher field information sent from the environment to human *kankeishi*.

CONCLUSION

In this chapter we have considered some of the basic aspects of Informatics, a new science dealing with the study of information as meaning, which draws on both natural and social science for its tools and is not limited by any previously defined area of study.

The basic thesis of Informatics is that information is integrally related to life and it is concerned with the meaning of information rather than merely with the carrier. The basic tools that are currently available are a new supplemented form of cybernetics and principle of self-organization.

Our cybernetics includes both Wiener's first cybernetics and Maruyama's second cybernetics as well as the supplementary ideas of phase transitions through dynamic cooperation and the holonic loop, which provide for self-organization and lead directly to the model of *kankeishi* as the processors. Informatics also includes the theory of hierarchical levels from social sciences in relation to the understanding of meaning.

This is not the present limit of our understanding of Informatics. It is merely the basics. Hata's work (Hata 1992) has already discussed the relation between the ego and the world (Umesau 1988, Yoro

1989, Shimizu 1989): meaning as dealt with by natural science (Yoro 1989); the difference between natural and social science (Kurimoto 1980, Yoro 1989); knowledge, models, and software (Sayeki 1983, Sakai 1988, Shimizu 1989); specific characteristics of information-value, openness, and closedness (Umesao 1988, Sakai 1988, Shimizu 1989); the organization theory of networking; information organizing theories (Sakai 1988); the information oriented society (Kurimoto 1980, Umesao 1988); and epistemological heterogeneity (Maruyama 1991) and the paradigm of complexity (Morin 1992). We hope to have the opportunity to present these in detail in a future paper.

REFERENCES

Chomsky, N. (1957) *Syntactic Structures*, The Hague: Mouton & Co.

Dilts, R., Grinder, J., Bandler, R. and DeLozier, J. (1980) *Neuro-linguistic Programming*, Cupertino, CA: Meta Publications.

Hata, H. (1992) *Johogakku Josetsu* (Introduction to Informatics), Tokyo: Chuo Bijutsu Kenkyujo.

Hiromatsu, W. (1982) *Sonzai to Imi* (Being and Meaning), Tokyo: Iwanami Shoten.

Korzybski, A. (1980) *Science and Sanity*, New York: Institute Censeman.

Kurimoto, S. (1980) *Imi to Seimei* (Meaning and Life), Tokyo: Seidosha.

Machalup, F. and Mansfield, U. (1983) *The Study of Information*, New York: John Wiley & Sons.

Maruyama, M. (1963) 'The Second Cybernetics', *American Scientist*, 51, 1963.

—— (1991) 'Epistemological Heterogeneity and Subsedure: Individual and Social Processes', *Communication and Cognition*, 24, pp. 255–72.

Morin, E. (1992) 'The Concept of System and the Paradigm of Complexity', in M. Maruyama (ed.) *Context and Complexity*, Berlin: Springer-Verlag.

Neisser, U. (1967) *Cognitive Science*, New York: Appleton.

Okazawa, K. (1989) *Johogakku Kogi Noto <3>* (Lecture note *<3>* of Informatics), Tokyo: Keibundo.

Polanyi, M. (1969) *Knowing and Being*, Chicago: University of Chicago Press.

Sakai, T. (1988) *Senryakuteki Sozo no tame no Joho Kagaku* (Information Science for Strategic Creation), Tokyo: Chuokoronsha.

Sayeki, Y. (1983) Ninchi-Kagaku no Tanjo (Birth of Cognition Science), in K. Fuchi (ed.) *Ninchi-Kagaku e no Shotai* (Invitation to Cognition Science), Tokyo: NHK Shuppan Kyokai.

Shimizu, H. (1989) *Seimei wo Torae-naosu* (A New Approach to Life), Tokyo: Chuokoronsha.

Umesao T. (1963) 'Joho Sangyo Ron' (The Information Industries), *Hoso Asahi*, 104, pp. 4–17.

—— (1988) *Joho no Bunmeigaku* (The Science of Information Cultures), Tokyo: Chuokoronsha.

Wiener, N. (1948) *Cybernetics, or Control and Communication in the Animal and the Machine*, New York: John Wiley.

Yoro, T. (1989) *Yuinoh Ron* (Brainism), Tokyo: Seidosha.

3 Epistemological types and creative environment

Magoroh Maruyama

SUPPRESSION OF EPISTEMOLOGICAL TYPES AND MENTAL HEALTH CONSEQUENCES

Heterogeneity of epistemological types among individuals exists in each country. Any epistemological type that is found in one country is found in other countries. Cultural differences consist in the way a type becomes dominant and utilizes, suppresses or transforms other types. Individuals, whose epistemological types differ from the dominant type, cope with the situation in various ways: (1) find a niche where the dominant type can be avoided; (2) camouflage one's own type; (3) become able to function in both the dominant type and one's own type; (4) reversible repression of one's own type into the unconscious; (5) irreversible repression; (6) become a rebel or a reformer; and (7) emigrate.

All these conscious or unconscious processes involve various degrees of stress, frustration, dissatisfaction or distortion of mental function, which can be considered as primary effects. Moreover, individuals whose epistemological types differ from the dominant type are discriminated against in job selection. Currently there is no equal opportunity for different epistemological types. The result is not only poor mental health for the individual but also waste of human resources for the society. There are secondary effects.

Epistemological types and their mixtures have been discussed in detail elsewhere (Maruyama 1974, 1979, 1980, 1981, 1993). Among the numerous types, the following four are found most frequently. Some of their characteristics are set out in Table 3.1. (For fuller characterization, see Maruyama 1980.)

These four types and mixtures between them account for about two thirds of the population in most of the cultures.

These four and other epistemological types are called 'mindscape types' (Maruyama 1980). This theory may appear to be a typology but

Table 3.1 Epistemological types

H-type	*I-type*	*S-type*	*G-type*
homogenist	heterogenist	heterogenist	heterogenizing
universalist	nominalist	mutualist	mutualizing
hierarchical	isolationist	interactive	interactive
classifying	randomizing	contextual	contextualizing
sequential	haphazard	simulataneous	simultaneous
one truth	subjective	poly-objective	poly-objective
eternal	temporary	stability	evolution
ranking	uniquing	cooperative	cogenerative

its purpose and use lie in interrelating seemingly separate aspects of human activities such as organizational structure, policy formulation, decision process, architectural design, criteria of beauty, choice of theories, cosmology, etc. It is relational, rather than classificational, and partly learned. Different cultures and professions exercise different pressures for or against some types in the process of acculturation, socialization, ostracism, marginalization, etc. Individuals also exercise self-selection, internalization, sublimation, attrition, alienation, repression, identification, etc.

As can be seen, the mindscape types are quite different from the Jungian, Jaspersian and other psychological typologies. They represent diverse epistemological meta-types. Furthermore, these mindscape characteristics provide a link between seemingly separate activities such as decision process, criteria of beauty, choice of science theories, etc. It is also important to point out that these four types do *not* line up on one scale, *nor* do they fit in a two-by-two table. They are more like the four corners of a tetrahedron (a pyramid-like shape with a triangular bottom). If anything, H and I are two sides of a coin, while S and G are the two sides of a different coin. However, the line H-I is *not* parallel to the line S-G. Therefore they cannot be put in a two-by-two table.

The preceding list of the characteristics of four mindscape types serves as a projective test. One can tell the mindscape type of a person by the way he or she reacts to the list: (1) if the person notices that the list is not exhaustive and the categories are not mutually exclusive, and tries to make an exhaustive and mutually exclusive list, then he or she is of the H-type; (2) if the person rejects the list as completely irrelevant, then he/she is of the I-type; (3) and if the person interprets the list as changeable depending on situations and circumstances, then the person is of the S-type or G-type.

The specific and concrete ways in which the mindscape types manifest themselves in various aspects of our thoughts and behaviour have been discussed in detail (Maruyama 1980, 1981, 1991a, 1993). Some examples are given in the next section.

Human values

(H) Values can be rank-ordered from the highest to the successively lower. Furthermore, the ranking obtained is valid for all cultures because human nature is universal. Values can be classified into neat categories. Universally valid scales of 'quality of life' can be constructed and applied to all individuals and all cultures. Personal integrity consists in adhering to higher values regardless of the situation and the context.

(I) Each person has his or her own value system, and each value is independent of other values. The meaning of 'quality of life' varies from individual to individual. Personal integrity consists in adhering to one's own value system regardless of what others say or think.

(S) Values are interrelated and cannot be separated into independent categories or rank-ordered. The meaning of each value depends on contexts and cultures, and cannot be universally defined. How a person behaves or should behave is determined by his or her relations with others, i.e., by the social situation and context. Likewise, the person's opinion is a contextual opinion, neither an abstract categorical principle, nor an individually isolated point of view which disregards interpersonal context. Personal integrity consists of behaviour and opinion which reflect the social situation and context. This is often misinterpreted as inconsistency, dishonesty or deception by those who have an H-type mindscape or an I-type mindscape.

(G) Similar to (S). However, values interact and generate new values and new meanings. Values, needs and meanings are redefined as new contexts arise. Personal integrity consists in inventing new patterns of interactive behaviour which generate benefit in new situations and contexts.

The concept of the individual

(H) The concept of the individual has many parallels with the concept of space (Maruyama 1981). In H-type mindscapes, the individual has boundary, identity and specialization, fits in a category and successively smaller subcategories, and occupies a position in a hierarchy. He can be defined in terms of the category, subcategories, specialization and hierachical position.

(I) Uniqueness independent of others.

(S) The individual is a node of interrelations with others around him/her. Each has a special way and meaning in relation with others, which becomes his/her individuality. Without such relations, there is no individuality. For example, young Japanese people tend to form groups. In each group, the individual fills a special function such as a car expert, a camera expert, a music expert, etc., for the purpose of being useful to other members and for being appreciated by them (Maruyama 1985b). There is no absolute leader: each becomes a leader for specific activities. This type of individuality is others-oriented: the specilization is developed to fill the needs of the group. Furthermore, it is convertible: it is easily changed when needs change. Such a concept of the individual as a node of relations with others has been named 'aidaschaft' (Maruyama 1984) in contrast to gemeinschaft und gesellschaft.

(G) Similar to (S) with the following differences. In (G), one must be useful as an explorer, path-finder and innovator. Each collects new information, checks on new trends, etc. There is a large market to meet this need of young people: there are small stores, small restaurants, etc., purposely inconspicuous, camouflaged as ordinary houses or something else, located in hidden alleys, which keep changing their merchandise, interior decoration, etc., to give the young people the excitement of discovery (Maruyama 1985b). The merchandise is not arranged neatly in shelves, but is mixed and piled in heaps. These stores are located in the periphery of busy areas.

Responsibility

(H) Responsibility is neatly divided among individuals without overlapping. To go beyond one's responsibility is considered to be trespassing, for example making a suggestion for another department.

(I) Each person sets his/her own sphere of responsibility.

(S) Responsibility is overlapping. For example, if there are five persons in a group, each takes 100 per cent responsibility for the work of the entire group, with the result that a total of 500 per cent is taken. In practical terms, each worker in an assembly line is capable of correcting errors which have been made by someone preceding him/her. This results in high productivity. For example in the assembly lines of a car manufacturer in Sweden, the unit in which an error was found must be taken out of the line and sent back to where the error was made. In modern car manufacturing, different types of cars are sequenced mixed on the assembly line: one car to go to France with yellow headlights; next car for England for left-hand driving, etc. Parts that are fed into the assembly line must also be sequenced accordingly. Taking one unit out of the sequence involves readjustment of the parts lines, and is costly. On each spot on the assembly line, the work is paced to leave extra seconds between units. The Swedish workers do knitting or reading to pace the waiting period (so many stitches or so many lines of text until next unit arrives). The Japanese workers keep checking and double-checking the unit on which he/she has just finished working.

(G) Similar to (S).

Social, cultural and psychological processes

In any large society, it is possible to find all types of individual mindscapes. Cultural differences consist in the way some types become dominant and influence other types. Individuals of non-dominant types undergo various cultural, social and psychological transformation:

Niche-finding During periods when the mainstream type was H, for example, during the period of Gothic architecture with principles of hierarchy, unity by repetition of similar or identical forms, tension between points, extension of lines and surfaces, and opposition between mass and space, between masses as well as between spaces, or periods when H-type thinkers such as Descartes or Kant dominated. Under such circumstances, individuals with other mindscape types may channel their activities into fields such as painting where their types are accepted and respected.

Masking Individuals with non-dominant types may disguise their types and practise them in a camouflaged form.

Subsedure Some persons become capable of functioning in two patterns: their own pattern in a private life, and in the mainstream pattern in public or professional life. Persons in subsedure are biscapal.

Suppression The non-dominant types may become unconscious or latent in individuals, either by external pressures such as acculturation, socialization, ostracism, marginalization or indoctrination, or by internal processes such as repression, sublimation, internalization or identification, but they can still be reactivated under favourable conditions.

Loss If the suppression goes a step further, the individual may become incapable of reactivating his/her own pattern. There may be an age limit beyond which the transformation becomes irreversible. The age limit may vary from individual to individual: some become fixated at an early age, while others have a later age limit or no limit.

Difficulty of communication between types

As for the communication between different mindscape types, I have discussed the problems in several articles (Maruyama 1979, 1985a). There are many types of distortions which occur. Dimension reduction may produce an internally consistent explanation and consequently a delusion of perfect understanding. Autodox is the conversion of a counter-argument into a proof of one's own theory. Further, a person's autodox may enable opponents to argue that his autodox can be expected by their theories and therefore theirs are correct. But psychologically most damaging is unawareness of misunderstandings on both sides which later leads to feelings of having been deceived, betrayed or insulted. For example, the same statement 'small is beautiful' may be supported by four mindscape types on different unstated grounds. H-type mindscapes can support it on the reasoning that since the entire region is homogeneous, nothing is lost by dividing it into smaller units. The I-type can reason that since all parts are different, it makes sense to let them be isolated. The S-type and G-type can support it because they see heterogeneity in the region, but on an unstated assumption that the different parts interact for mutual benefit. In my work in urban and regional planning, I found it useful to sort out different mindscape types behind a seeming agreement, in order to avoid later resentments and hostilities resulting from the delusion of agreement. In other cases, seeming disagreement disappeared when both sides became aware of mindscape differences.

Mental health consequences

Individuals, whose mindscape types differ from the dominant type, experience various types and degrees of stress, frustration, dissatisfaction or distortion of mental function. If one is confined in a niche, he/she must live in a small psychological and social world. If one camouflages his/her own type, he/she must be always on guard. Even if one is able to operate in two mindscape types, he/she faces the frustration of not being understood by the dominant type. Repression of one's own type is unhealthy by itself. But it may become pathological when one becomes unable to tell what his/her own type really is, i.e., one assigns an incorrect truth value to himself/herself. This condition was considered to be shizophrenogenic (Bateson *et al.* 1956). But even when the condition is not so severe, it is very common among the individuals of nondominant epistemological types to feel lonely, misunderstood, unappreciated, unfairly treated, rejected, or to suffer from the feeling of failure or low self-esteem. Furthermore, in the school situation, if the teaching method is based on one epistemological type, children of other epistemological types may not learn well, and may be considered unintelligent.

CREATIVE ENVIRONMENT AND MENTAL HEALTH: COMPARISON OF DENMARK, SWEDEN, USA AND JAPAN

There are three *fallacies* regarding creative environment: (1) creativity as a cause of mental health or mental illness; (2) creative activities as a cure of mental illness; and (3) the same environment as uniformly creativity-conducive for all individuals.

Mental health is a matter of match or mismatch between the individual's own epistemological type and the type which happens to be dominant in the environment. Insanity is not inherent in creativity per se.

In my earlier work (Maruyama 1959) I pointed out that individuals with high communicative need in factual information exchange suffer in Denmark, but thrive in Sweden. Hendin (1964) pointed out that Swedes were performance-oriented while Danes were nurture-oriented, and consequently low performance was an important cause of suicide in Sweden, while loss of dependency relations such as death of a loved person was an important cause of suicide in Denmark.

In subsequent years I developed a theory based on epistemological heterogeneity among individuals in any given country, called 'mindscape theory' (Maruyama 1974, 1980, 1991a, 1993). In this chapter I would like to re-interpret the matter of mismatch, incorporating the concept of epistemological types.

In the Danish culture (Maruyama 1961) the main purpose of interpersonal communication in daily life is maintenance of familiar atmosphere and affect relations. For example a small group of friends often sit together in the same café, eating the same pastry week after week, making the same or similar gossip. Subtle variations are considered interesting. For example everyone in the group knows that Mr X ties his left shoe first, then his right shoe. One day he reverses the sequential order. This becomes a big news. Less subtle information is avoided because it may disturb the familiar atmosphere. It is impolite to explain things, because such an act assumes that someone is ignorant. It is also impolite to ask questions on anything beyond immediate personal concern, because the respondent might not know the answer. It is often considered aggressive to introduce new ideas. One prefers to repeat the same or similar old jokes. Discussion on international politics or economics was a taboo in the 1960s and 1970s except in marginal enclaves which were niches for those who avoid the mainstream mindscape type. In the late 1980s and the 1990s this taboo may have been broken, because Denmark became involved in questions on the EC. Safe topics of intellectual conversation were and still are art, literature and music, on which one can disagree without embarrassment, because people are expected to have different tastes. Even insults are made implicitly rather than explicitly. The finest insult is the one that is not suspected as an insult by the person who is insulted. It does not have to be understood by third persons. An insult which is not understood by anyone is the most refined insult. There are many tales. For example, a Danish family was travelling on a train in Italy. They delighted in insulting, in Danish, an ugly man sitting on the train. As the train pulled into Rome, the man came up and introduced himself as Danish. He was not angry. He was a Dane, and understood the psychology of Danes. He probably shared their delight vicariously.

In contrast in Sweden, the purpose of daily interpersonal conversation is transmission of new information or frank expression of feelings. One prefers to remain silent unless he/she has an important message, while in Denmark one must keep talking. If you have a stomach ache, in Denmark you should not mention it. In Sweden you mention it and they will later ask you how you feel. In the US someone will give you a medication and everybody forgets about it. In Japan, others may talk about their experience of a stomach ache.

The dominant mainstream mindscape in Sweden is a mixture of H- and G-mindscape types, while an S-type with a shade of I-type characterizes the Danish culture. Other types either form their own enclaves or emigrate. Peter Freuchen, a Danish explorer who lived among Inuits and died in Alaska, said that all Vikings had left Denmark. In 1980s I interviewed workers from many countries working in a large factory in Sweden. Among them was a foreman from Denmark. He was happy there, and said that there were two kinds of Danes in the factory: those who liked to live in Sweden and those who did not, and the latter went back to Denmark after a short period (Maruyama 1994a). Søren Kierkegaard was very Danish in his lonely sufferings, but was very un-Danish because he expressed them. Actually, he is appreciated more by foreigners than by Danes. He was of I-type mixed with H-type. For him, interpersonal communication was impossible except through God, while Danes say: 'I do not understand myself. Why should I try to understand others?'

Creativity consists in generating new patterns. Genuine new patterns, different from new combination of old patterns, occur by interaction among heterogeneous elements as demonstrated in the second cybernetics (Maruyama 1963). A fallacious notion that randomness is a source of creativity is held by a considerable number of present-day European architects and music composers (Maruyama 1981) and North American art teachers (Maruyama 1972, 1974). Randomness is the opposite of pattern (Shannon and Weaver 1949).

Interaction of ideas necessary for creativity can occur either among heterogeneous individuals (Maruyama 1989) or the mind of one person with a G-type mindscape (Maruyama 1972, 1974, 1980, 1989). Even persons who can generate new patterns within their own mind can benefit greatly by interaction with heterogeneous individuals. In addition to creativity per se, creative individuals need to channel their output, not only for income but also for the feeling of accomplishment, freedom of expression, and appreciation by others. A creative individual who is forced to be isolated or deprived of opportunities for interaction and/or outlet can easily feel that his/her lifetime work has been wasted and there is no meaning in life. This, of course, causes mental health problems.

Deprivation of opportunities occurs frequently, and one must say regularly, when the individual's mindscape type differs from the dominant 'mainstream' type. In North America, monopoly is prohibited in business. However, in academic departments, dominance by one theory or one methodology often perpetuates and reinforces itself by their hiring procedures. There is no anti-monopoly law, epistemological equal opportunity or fair employment practice (Maruyama 1992) from the point of view of epistemological types. In this sense the North American academic system is of H-type, even though there are many G-type individuals in it. On the other hand in Japanese academia, its overprotective 'kindergarten' mentality and over-organization act as a disincentive and deterrent to creative vitality. The Japanese academic system is of S-type, and G-type individuals prefer to work in foreign countries.

Edgar Morin describes (Morin 1987) how, in the European academic and intellectual environment, different theories oppose one another without annihilating any opponent. In the USA, the situation is entirely different. Fair employment and equal opportunity regulations exist with regard to race, sex and religion. Vacancies must be advertised widely to attract applicants of all races, sexes and religions. However, very often the person to fill the position has already been chosen, and the advertisement is only a pretence. The job description is written in such a way as to fit exactly the person, but exclude other possible applicants. A problem occurs when some other applicants show up who meet the job description. Therefore a job description often includes an escape clause such as 'and otherwise to meet the specific needs of the department' (Maruyama 1992). Hence the fair employment practice is circumvented even with regard to race, sex and religion. With regard to epistemological types, monopoly is practised quite openly. A sociology department debated whether it should fill a vacancy with a Marxist or an anti-Marxist. Applicants who were neither Marxist nor anti-Marxist were not considered at all (Maruyama 1978).

With regard to opportunities for publication in research journals, the theoretical and methodological monopoly is even more accentuated. The same is often true with regard to the opportunities to present papers in conferences. Individuals with non-dominant epistemological types are deprived of opportunities for outlet, communication and interaction.

If there is no academic anti-monopoly law, there are plenty of what is equivalent to non-tariff barriers against interdisciplinary work (Maruyama 1992). One of them is disciplinary contents requirement (Maruyama 1991b) which is an academic counterpart of the local contents requirement in manufacturing by foreign firms. Foreign firms who want to manufacture automobiles in the USA are required to buy parts from American firms. This is the local contents requirement. If one wants to publish an article in an academic journal, it is usually required that a short review of other researchers' work in that field should be included in the article. This requirement is an obstacle to manuscript submission from outside. Interdisciplinary exchange is an important part of creativity. From this point of view, research journals in the USA constitute an unfavourable environment for creativity. Of 160 articles I published, most of them appeared in European journals.

In Japan, overprotection and overorganizing have prevailed, even though these tendencies are gradually decreasing. In conferences, there used to be almost no active discussion. The chairperson tended to use 20 or 30 minutes for his or her summary of what the speakers had said which everybody had heard. This is the kindergarten mentality. This left no time for discussion. If there was some time left, some character in the audience would stand up and give a long speech instead of asking a question.

Recently I was surprised by an incident. A European colleague told me that he planned to be in Tokyo in October for a conference, and would have one day free, and would like to visit my university. I therefore organized a colloquium on that day. On the day of his arrival in Tokyo, I called the conference office to check whether the participant had arrived. A man answered and accused me of not having obtained his permission. I did not know what he meant. He said that his university office was instrumental in issuing a document for my colleague's visa, and therefore his office was responsible for my colleague's whereabouts. He also added that it was an international common sense that I should obtain his permission. I said that I had lived in many countries and had never heard of such a requirement. He said that if I did not agree to his procedure, he would sue me. In order not to waste any more time, I sent him a fax requesting his permission. Then he became happy and gave me his permission. I wondered why he was so authority-hungry and possessive. As a possible reason I thought the conference might have paid my colleague's travel expenses. Later my colleague told me that the conference did not pay his expenses, but showed their authority to 'permit' him to attend the conference. This show of authority is rare nowadays in Japan, but still exists. The following example is still very common, however. Suppose some funds are made available to subsidize a publication or a research project. Then the priority is given to those who have never published before and have little motivation to do so. The authority would ask them 'Please publish' or 'Please do research'. Sometimes it is even explicitly announced that those who have published or done research are inelligible. Once the subsidy is given to an individual, his/her performance is seldom evaluated. Inclusion of unmotivated persons in research projects is proving to be a waste of money and supervisory time and effort. This practice acts as a disincentive and deterrent to creativity. But a mood for reform is gaining momentum. There may be some tangible change in the near future. There is, however, one important advantage in Japanese academia. It is free from domination by one epistemological type, one theory or one methodology. One can get anything published. Japanese publishers are willing to print a book if 500 copies of it can be sold in 3 years. In a way Alvin Toffler made use of this system. A part of his new book *War and Anti-war* had been published in Japan, which was translated back into English and was read by Pentagon officials much earlier than the publication of the book in the USA.

Each environment has its own characteristics. Whether it is mentally healthy or unhealthy depends on the individual mindscape types.

CONCLUSION

There are many individual types in each culture, and any individual type that is found in one culture can be found in other cultures overtly or covertly.

Cultural differences consist in the way some type becomes dominant and suppresses, transforms or utilizes other types. Individuals may find niches to avoid the dominant type, camouflage their own types, operate in two types (their own and the dominant type), repress their own by socialization, acculturation, identification, sublimation and other processes, or become reformers or emigrate. The repression may be reversible or irreversible. There may be individually varying age limits for reversibility. Some psychological aspects are more subject to suppression or repression than others. Epistemological types are vulnerable to political and educational pressure. Equal opportunity for different epistemological types is not yet practised in education and employment, resulting in mental health problems due to deprivation of social contacts and activities, self-devaluation and many types of frustration.

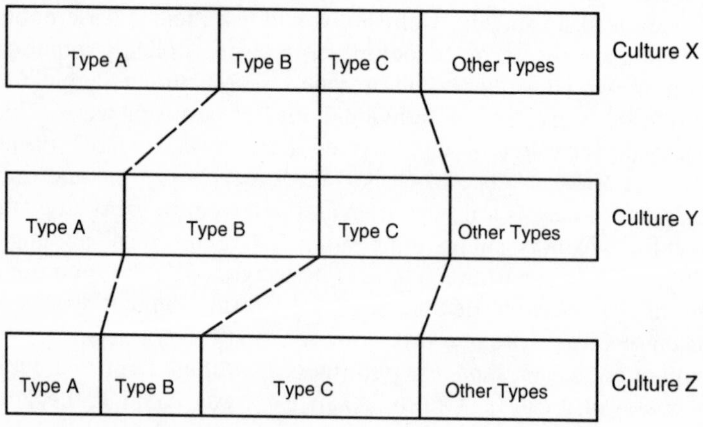

Figure 3.1 Heterogenetic view of cultures

REFERENCES

Bateson, G., Jackson, D., Weakland, J. and Haley, J. (1956) 'Toward a Theory of Schizophrenia', *Behavioral Science*, 1, pp. 251–64.

Hendin, H. (1964) *Suicide and Scandinavia*, New York: Grün and Stratton.

Maruyama, M. (1959) 'A Critique of some Widely held Assumptions on the Relationship between Culture and Mental Health', *Revue de Psychologie des Peuples*, 14, pp. 273–6.

—— (1961) 'Multilateral Mutual Causal Relationships among the Modes of Communication, Sociometric Pattern and Intellectual Orientation in the Danish Culture', *Phylon*, 22, pp. 41–58.

—— (1963) 'The Second Cybernetics: Deviation-amplifying Mutual Causal Processes', *American Scientist*, 51, pp. 164–79, 250–6.

—— (1972) 'Human Futuristics', *Co-existence*, 4, pp. 2–19.

—— (1974) 'Paradigmatology and its Application to Cross-disciplinary, Cross-professional and Cross-cultural Communication', *Cybernetica*, 17, pp. 136–56, 237–81.

—— (1978) 'Seven Moves in Seven Years', *Chronicle of Higher Education*, November 20, p. 18.

—— (1979) 'Trans-epistemological Understanding', in R. Hinshaw (ed.) *Currents in Anthropology* (Sol Tax Festschrift), Den Haag: Mouton.

—— (1980) 'Mindscapes and Science Theories', *Current Anthropology*, 21, pp. 589–99.

—— (1981) 'Denkmuster: Metaprinzipien der Umweltgestaltung', *Garten und Landschaft*, October issue, pp. 806–15.

—— (1984) 'Alternative Concepts of Management: Insights from Asia and Africa', *Asia Pacific Journal of Management*, 1, pp. 100–11.

—— (1985a) 'Mindscapes: How to understand Specific Situations in Multicultural Management', *Asia Pacific Journal of Management*, 2, pp. 125–49.

—— (1985b) 'The New Logic of Japan's Young Generation', *Technological Forecasting and Social Change*, 28, pp. 351–64.

—— (1989) 'Practical Steps for Interactive Inventions', *Technology Analysis and Strategic Management*, 1, pp. 423–30.

—— (1991a) 'Epistemological Heterogeneity and Subsedure', *Communication and Cognition*, 24, pp. 255–72.

—— (1991b) 'Disciplinary Contents Requirements: Academic Non-tariff Barrier in Interdisciplinary Communication', *Human Systems Management*, 10, p. 55.

—— (1992) 'Anti-monopoly Law to Prevent Dominance by One Theory in Academic Departments', *Human Systems Management*, 11, pp. 219–20.

—— (1993) 'Mindscapes, Individuals and Cultures in Management', *Journal of Management Inquiry*, 2, pp. 140–55.

—— (1994) *Mindscapes in Management*, Aldershot: Dartmouth.

Morin, E. (1987) *Penser l'Europe*, Paris: Gallimard.

Shannon, C. and Weaver, W. (1949) *Mathematical Theory of Communication*, Urbana, IL: University of Illinois Press.

4 What can we learn from biological networks?

Vera Calenbuhr

1 INTRODUCTION

Although being aware of the limitations of rational arguments in economics, most managers nevertheless would maintain that any economic endeavour is governed to a large extent by rational thinking. Many unpredictable or incomprehensible events are generally dealt with using intuition or more or less spontaneous decisions based on the manager's experience, skills and interactions with other people. This can be a good strategy in many cases, but the question arises whether one can do better, and if so, one would like to know, where this rationale stems from.

The foregoing applies not only to the context of economics, but to more general situations where groups of people interact. The members of a group usually believe that their actions are based on either personal decisions, or are influenced by other people or circumstances. Some of them believe that whatever they decide or do is done consciously.

However, groups of human beings are also capable of displaying collective behavioural patterns, e.g. collective decisions, in which the members are not at all aware of being involved in the whole process. A simple example can often be observed at a pedestrian crossing. Usually people wait and become impatient to cross the street. Occasionally, one member of the group makes a timid attempt to disobey the red light and to walk across the street. Often, however, the remaining people, who prefer to wait, discourage the person tempted to cross. From time to time there may be new attempts. Suddenly, the whole group disobeys the red light and crosses the street. There are many other examples like this and they are often based on imitation behaviour: 'I will wait if the others wait, and I will cross if the others begin crossing.' In general: 'I do what my neighbour does.'

It is important to note that the individuals in the traffic light example are unaware of making a collective decision. Neither do they consider themselves as being part of an interacting group. Nevertheless, the individuals in the group interact and are able to display large scale behaviour which was neither planned nor intended.

This example shows that human groups have the potential to display collective patterns which can in many cases be interpreted as collective decisions. In some types of groups these patterns may be welcome, even wanted, but they could also be dangerous in other cases. One may wonder whether this potential can be beneficial by having people interact in particular ways. The benefit would be derived from the collective intelligence of groups.

Although the traffic light example is very instructive, there remain several objections. First of all, it may be a unique example. Further, although one easily admits that the people in the example were indeed involved in a collective decision process, there remain doubts whether this decision has generated intelligent behaviour. Several questions arise immediately. First of all, one would like to know why we are so optimistic that groups of interacting people can display certain types of collective intelligence. Further, we would like to know whether the collective patterns are superior to other patterns of behaviour. In the following, we will discuss some self-organization processes in biological networks that lead to intelligent behaviour. As the actors in these networks are generally, molecules, cells, or animals (e.g. insects), the intelligence of these systems cannot be rooted in the intellectual capacities of the individuals. And in fact, this intelligence is a collective property. Given that many biological systems can display intelligent behaviour without the need for centralized control mechanisms, it is tempting to learn from biological design in order to implement certain of these structures in human-made contexts. Once these structures are implemented, one should expect similar types of behaviour as in the original context. One possible man-made organization where one could implement such structures are enterprises at the level of the interaction schemes of the people working there.

We shall not argue that human group behaviour follows the behaviour of enzymatic or immune networks. However, there are some general characteristics shared by many different types of networks. Our aim here is simply to turn the attention to the possibility that this type of intelligence could be an unexploited potential in groups of humans; we want to draw the readers' attention to some points of view which may help to interpret human group behaviour in a new perspective. We are still awaiting most of the solutions. In general it is not obvious at which scale one should start to do modelling of human group behaviour. A group capable of taking a collective decision may consist of only four or of one hundred people. The point that we want to make here is just to present a philosophy, a way of seeing things that has proved to be successful in the physical and to a certain extent in the life sciences in explaining complex behaviour.

Before going any further let us briefly summarize what and how we are going to proceed in our discussion. First of all we must accept that there exist certain types of collective intelligence in nature. The simplest way to do that is to look very carefully at the architecture of biological systems. In section two we shall do precisely this: by presenting some design features of biological systems we will appreciate where the fundamental differences between natural and human-made design lie. This discussion will take us to one of the key mechanisms responsible for the organization of biological systems, namely positive feedback. In section three we will deepen this aspect by juxtaposing positive and negative feedback and relating them to innovation and homeostasis. In section four we will discuss examples taken from the world of social insects to see in action the mechanisms presented so far. In section four we will also introduce the notion of internal and external coherence, which will be important for what follows next. So far we have never left the save grounds of biology where all the mechanisms discussed so far work very efficiently. So far everything sounds quite nice. But, in the end we would like to know whether there is really a chance to implement these mechanisms at the level of human group behaviour. We will discuss some aspects of this question in section five, although we have to admit that we are not able to give final answers at present. However, as was stated above, the goal of this discussion is not to present blueprints of well tested algorithms but to provide some ideas of how one can see things in a new perspective.

Whenever one tries to transpose ideas from one field to another, or whenever one recognizes common principles in seemingly different phenomena one wonders whether there are any deeper reasons for these similarities. Do similar circumstances lead to similar solutions? A deeper inspection may reveal that the suspected similarities exist only superficially. In other cases there are really common principles involved. We shall discuss some questions of this type that originate from the foregoing discourse also in section five.

Before going into the detailed discussion of the different aspects mentioned so far, it is important to put this account into a more general framework. It is also necessary and helpful to mention those works that have had a strong influence on the present discussion. Further, the reader may be interested in what type of mentally related models exist already. As we will also see later on, the ideas put forward here originated to a large extent during the author's phase of modelling social insect behaviour. Some of the ideas related to social insects can be found in Deneubourg and Goss (1989), Calenbuhr and Deneubourg (1991) and Calenbuhr (1992).

The study of systems governed by non-linear dynamics, or complex systems' theory is not only concerned with biological systems, but also and mainly with physical and chemical systems. Only very recently has it become clear that non-linear dynamics plays a tremendously important role not only at the physico-chemical level of biological processes, but also at the level of populations (May 1973, Murray 1989) and group behaviour (Deneubourg and Goss 1989). Nevertheless, complex system's theory has already found its way into the social, economic and political sciences (see Haken 1977, for some general ideas, and Weidlich and Haag 1983, Ebeling *et al.* 1991, as well as Silverberg 1991, for more detailed accounts). Most of these considerations can be found in the domain of macro-economics and are somewhat different from what is proposed here, which aims basically at implementing biological design features at the group level in inter-human relationships in, say, enterprises.

Schumpeter's (1919, 1947) view of an economic system and its change inspired quite a number of reseachers to study economic development similar to biological evolution. Many interesting papers in which the economy is seen as a complex evolving net can be found in the proceedings of an interdisciplinary workshop organized by the Santa Fe Institute (Anderson and Arrow 1988). Many of the models in this book also deal with the interesting behaviour obtained, when one removes the constraint of equilibrium. Later on, we will see that self-organization phenomena are only possible if the system under consideration is out of thermodynamic equilibrium (Glansdorff and Prigogine 1971, Nicolis and Prigogine 1977, Haken 1977). Georgescu-Roegen (1971, 1976) and Boulding (1978, 1981) discussed the openness of the economic system with respect to energy flow. They realized that a continuous supply of energy is necessary to maintain the processes going on inside the system. These ideas can even be traced back to Lotka (1924) and Marshall (1890).

Goodwin (1951) has shown that self-sustaining business cycles are only possible if non-linear interactions are present. For a long time irregularities in economic time series were interpreted as being caused by noise. Some references to economic models that generate chaos can be found in Brock (1988) who did time series analysis on empirical economic data. The proof for the existence of chaos in empirical data was yet very difficult, because the time series were not long enough. Nevertheless Brock showed that certain time series data could only be explained if there were non-linear interactions.

Huberman and co-workers have been developing models for co-operative behaviour in humans for many years (for a recent account of this approach see Glance and Huberman 1994, and references therein). In a sense, what we have in mind here is related to these models. However, while Huberman tries to incorporate consciousness, will and reflection in his models, we propose here to also investigate those aspects of human group behaviour which are not determined by these factors. Both conscious and unconscious elements always play an important role and perhaps it is not even possible to separate these two aspects. However, it is important to be aware that there are (at least) these two components to human behaviour and it is equally important to appreciate what the unconscious compound can achieve at least in principle. We do not yet know the answer, but perhaps the biological examples discussed so far help to increase interest in these aspects related to unconscious behavioural components.

2 ON BIOLOGICAL NETWORKS

Biological systems are distinguished by the fact that they are complex built, i.e., made up of several subunits and subsystems, and that they are highly reliable and fault tolerant. It is important to note that a biological system is in many cases capable of responding adequately to unforeseen situations.

The foregoing characteristics reflect in some respects what one would expect from an intelligent system. Therefore, seen from outside, a system that displays these characteristics would be termed intelligent. Operational reliability, fault tolerance and flexibility are characteristics that are not only required of a biological system but also of a technical system and most other complex structures or organizations in modern life such as enterprises or other groups of people.

In most cases the characteristics are difficult to achieve – if they can be achieved at all. In many cases nature has brought forth physiological- and information-processing systems with remarkable properties. Interestingly, the simplicity and robustness of biological design has already inspired engineers to learn from biological systems and to implement biological principles at a technical level. Most of these solutions, however, can be found in the context of static problems (profiles of airplane wings, fasteners based on the burr principle, parts of bridge building units). These static features of biological design are not the subject of our discourse. More interesting for our discussion are dynamical systems. Dynamical phenomena can be considered as behaviour in the widest sense of the term. Behavior thus refers to the way in which an individual interacts with other individuals and the environment. Individuals are considered to be the subsystems (molecules, enzymes, cells, insects, animals, humans) of a larger system, which one generally refers to as the society. Using this definition, physiological and biochemical systems belong also to the class of dynamical systems whose behaviour we shall investigate. The above-mentioned characteristic properties, i.e., reliability, fault tolerance and flexibility, can be found in the most pronounced way at this dynamical level.

The basic question that we are going to investigate is how systems, that are made up of many (simple) subunits, can display large scale coherent behaviour and where the reliability of such systems is rooted. Moreover, (in section five) we discuss some problems of how biological design can be transferred to the level of human conduct.

It is extraordinarily important to appreciate the conceptual difference between biological and most man-made design. The comparison between a (classical) computer program and the operation of a biological system may serve to epitomize this difference. (Classical) computer programs only carry out what has been conceived by the designer, which generally reflects our way of dealing with a problem: namely to appreciate the problem, decompose it into several smaller parts and to conceive solutions that are inspired by the idea that all relevant cases can be foreseen. This is a centralistic point of view. Compared to the organization of an enterprise this comparison is certainly exaggerated. The caricatured attributes of this description nevertheless underline the principal organizational fact, namely a top-down architecture.

However, complex systems cannot only be controlled in a top-down and principally central manner, but they have the potential, at least to a certain degree, to form hierarchical structures due to the system's inherent dynamics. And these hierarchical structures display ordered, coherent and functional features. Let us now see how such hierarchies are formed.

The operational reliability of biological systems stems from the fact that the system's subunits (enzymes, cells, individuals) are so numerous that it generally does not matter if some of them fail. The sheer number of subunits alone, however, is not yet sufficient to ensure reliability and fault tolerance. (And this is also what saves us from running into an intractable dilemma at the level of an organization in which human beings are involved.)

What is further needed is that the subunits interact with one another in such a way that a structure in the temporal as well as the spatial domain can form. (Such a structure can be a decision, the formation of an opinion or the occupation of seats in a theatre.) The formation of such a structure requires that the system be in a thermodynamical non-equilibrium state and that the interactions between the subunits be non-linear. Both requirements are fulfilled in biological systems. A certain structure can then in turn interact with other system subunits. (We recall that in section five we will discuss where to look for non-linearities and non-equilibrium conditions at the level of interactions between humans.)

It is important to note that a structure as such does not only represent an interesting physical phenomenon, but that it plays a role in the workings of a whole, which gives us – the observers – the impression that there was goal-oriented behaviour. (Here, we use a neutral formulation for goal-oriented behaviour, as the phenomenon of teleonomy – which is the technical term – is a highly debated and contentious issue in contemporary biology.)

In general, several structures can be formed (multistability). The selection of a structure occurs in many cases through interactions with the environment so that in a sense a structure reflects environmental characteristics and constraints. Moreover, a certain solution can also be influenced by the history of the system as well as being selected by the effect of noise. It is important to stress that a system can be perturbed by the environment and switch from one state to another. This also is a way of interacting or even responding to the environment.

Such a structure means nothing else than that many subunits behave in the same way. They show a large scale coherent behaviour. This means that the large number of subsystems can be described by a small number of variables, the so-called order parameters. It is possible to have a whole series of transitions where a large number of individuals (subsystems) behaves collectively and can be described by such an order parameter. In that way it is possible to form a hierarchy of behaviours, where the next higher level is characterized by the fact that we can find order parameters, which describe the collective behaviour of the next lower level. By going upwards in the hierarchy we can cross several levels of description starting from the microscopic level ending up at a macroscopic level. For long the conviction was held among scientists that it is necessary to integrate the microscopic behaviour to obtain macroscopic behaviour. While it has also been believed that it would be necessary to include an ever larger number of variables in passing from the microscopic to the macroscopic level, recent advances in the theory of non-linear processes have shown that the slaving principle (Haken 1977, 1983, Haken and Mikhailov 1994) or mode selection process (Nicolis and Prigogine 1977), which enable us to describe the collecive behaviour of many individuals, provide simpler alternatives.

What is important for our discussion here is that the foregoing mechanisms do not only operate if photons, molecules or cells are involved, i.e., they do not only operate in physical and chemical systems, or biochemical, and cellular systems, but also in social systems (Weidlich and Haag 1983, Deneubourg and Goss 1989).

It is the hierarchy of structures which are formed in interaction with the environment that give biological systems such a great flexibility. The order parameters at different levels of organization interact with the environment and exert an influence either on the upper or the lower levels of organization. In either case we have to deal with a few variables. If there was no hierarchy formation we would not even be able to deal with the system, because its description would require too large a number of variables. Biological systems theory is to a large extent a matter of self-organized hierarchies. Not much attention has been paid to this aspect in man-made organizations. Human-made organizations are a matter of imposed-organized instead of self-organized hierarchies. Self-organization leads to flexible structures, while imposed organization leads to rigid structures. In nature there exist already systems that are capable of generating coherent collective behaviour without central coordination. A system consisting of simple individuals (system subunits), that are built such that the group they are forming is capable of adapting to many different situations determined by the environment, is not only simpler and more fault-tolerant than a centralized organization, but can also be much more flexible.

Non-linearities have been considered an exception for a long time in engineering as well as in economics. Later it was recognized that they are not only ubiquitous but constitute in many systems the normal case. Still, one tried to suppress them and hoped to be able to control the system in the linear domain. Only very recently it has been recognized that nature uses those dynamical features resting on non-linearities as building blocks to build the control elements of a flexible, reliable and independent system. Nevertheless, the author does not wish to give the impression that all imposed organization is inferior. There are situations where only an extreme rigidity of the system's hierarchy leads to a viable organization. The command structures on ships and planes are good examples. Cases where members break out of this structure can be very dangerous. In other cases the courageous initiative of one or a few crew members, e.g. in plane crashes, have often proved to be the only solution. What is proposed here must not be interpreted as a kind of propaganda for a new idea. On the contrary, it is intended to point to some aspects of behaviour that have been almost completely ignored so far, but which prove to be an extremely useful alternative in certain systems.

In the following we shall try to look at some forms of biological design in more detail and investigate to what extent they may be transferable on to levels of human-made organizations. The above list of mechanisms (which is by no means complete) that give rise to the formation of structures in systems far from thermodynamical equilibrium are the subject of the theory ('theories' would perhaps be more appropriate) of self-organization or non-linear dynamics.

These mechanisms alone, however, do not suffice to give rise to coherent collective behaviour. It is equally important, that – in biochemical reaction networks for instance – several reactions can coexist without disturbing each other. In other cases it may just be necessary that reactions influence each other in a certain fashion. In order to guarantee the correct mutual relations between many reactions a fine parameter tuning is needed. In many cases, however, the environmental conditions are not sufficiently constant to assure this fine tuning.

Here, something else comes to bear, namely a system-architecture that establishes the correct mutual relations among the subunits. These relations at each level of organization constitute the network structure of the system. It is the right network structure which attributes to the system a certain autonomy but not autarky from the environment. I shall call this form of architecture internal coherence. Much of what will be investigated in the following can be found at this level. What is important for an organism is that it not only be well adapted to external environmental conditions but disposes equally well of an internal coherence.

3 POSITIVE VS NEGATIVE FEEDBACK = HOMEOSTASIS VS INNOVATION

The notion of equilibrium pervades our conceptions of systems in many cases. In general, one tries to keep the system within certain limits (homeostasis). Hence, equilibrium and homeostasis are not surprisingly characteristic of modelling engineering and economic problems. If changes of the state of the system are wanted, decisions become necessary which are usually taken by some individual or a computer program, which is prepared for a certain number of conceivable cases and which reflects of course the conception of its designer.

In no case, however, does one wish to confer a decision to the system proper. One may ask why this is so? Before trying to give an answer we have to remember what kind of behaviour we have in mind. Namely, how a process of decision formation can be understood at the basis of unintended group behaviour. The type of problem that we are interested in is, for example, the decision of a group of people to cooperate in a particular way, but also the selection of a particular fashion colour. By knowing which constellation of people in a network of relations can give rise to collective behaviour one can take advantage of the system's stability, innovations and flexibility. By knowing which interrelationships are favourable, we may not always find the best solution, but we can ensure a good working model. We will discuss examples in the context of social insects below. Let us now return to our basic problem: why should one not leave a decision up to the system, e.g. a group of human beings? We suspect that one of the reasons is that we are so used to the concept of a top-down architecture that we do not even see that there are alternatives. Another reason is possibly that even in those cases where we perceive alternatives it is extremely difficult to allow for some change since there is too much system-inherent inertia. The last statement stems from our appreciation of the fact that people tend to conceive of change as always being inextricably connected to structural change. What we advocate here, however, can be achieved by just removing constraints.

We have already discussed the importance of non-linearities, i.e., positive feedback, in the foregoing sections. Very often one associates exclusively destabilizing effects with positive feedback. One overlooks completely, however, that it can play an important role in complex regulation mechanisms. While negative feedback ensures homeostasis, positive feedback plays an innovative role in the selection of different possible solutions. It helps thus to control the activities in, say an ant society or an enzymatic network or a group of people. Again, while negative feedback plays a conservative role, positive feedback is associated with innovation. Negative feedback is a damping process, while positive feedback amplifies.

Positive feedback is a necessary condition for the formation of so-called 'emergent properties', i.e., the coordination of many (simple) subunits that display a coherent pattern whose temporal and spatial scales exceed the scales of the individual subsystem by orders of magnitude. Actually, the large-scale collective pattern results from the individuals' behaviour in a way that is not immediately intelligible but can only be understood through detailed modelling of the process.

4 THE PRESENTED MECHANISMS AT WORK: EXAMPLES FROM SOCIAL INSECTS

So far we have presented some of the mechanisms that lead to self-organization processes. In order to get a better understanding of these abstract ideas, we shall have a closer look at examples of biological organization. Social insects are particularly interesting in this respect, because we find in operation all the factors discussed before. Here, we see in a transparent way what is meant by internal coherence and how several hierarchical structures are formed. Social insects have always attracted people's attention because of their seemingly random, yet highly coordinated organization. Ant societies are a marvellous example which elucidates the concept of decentralized organization and its efficiency in solving logistic problems.

Many logistic problems presented here can be interpreted as task allocation problems. There are two important aspects of task allocation problems which are solved by self-organization processes simultaneously. First, it is necessary to know who and how many have to do what in a particular place. Second, it matters how the task is done. The problem of assigning the right proportion of the workforce to the right places as well as the dynamics, that is the 'how' of the process are generated by the examples we discuss now. The system's proper dynamics finds a solution to the 'how'; a solution that does not have to be implemented explicitly by the designer (i.e., nature in this case) of the system. Here lies the strength of this approach. Moreover, we pronounce that the methods put forward here can be used to find good solutions (near optimal) to the first aspect of task allocation problems by using less computational effort than classical methods.

Before starting the description we would like to add one further remark. After reading this section the reader will wonder whether it is possible to conceive systems using biologically inspired design that equal biological systems' perfection. The doubts are justified. However, on one hand it may not be necessary to achieve this perfection and on the other hand one should not be too ambitious right at the beginning. This is the more the case taking into account that we have used a totally different philosophy for a long time. Nevertheless, it can be instructive to appreciate the remarkable degree of internal and external coherence achieved by biological systems. The performance of enzymatic networks, the immune system or social insects (the chosen example here) should give us a clear indication that it is not only the human brain that is capable of solving complex tasks. This hypothesis may seem daring at first sight. It loses all its boldness, however, when witnessing the performance of model systems that can solve similar tasks on a computer screen. Sophisticated models can at least achieve semi-quantitative agreement with experimental results. After such a demonstration the foregoing statement will no longer be considered inadequate. To avoid any misunderstandings: the code of these computer programs describes the kind and strength of the relations between the insects, i.e., the communication network, in terms of differential equations. The decisions taken by the groups are entirely governed by concentrations, numbers of individuals etc. There are nowhere binary decision trees or the like.

Social insects represent an instructive example of a decentralized operating system, consisting of many simple subunits, and displaying the emergence of coherent collective patterns at spatial and temporal length scales that exceed the characteristic scales of the subunits by far. The first question that we want to address is how social insects can generate such behavioural patterns. We will start with a simple example, namely the buildup of a chemical trail.

Imagine there are some ants moving about randomly and exploring the environment of the nest. As soon as one individual finds a food source, it will return to the nest laying a chemical. The odorous substance used to mark the trail is called pheromone. Upon arrival at the nest the ant will return to the food source and so on. Other individuals that find the scent trail, will be guided either to the food source or to the nest (where they return and walk then to the food source). Successful ants, i.e., those that have found food at the source will always return to the nest laying a chemical trail. If the food source becomes exhausted the trail is no longer reinforced. Also, crowding at the food source leads to a situation where some ants do not find food. They also do not reinforce the trail in turn. The trail is thus reinforced by trail laying ants and decreases in strength due to the evaporation of the pheromone. There are two interesting aspects. First, the ant colony shifts from exploration mode to exploitation mode through the formation of a trail. Hence, one single ant can induce the change. The exploration mode is characterized by the problem of searching the terrain in the most efficient way. This can only be achieved if all the individuals are widely dispersed. The exploitation mode is characterized by the problem of leading a sufficient number of individuals to the locus of the food find. Hence these modes are characterized by two entirely different requirements. The second aspect is related to the dynamics of the scent trail. The trail provides not only an orientational cue, but reflects through its dynamics the state of the food source.

We continue the first example of trail formation by discussing the exploitation of two unequal food sources. Imagine ants moving back and forth between the nest and a food source following a chemical trail. The ants reinforce the trail as a function of the quality of the food source. They lay more trail pheromone when the source is richer. In that way the food source providing more and better food will be associated with a stronger and more persistent trail. In the end the reinforced trail will be used almost exclusively. In very much the same way the stronger trail will become less attractive to the ants when there is crowding at the better food source so that ants have to return without success (as in the previous example). The trail will also become less attractive as it is less reinforced when the food source becomes exhausted.

This is a beautiful example of how a mechanism of positive feedback regulates recruitment behaviour: the better the food source the more the trail is being reinforced and the larger the probability that this trail will be selected. The stronger the trail the larger the probability of reaching the food source. Mechanisms of that type can be found in almost all phenomena that show multistability and time dependent environmental parameters. Therefore this scheme can be considered quite general. The first example is described in detail in Calenbuhr (1992), where it is shown how the whole dynamics can be basically related to the trail-following mechanism of the ants. Many other interesting cases are discussed in Deneubourg and Goss (1989), where the second example is summarized, as well as in Franks (1989) and Calenbuhr and Deneubourg (1991, 1992). The ideas put forward in this article emerged to a large extent when the author was working with J.L. Deneubourg, the principal theoretician of self-organization in social insects. The application of ideas from complex systems theory to social insects started during the 1970s in the same place in the Brussels school of thermodynamics and self-organization.

Another equally important aspect that we are going to discuss now is the relationship between the individuals and their environment.

This factor will bring us closer to an understanding of the flexibility of biological behaviour. The above description of the recruitment of an insect society is not only a very interesting regulation mechanism but constitutes also a communication system. Information about the food source is conveyed by the trail. The delicate balance of exploiting the food source on the one hand and the reinforcing of the trail on the other, as well as many other environmental factors generate a mirror image of the whole situation. This mirror image in turn serves the individuals for orientation and their behaviour modifies the mirror image subsequently.

The technique that nature uses in this example is the following: many individuals contribute to the building up of a mirror image of the environment. This mirror image provides orientational cues for the individuals. In order for the whole process to function all the different rules of the game must fit together. This then is probably the most severe problem as far as the application of biological design to other problems is concerned. The rules of the game have to be complementary to many different environmental situations. For nature, which constitutes a large laboratory with as much time as is needed, this is in general no problem.

For a manager, however, the adequate solutions are not at all obvious. This is precisely the reason why it is worth finding out about nature's ways. In order to show that this is really possible it may be noted that a perfect complementarity can be achieved with a very small number of rules.

In the case of social insects about five rules are sufficient to understand the principal classes of behaviour that rely on chemical communication. Moreover, we should emphasize that all of these rules are of a simple nature (Calenbuhr 1992).

5 FROM BIOLOGICAL NETWORKS TO HUMAN GROUP BEHAVIOUR

Learning from biological design sounds nice but one may ask whether it is not just wishful thinking. Most people making remarks in this direction have in mind that biological systems have evolved in the course of a long evolution and that groups of human beings are quite different things than groups of cells or insects. Both objections are correct and justified. We therefore have to verify whether they are relevant to our case or whether they are not mere reflections of human bias.

So far we have discussed several examples of how systems made up of several subunits can show collective behaviour patterns without a central control. The collective behaviour resulted from the communication between the subunits – each of which acts according to the locally available information. The natural question that arises at this point is whether it is possible to learn from such design principles and implement them at a level where humans interact. It is also of utmost importance to be aware of precisely what we can take out of the biological context and transpose to another one.

In the ant example discussed before all individuals obeyed the same rules. In reality the situation is a little bit more complicated. There are individuals that dispose of a set of rules that can differ significantly from that of other individuals. The ways in which the individuals interact with one another define a network. This network can be quite small, but it can also be large. We shall not go into the subtleties of the discussion of how subsystems (subnetworks) like those ants that participate in the exploitation of the food source are related to those that are engaged in nest building activities. Suffice it to say that different subnetworks can be combined. Seen that way, it appears quite natural that the ant society is only a part of a still larger network which is defined by the society's environment, which in turn is embedded in the ecosystem.

In principle one would like to model the whole big network. This, however, is impossible (which is not surprising). This whole section so far would then also be totally meaningless if it were not for this remarkable capacity of hierarchy formation in such networks which allows the elimination of many variables and to study properties of the network which can be described by only a few variables. In the ant example above it is sufficient to model the behaviour using the number of individuals at the source and those in the nest as the only variables.

Let us next discuss some of the necessary ingredients to have self-organizing effects again, but this time in the context of human behaviour. These two ingredients are non-linearities and non-equilibrium conditions. What does non-linearity mean? In popular terms it means that the whole is more than its parts. Although this is a very beautiful formulation (and a correct one, too) it has too much philosophical flavour for our discussion here. Therefore let us look at two examples taken out of everyday life. We will first describe a non-linearity at the level of the interactions between group members. Imagine there is a cinema which announces a new film. Imagine further that it is a film that many people will probably like but that they would not admit that they like. It could be a comedy which is not located at, say, a higher intellectual level. We all know films like this. People get informed about the film only by passing by the cinema and seeing the poster announcement. In that way the number of people who know about the film will be a linearly increasing function. Imagine now, that there is another film announcement. This time the film was made by a famous director and it is a 'must' to see it although many people would actually not really like it. This time it is quite fashionable to know about the film and spread the news. So the next morning I will tell my colleague that there is this new film. He in turn will tell it to other people who also spread the news and so on. In this way the number of people who know about the film will increase non-linearly. This type of non-linearity is what we have encountered in the first ant example above, i.e., the buildup of a new trail. Moreover, whether the people like the film or not is irrelevant. What matters is whether or not they communicate their knowledge.

Now there is also another type of non-linearity which operates not at the level of the interactions between the individuals but at the level of the individual itself. It is related to the notion of stimulus–response. Imagine that I am being offered a particular job. If I were offered twice the amount of money (or three times as much), would I be motivated twice as much (or three times as much) to take it? We all know that this is not the case. Although stimulus–response relationships vary from person to person they tend to be of the same form but only with different weights. This is not only true for physiological stimulus–response funtions like, for example, the objective loudness of an audible signal and the personal impression of loudness, but also in totally different contexts (although this is only true for very simple and standardized situations). All these stimulus–response relationships are non-linear (many examples can be found in Stevens 1975). We have encountered this second type of non-linearity in the second ant example above.

The next problem to discuss is the condition of non-equilibrium. A general definition of what non-equilibrium means at the level of human behaviour is certainly very difficult to find. We are not aware of any research in this direction. It is absolutely necessary to become aware of the fact that the non-equilibrium situation has not necessarily to be searched for at the level of the individual. Nor does it necessarily reside in the mind of an individual. Imagine the following situation (again a cinema example). People enter the cinema and look for a seat. At the beginning there will be a certain average inflow of people into the cinema. As long as there are still many unoccupied seats the situation in the cinema will not hamper the inflow of people.

If there are no more new people arriving, we would intuitively speak of an equilibrium situation. As long as there were people streaming into the cinema, there was non-equilibrium. This is only meant to be an illustrative example. In general, flows are a good indicator of processes taking place under non-equilibrium. The flow of ants in the examples above is driven by the presence of food.

Another important question is not what we can or could learn from biology in principle, but what we should learn.Would it be clever to learn from ants how to build streets? Perhaps not, because we are living in a different world. However, it seems plausible to take some abstract ideas out of the context of ant trail formation and to implement them in a different context. For example, it was found that trail fidelity plays a very important role. Ants that are not sufficiently good at following a chemical trail are probably not good foragers. However, it was shown that too high a fidelity is not good either (Deneubourg *et al.* 1983). A certain amount of noise (ants that happen to leave the trail) may find another food source. It was found that there exists an optimal noise level. This shows us a very important feature. A certain failure rate can turn out to be useful elsewhere. Too rigid a structure does not provide the freedom to search for innovations!

Engineers have often copied biological design features, albeit mostly static architectures. As was mentioned above, hollow bridge building units are directly copied from bird bones. In the case of sonar one has exactly replicated what was developed by bats a long time ago. This last example, however, is very interesting for another reason. American, British and German engineers, who developed sonar independently during World War II were not at all aware of the echo location mechanisms in bats and found nevertheless a technical solution which resembled the biological one to a considerable degree. Moreover, during the development the engineers independently encountered similar problems that seemed to have posed major problems during the biological evolution. The point we want to stress here is the following. Although biological evolution, engineering problems and human group behaviour are much different there is one interesting common feature. The foregoing case as well as many others show that similar problems and constraints seem often to give rise to similar solutions.

All the foregoing is good news. First, although it may often not be advisable to copy exactly the biological solution, it may be advantageous to learn from it. Second, although it may appear impossible to design systems that are as perfect as biological ones, we save a lot of experimentation just by looking at nature. Third, if it is true that similar problems and constraints lead to similar solutions (and there are many reasons to have faith in this suspicion) then we know that we are well advised to look for similar solutions in nature.

6 CONCLUDING REMARKS

It is now time to become aware of the self-organization potential of a system and to rely no longer exclusively on one's own intelligence but also on that of a system. This means that the system is not controlled from the outside and from above but that the system solves a problem due to its intrinsic dynamics and in interaction with its environment.

The most severe problem in that enterprise resides not in the task itself but in mankind's difficulty of admitting that not only an individual but also groups of individuals can achieve intelligent and useful solutions. As long as the members of such a group are humans, there seems to be no problem in principle. Not only modern management makes use of this insight but in many other forms of human conduct we find applications of these ideas. However, they still rely on the tacit assumption that the problems to be dealt with can be solved by conscious reflection. If one is to confide in the self-organization potential of a group of people at a level where their behaviour could equally well be obtained by a group of insects, robots, or other individuals (i.e., we no longer consider the results of a process based on ratio but instead one that is based on the pure dynamics between the interacting members of the group) one tends to be sceptical. There may be several reasons for that. First, one is simply not accustomed to such an operating mode. Therefore one intuitively tends to dismiss these ideas until they haved proved to be superior. To perform the proof, however, one has to allow the new ideas to contend with the prevailing working mode. In general, it takes a long time to overcome the friction and inertia in an established system. Another reason is that one is intuitively reminded of raging groups of people raiding innocent neighbourhoods of football stadiums or civil war scenarios where people have lost control over their actions.

Experience teaches us that people can do harm to other people, animals or the environment independently of the way they are organized. We should therefore not be misled by some seemingly poignant examples and dismiss the ideas presented in this article as simply dangerous.

The case which we wanted to advocate here is simply stated. It is based on the recognition that large organizational structures such as enterprises are in many respects similar to complex biological systems and are therefore subject to dynamical processes characteristic of these systems. Biological systems are in many cases organized in a bottom-up architecture, while most man-made design, whether it be technical processes or the organization of an enterprise is mostly top-down organized. Biological systems are very often based on bottom-up architectures which renders them fault-tolerant, reliable, robust and intelligent. We should consider whether we can afford to neglect such a potential that can be activated just by removing constraints.

ACKNOWLEDGEMENTS

I am intellectually indebted to J.L. Deneubourg. Financial support from the Stiftung Volkswagenwerk and the Fritz Thyssen Stiftung over the years is gratefully acknowledged.

REFERENCES

Anderson, P.W. and Arrow, K.J. (eds) (1988) *The Economy as an Evolving Complex System*, SFI Studies in the Sciences of Complexity, Reading, MA: Addison-Wesley.

Boulding, K.E. (1978) *Ecodynamics: A New Theory of Societal Evolution*, Beverly Hills: Sage.

—— (1981) *Evolutionary Economics*, Beverly Hills, CA: Sage.

Brock, W.A. (1988) 'Nonlinearity and Complex Dynamics in Economics and Finance', in P.W. Anderson and K.J. Arrow (eds) *The Economy as an Evolving Complex System*, SFI Studies in the Sciences of Complexity, Reading, MA: Addison-Wesley.

Calenbuhr, V. (1991) 'Pattern Formation via Chemical Communication: Collective and Individual Hunting Strategies', in J. Billen (ed.) *Biology and Evolution of Social Insects*, Leuven: Leuven University Press.

—— (1992) *Collective Behaviour in Social and Gregarious Insects: Chemical Communication and Self-Organization*, PhD Thesis, Free University of Brussels.

Calenbuhr, V. and Deneubourg, J.L. (1991) 'Chemical Communication and Collective Behaviour in Social and Gregarious Insects', in W. Ebeling, M. Peschel and W. Weidlich (eds) (1991) *Models of Selforganization in Complex Systems – MOSES*, Berlin: Akademie Verlag.

Deneubourg, J.L. and Goss, S. (1989) 'Collective Patterns and Decision Making', *Ecology, Ethology and Evolution*, 1, pp. 271–95.

Deneubourg, J.L., Pasteels, J.M. and Verhaeghe, J.C. (1983) 'Probabilistic Behaviour in Ants: A Strategy of Errors', *Journal of Theoretical Biology*, 105, pp. 259–71.

Ebeling, W., Peschel, M., Weidlich, W., (eds) (1991) *Models of Self-organization in Complex Systems – MOSES*, Berlin: Akademie Verlag.
Franks, N.R. (1989) 'Army Ants: A Collective Intelligence', *American Scientist*, March–April, pp. 138–45.
Georgescu-Roegen, N. (1971) *The Entropy Law and the Economic Process*, Cambridge, MA: Harvard University Press.
—— (1976) *Energy and Economic Myths*, New York: Pergamon Press.
Glance, N.S. and Huberman, B.A. (1994) 'The Dynamics of Social Dilemmas', *Scientific American*, 3(270), pp. 58–63.
Glansdorff, P. and Prigogine I. (1971) *Thermodynamics of Structure, Stability, and Fluctuations*, New York: Wiley-Interscience.
Goodwin, R.M. (1951) 'The nonlinear Accelerator and the Persistence of Business Cycles', *Econometrica*, 19, pp. 1–17.
Haken, H. (1977) *Synergetics. An Introduction*, Heidelberg: Springer Verlag.
—— (1977) *Advanced Synergetics*, Heidelberg: Springer Verlag.
Haken, H. and Mikhailov, A.S. (eds) (1994) *Interdisciplinary Approaches to Nonlinear Complex Systems*, Heidelberg: Springer Verlag.
Lotka, A.J. (1924/1956) *Elements of Mathematical Biology*, New York: Dover.
Marshall, A. (1890) *Principles of Economics*, London: Macmillan.
May, R.M. (1973) *Stability and Complexity in Model Ecosystems*, Princeton, NJ: Princeton University Press.
Murray, J.D. (1989) *Mathematical Biology*, Heidelberg: Springer Verlag.
Nicolis, G. and Prigogine, Y. (1977) *Self-Organization in Non-Equilibrium Systems*, New York: Wiley & Sons.
Schumpeter, J. (1919) *Theorie der wirtschaftlichen Entwicklung*, (English translation, (1934) The Theory of Economic Development) Cambridge, MA: Harvard University Press.
—— (1947) *Capitalism, Socialism and Democracy*, New York: Harper & Row.
Silverberg, G. (1991) 'Selforganization, Technical Change, and Economic Evolution', in W. Ebeling, M. Peschel and W. Weidlich (eds) *Models of Selforganization in Complex Systems – MOSES*, Berlin: Akademie Verlag.
Stevens, S.S. (1975) *Psychophysics*, New York: John Wiley & Sons.
Weidlich, W. and Haag, G. (1983) *Concepts and Models of a Quantitative Sociology*, Heidelberg: Springer Verlag.

Part II

Organizational behaviour and the management of the firm

5 Japanese management as a set of cybernetic principles of managing human systems

Tetsunori Koizumi

INTRODUCTION

As the products of the Japanese economic machine flood foreign markets, such tongue-twisting Japanese terms as *keiretsu*, *kanban* and *kaizen* now find increasing references in newspapers, magazines and business textbooks published in countries outside Japan. It is not surprising, then, that some commentators and politicians back in Japan proclaim that Japanese management, or 'Japanese-style management' as some prefer to call it, as represented by a set of business practices associated with these terms, is a distinct product of Japanese culture with universal relevance. And why not? While Japan's proud cultural products such as *kabuki* and *sumo* have yet to establish foreign operations despite a popular following among foreigners, Japanese business firms – large and small – are now engaged in direct production of their highly popular products all over the world.

What we propose to do in this discussion is to examine whether Japanese management is indeed an exportable product of Japanese culture which has some universal relevance in the lands beyond the seas surrounding this island nation. Part of the answer to this question no doubt depends on what we mean by 'Japanese management', i.e., whether we regard Japanese management as a set of business practices promulgated by successful Japanese business firms or as a set of organizing principles of human systems in general. It behoves us, therefore, to make it explicit in the first place what is meant by Japanese management before we turn to the task of examining the sense in which it can be judged as containing universally applicable principles of human systems management.

JAPANESE MANAGEMENT AS A SET OF BUSINESS PRACTICES

In order to answer the question of whether Japanese management is an exportable product of Japanese culture, or 'a civilization' as one author suggests (Hamaguchi 1987), it is essential that we distinguish between the narrower conception and the broader conception of this term. In the narrower conception, Japanese management refers to a set of business practices which have gained a wide recognition abroad by the remarkable success of the Japanese economic machine in the global marketplace in recent years. On the other hand, it is possible to conceive Japanese management in a much broader context as defining a set of organizing principles of human systems in general.

Much has already been discussed, written, and known about Japanese management in the sense of a set of business practices. While different authors emphasize different aspects, it is useful to summarize Japanese management in this narrower conception in terms of the three Japanese terms mentioned at the outset: *keiretsu*, *kanban*, and *kaizen*.

The term *keiretsu* points to the importance of 'networking' as a fundamental principle of organizing economic life in Japan. The networking principle implied by this term may take the form of a group of firms organized around the main bank, or a group of parts suppliers organized around the main manufacturer. It is important to recognize the systemic nature of *keiretsu* as a networking of business firms. Whether the networking is based on explicit contract or implicit understanding, 'the firm as a nexus of treaties' seems to be a fair description of the manner in which the Japanese firm operates (Aoki *et al.* 1990).

As is well-known by now, *kanban* has a specific origin as a just-in-time system of inventory management. But it is possible to interpret the term as referring to a resource-management system by which the Japanese firm maintains efficiency of multi-staged production processes by economizing the use of resources, including space and time. It is, in fact, a cybernetic system of managing a diversity of resources involved in the production of products in that the idea of 'communication and control' is very much at the core of this system.

The term *kaizen*, narrowly conceived, refers to constant effort to improve the operation of a production plant. However, *kaizen* can also be broadly interpreted as a practice of self-managing a business organization, for it usually involves the practice of wide-spread worker participation as represented by QC movements.

Japanese management as a set of business practices has come to attract increasing attention around the world mainly because of the enormous success the Japanese economic machine has accomplished in recent years. To be more specific, these practices have proved to be effective in economizing the use of resources, reducing transaction costs, and improving the quality of products (McMillan 1992). Indeed, these practices have already been exported to other countries as Japanese transplants have been practising them in the running of their operations abroad.

JAPANESE MANAGEMENT AS A SET OF CYBERNETIC PRINCIPLES OF MANAGING HUMAN SYSTEMS

If the individual human being is a system, as argued by Parsons and other structural sociologists, defined in the space of interaction between motivational orientation and value orientation (Parsons and Shils 1952), then the question of management is a universal concern for any organization as a human system consisting of individuals, each endowed with these often conflicting orientations. In addition to the internal conflict and friction inherent in any human system, the need for management also arises from the fact that human systems operate among, and along with, natural systems which are subject to a natural tendency to decay and disorder, reflecting, as they do, the second law of thermodynamics. While human systems get around the tyranny of the second law of thermodynamics and try to maintain their viability by constant intake of information from the environment, they are nevertheless subject to the forces of decay and degeneration in the form of generational changes within the organization, which lead to loss of institutional memory, as well as changes in technology, values, and other environmental factors taking place outside the organization, which lead to obsolescence of institutional knowledge.

Japanese organizations, including business firms, employ a certain set of practices which can be construed as defining a set of cybernetic principles of managing human systems in general. In the first place, there is a universal concern expressed by Japanese organizations over human development as reflected in such practices as lifetime employment and seniority-based promotion. While such concern translates itself into the practice of age-specific on-the-job-training in the narrow context of business organizations, it embodies the idea of on-the-job-development when viewed in the context of human systems management. This idea is based on a view of human nature that the individual human being is a self-organizing system in the sense that he/she is in constant search for the appropriate role for him/her at each stage of his/her human development.

The second important characteristic of Japanese management in this broader conception as a set of cybernetic principles of managing human systems is the idea of an organization as a self-managed system. This idea translates into common understanding by the Japanese that an organization is, in general, a system whose operation is defined by a nexus of mutual obligations among its members. Thus, the firm is regarded as being jointly owned by the employees rather than by the shareholders. As a consequence, the idea that labour represents an opposing interest from management is replaced by the idea that all members of the firm are 'associates' and, therefore, need to be involved in all aspects of its operations.

The practice of cross-holding of shares among *keiretsu* firms, which has become a subject of criticism by foreign firms and governments in recent years as a practice which excludes shareholders outside the *keiretsu* group, can also be regarded as reflecting this notion of an organization as a self-managed system. The cross-holding of shares indeed resembles a system of 'hostage exchange', as one author suggests (Ito 1991). But it is an effective system of self-management for *keiretsu* firms in that it allows them to concentrate on what they are supposed to be doing in the first place – engaging in R&D activities, planning for efficient production and distribution, and cultivating new markets – by minimizing outside intervention of other stakeholders in the running of their business.

The cross-holding of shares and the exchange of personnel among *keiretsu* firms are but two examples which illustrate the importance the Japanese attach to the idea of networking in managing human systems. Needless to say, any human system is a cybernetic system in the sense that some degree of steering and control is unavoidable. Steering and control can be accomplished by resorting to negative feedback coming from top management. But it can also be accomplished by positive feedback such as QC circles, nightly rounds of drinking, and joint recreational activities. In short, the idea that an organization is a self-managed system defined in the space of mutual obligations among self-organizing individuals summarizes what Japanese management is all about as a set of cybernetic principles of managing human systems.

IS JAPANESE MANAGEMENT EXPORTABLE?

Given that Japanese management can be given a broader interpretation as referring to a set of cybernetic principles of managing human systems, the answer to the question of whether Japanese management is exportable depends on how we assess the extent to which the world as a social system is amenable to these cybernetic principles. In other words, it depends on the degree to which Japanese management is culture-specific.

The importance Japanese management places on 'networking' – among individuals as well as organizations – has prompted many commentators to characterize it as a product of a group-oriented culture. From a historical perspective, Japanese management can be regarded as an evolutionary product of 'rice culture', as one author suggests (Hayashi 1988). Group endeavour, lack of division of labour, repetition, imitation as a key to success, diligence and consensus decision making can all be regarded as 'successful' practices which have evolved out of Japan's rice culture. What is not to be neglected in this connection is the legacy of Confucian culture in Japan, for society, in the Confucian conception, is a system of well-defined networks of mutual obligations (Koizumi 1989).

To the extent that the idea of a society as a system of well-defined networks of mutual obligations is universal, it is not surprising that Japanese management is to be found in other societies. Thus, Maruyama finds Japanese management, or what he terms 'Asian and African model of management', as a prevailing mode of managing human systems in these parts of the world (Maruyama 1984). On the other hand, the same model encounters a less receptive audience in countries in North America and Europe with different cultural traditions.

What is perhaps more important in examining the exportability of Japanese management is to recognize the fact that the world can no longer be neatly divided into cultural zones following different management principles which have emerged out of different cultural traditions. Indeed, what has happened in recent years, and is happening today, in the world around us is nothing short of revolutionary in all areas of social life. In the area of economic life, newspapers are full of stories every day of direct investments, strategic alliances and joint ventures. We are even told of instances where former rivals in the same industry are joining hands in strategic alliances and joint ventures across national borders. This is a brave new world for Japanese management even in its narrower conception as a set of business practices. The idea of an organization as a self-managed system by self-organizing individuals will be severely tested by the challenges of having to manage a multi-cultural workforce, to comply with rules and regulations of foreign lands, and to live up to the international standards of good behaviour as a global organization.

CONCLUSION

Japanese management as a set of cybernetic principles of managing human systems can be regarded as a mode of adaptation which has proved to be successful for Japanese organizations in the last several decades, especially in the realm of business and economics. But it is a mode of adaptation which has evolved out of a specific cultural environment. As such, its relevance is limited to local conditions and cannot, by itself, be claimed to have universal relevance.

Does this mean that Japanese management is just a passing fad whose effectiveness is being eroded by the ever-expanding scope of 'internationalization' for Japanese organizations? While representing conventional wisdom in a specific cultural environment, Japanese management does contain some universal elements as the principles of human systems management. For example, there is the idea of exploiting positive feedback rather than negative feedback in motivating individuals. Then, there is the idea that an organization, or a human system, defines an environment for human development for self-organizing systems called human beings. Whether these ideas will have lasting values will largely depend on whether Japanese organizations will be able to perpetuate their practices in the world where the idea of an organization as a self-managed system is being challenged by the idea that an organization is at best a loose coupling of diverse interest groups. To the extent that they are successful in perpetuating these practices, *keiretsu*, *kanban*, and *kaizen* – along with *karaoke* – will find their way into foreign language dictionaries.

REFERENCES

Aoki, M., Gustafsson, B. and Williamson, O.E. (1990) *The Firm as a Nexus of Treaties*, London: Sage.

Hamaguchi, E. (1987) 'Japanese Management as a "Civilization"', *MITI Journal*, 1, pp. 46–8.

Hayashi, S. (1988) *Culture and Management in Japan*, Tokyo: University of Tokyo Press.

Ito, K. (1991) 'In Defense of Japanese Management Practices', *Economic Eye*, Autumn, pp. 19–22.

Koizumi, T. (1989) 'Management of Innovation and Change in Japanese Organizations', *Advances in International Systems Management*, pp. 245–54.
McMillan, C. J. (1992) 'Japan's Contribution to Management Development', *Business in the Contemporary World*, 4(2), pp. 21–33.
Maruyama, M. (1984) 'Alternative Concepts of Management: Insights from Asia and Africa', *Asia Pacific Journal of Management*, January, pp. 100–11.
Parsons, T. and Shils, A. (1952) *Toward a General Theory of Action*, Cambridge, MA: Harvard University Press.

6 Group decision making in the 'self-organization' perspective

Haruo Takagi

INTRODUCTION

The aim of this chapter is to report the results of a series of observation studies I carried out on group decision-making meetings. These studies were formed to acquire the knowledge of structure and process of meetings, which should be taken into account in designing computerized group decision support systems.

I recognize how important this form of group activity as a management device is to Japanese business, which places emphasis on consensus among people. Group decision-making meetings are carried out in all types and levels of Japanese business organizations. Its intellectual productivity has a significant effect on the overall efficiency of the business.

The use of latest information technology to develop group decision support systems is promising to raise the intellectual productivity. For this end, we should have a correct knowledge of what kind of structure and mechanism will see progress made in this style of group activity (and especially in communication among participants). We should also have an accurate understanding of what aspects of group activity should be controlled to raise the intellectual productivity of meetings. Without this knowledge, it would be impossible to devise methods of raising the intellectual productivity, and any group decision support system that is not founded on this knowledge is meaningless.

I shall first look at what kinds of research on the meeting process and its control have been conducted in the organizational behaviour research area, which is my speciality. Then, I shall introduce the self-organizing perspective of the social system as a new theoretical framework (meetings are small social systems). Finally, I shall detail the results of my research using this framework, which show that the knowledge is available to use for raising the intellectual productivity of meetings.

HISTORICAL OVERVIEW OF RESEARCH ON THE PROCESS AND CONTROL OF MEETINGS

Research on group dynamics within small groups has been carried out since the early stages as a part of research on organizational behaviour. This area of research, founded by Lewin (1951), flourished mostly in the United States, and was very actively pursued during the 1950s and 1960s. Research did not specifically focus on forms of meetings within business organizations, rather, it looked at the behaviour of small groups at the work place. Many theories have been formulated as to why members of an observed small group interact with each other in the way they do, including Bales (1950), Homans (1950, 1961), Thibaut and Kelley (1959), Cartwright and Zander (1968). It can be said that these studies generally leaned more towards gaining a theoretical understanding of the social and emotional interaction process within the small group, than towards examining the efficient and effective actions of the meeting to achieve set goals.

It was not until the 1970s that the focus of research turned to the efficiency or effectiveness of meetings. The term 'group decision making' became popular, and research began to look at the process of group decision making as an effective means of solving problems, rather than concentrating on building theories to explain how small groups develop the process of dynamic behaviour. What turned many researchers'eyes in this direction was research into the non-productive processes (referred to as 'groupthink') of a national security conference convened by President Kennedy to plan the Bay of Pigs incident in Cuba in 1961 (Janis 1972, 1982, Janis and Mann 1977).

Following this, a considerable amount of research indicated that meetings in which the agenda and progress of discussion are set beforehand in a way are more effective than normal meetings which progress through natural interaction during the discussion (early studies include Van de Ven and Delbecq 1971, 1974, while recent studies include Schweiger *et al.* 1986 and Schweiger and Sanberg 1989). These studies reported that for efficient and effective group decision making, meetings could achieve much more if the processes necessary for making decisions were properly structured, than if the flow of dicussions was left to spontaneous and dynamic interaction among participating members. There have been several proposals regarding methods of structuring meetings to facilitate effective group decision making (e.g. Brightman 1988).

In general terms, I can say that the underlying pattern in research on meetings for group decision making to date is that setting a structure in which the self-control of members with respect to problem solving does not increase is an important means of raising the effectiveness and efficiency of meetings. Thus the line of research has shifted towards the structuring of the meeting process.

However, one cannot but say that this pattern is only indirectly linked to the primary aim of group decision-making meetings. If the meeting is positioned as a mechanism for collaborative work to develop new ideas, and not simply as a means of passing on or sharing information, there is a need to find a direct method of raising the intellectual productivity of the meeting, that is, a direct method of creating information. In my view, the studies on meetings that I have outlined above have their foundation in the idea that intellectual collaborative work in itself cannot be structured (Brightman 1988 and Schrage 1990 expressed this opinion), so they have tended not to take this up as a research theme. It can therefore be said that the research conducted thus far has been indirect research that structures the process of meetings in which intellectual collaborative work progresses smoothly.

SELF-ORGANIZATION FOR INTELLECTUAL PRODUCTIVITY IN MEETINGS

It goes without saying that raising the intellectual productivity of group decision-making meetings is a vital theme for business today. While research that can directly contribute to this end is absolutely essential, research to date has not had the theoretical framework which would allow it to take up the intellectual productivity of meetings. This framework is now necessary, and I believe that we should focus our attention on 'self-organization' as a highly convincing perspective for its construction. Discovery of self-organization in studies on immune systems in living matter in recent years and also in studies on heat convection has greatly stimulated research in Japan not just in the natural sciences area, but in the social sciences as well. Its theoretical effectiveness has attracted much attention (Nonaka 1985, Imada 1986, Imai 1986).

The self-organization theory of the social system presented by Imada (1986) in particular is an extremely important study into the small social system of the group decision-making meeting. The reason is that the self-organization perspective is defined as 'a nature whereby as the social system interacts with the environment, human activity, which is a system component, alters the structure of the system itself and creates a new order' (Imada 1986). To develop the group decision-making meeting as a device for creating knowledge or ideas to facilitate problem solving, the meeting must be structured in a way that can create from the interrelationship among participants something which each participant did not have before. Considering the preceding research on self-organization, creativity at meetings, which are small social systems, can be pursued within self-organization.

What we should note here is that the idea of self-organization does not contend that we ought to find the best (i.e., one fixed) structure for the intellectual production activities of group decision-making meetings. Rather, it teaches us that to raise intellectual productivity, the structure itself should be constantly changed. It can be said that this reveals the limits of the research on the process and control of meetings mentioned in the last section. This indicates that research should shift direction to the line of thinking that structural change during the meeting process is necessary for intellectual productivity.

To my knowledge, self-organization at meetings occurs daily, but to different degrees. Even at ordinary meetings that are not of any great importance, participants are constantly aware of the aim and process of meeting. They often seek to engage in debate by stating their respective views on the aim and process of the meeting. And if the discussion fails to make favourable progress, they seek to hold discussions to re-examine the aim and process of the meeting. These two facts can be seen as being equivalent to the 'self-reference' and 'self-examination' raised by Imada (1986) as important aspects of self-organization.

The central action of self-organization is applying self-reference and self-examination to the 'rules' of the social system. Rules govern the actions of a social system (meeting), and they are the way in which meetings proceed. Even at ordinary meetings, a great deal of time is spent discussing the meeting process (rules). Therefore, research on how self-organization is activated in meetings is extremely important.

We can also see the validity of the self-organization perspective for research on meetings from the following points. In the research area of family therapy, which is thought to bear no relationship to research on business phenomena, the family is taken as a system (i.e., a small social system). Researchers study paradoxes within conversations among family members to assist in the therapy of psychopathological symptoms in the family (Hoffman 1981). One of the major elements of this research is the double-bind theory developed by Bateson

(1972, 1979) and collaborating researchers (Watzlawick *et al.* 1967, Watzlawick *et al.* 1974). This theory is a formula for the occurrence of psychopathological symptoms among family members owing to the continuous presentation of two paradoxical instructions and the double punishment that comes as a consequence.

I see this theory as indicating the circumstances under which self-organization will cease to occur in the social system of the family. That is, 'self-referring' statements among family members create paradoxes in communication, but it is thought that binding through the presentation of double punishment stops the 'self-examination' of the paradoxes by family members. This finally makes members themselves unable to talk about and improve the family relationship (system structure) itself. We can say that holding back self-organization in this form is creating psychopathological symptoms within the family.

Although the terminology differs, research in the family therapy area is based on views that run parallel to the self-organization perspective in the social sciences area. I believe that research on self-organization itself is possible even at meetings, which are small social systems on the same level as families. I also believe that it is highly possible to grasp self-organization as the central activity of intellectual productivity of meetings.

OBSERVATION OF SELF-ORGANIZATION AT GROUP DECISION-MAKING MEETINGS

In this section and the next I shall report on the results of my observation of group decision-making meetings. This section will cover research which recognizes the existence of self-organization in the process of the group decision-making meeting, while the next section will cover analysis on how self-organization at a meeting is related to the meeting's intellectual productivity.

First I shall describe my research which recognizes the existence of self-organization in the process of the group decision-making meeting. This was conducted by way of observing meetings. The meetings I refer to here were group discussions at a management development programme using the case method conducted in a certain company. I videotaped the two-hour group discussion which preceded the class discussion. This VTR recording was the subject of my observation research.

First, the instructor handed out to the participants a case (a documented example of real business operations) and questions (what kind of management issues emerged in the example and how would the participants evaluate the actions of people concerned). The participants were asked to study by themselves prior to group discussion (they were required to read the case and compose their own thoughts and opinions). The participants were then divided into eight groups of six or seven people for group discussion. The theme of the group discussion was the same as the questions for individual study, which had already been handed out to the participants. The groups were to form a group solution or conclusion that took in the view of each group member. The instructor did not stipulate any particular way in which the discussion was to proceed; participants were generally free to follow their own course.

The importance of these meetings lies in the fact that reaching a conclusion by discussing and analysing a case within a group is essentially the same as reaching a conclusion at a strategic or planning meeting within a real corporate setting. So even though the meetings were a part of a management development programme, they were able to reproduce fairly accurately the process of an actual group decision-making meeting in a real business setting.

I used the following two methods to analyse the discussions of the eight groups which I videotaped. The first method is that I recorded in broad outline the two-hour discussion of each group, paying attention to what was discussed (whether the members were discussing the meeting process, or discussing the contents of the case). The second is that I observed and recorded precisely who was saying what to whom for one minute in every five, as in the sampling method used in work study.

I could grasp the following points from the observations using the first method. Each group discussed, alternately, rules for the meeting process, and the actual contents of the case (according to the decision on rules for the meeting process), with a certain amount of time allocated to each. When the discussion moved from the content of the case to the rules governing the meeting, the participants in most cases discussed a review of and amendments to the rules that they had been following until then. From this, we could observe in the meeting self-organization in the sense that the members were applying self-reference and self-examination to the rules of the social system as pointed out by Imada (1986).

By analysing the observations using the second method for parts to which the results from the observations with the first method could not be applied, I could pin-point the following three settings. The first is where an extremely confused discussion was maintained when utterances connected with rules of the discussion and utterances connected with the case became entangled. Several group members tried to discuss the case, thinking that discussion on the rules had been settled, but other members tried to continue discussing the rules, unaware that this discussion had already been settled. The reason for this is that both sides had a different awareness about what was being discussed (i.e., individual members' awareness about the meeting process), and because of this difference, self-organization as it should be did not easily occur.

The second setting is where discussion moved to the case before debate over discussion rules had reached a proper conclusion. Then, a tense confrontation occurred between members who had formed two sides during discussion over interpretation of a certain fact within the case. At that time, a member from one side suggested that the group have a break, to which everyone agreed. Once outside the group's room, the members chatted informally about the two sides' different ideas on the meeting process. Another problem in this setting is the difference in the idea that each member had about the discussion rules when each of them spoke. We can see this as an example in which a certain member who noticed a difference in what each member believed were the rules for the meeting process gave rise to self-organization.

The third setting is where a long time was spent talking about the facts of the case with nothing said whatsoever about discussion rules. From the start to the end the discussion was lifeless. In this setting self-organization was not demonstrated at all.

At least from these observations, it can be said that self-organization exists in the processes of the group decision-making meeting. Self-organization here is the changing, by the meeting members themselves, of the rules which stipulate the activities of the meeting-type social system. The key point is that rules stipulating the meeting process do not remain fixed, but are constantly changed or revised by the members.

This is the point that must be emphasized in research on the intellectual productivity of meetings. Research which searches for and tries to give structure to the best possible meeting process (i.e., a fixed process) serves only finding a way to obstruct the meeting's move towards self-organization. Rather, the research that ought to be carried out is research to determine how such a move towards self-organization relates to intellectual productivity, and how we can manage this self-organization to raise intellectual productivity. The research covered in the next section has been conducted with a view to this.

ANALYSIS OF THE RELATIONSHIP BETWEEN INTELLECTUAL PRODUCTIVITY OF A MEETING AND SELF-ORGANIZATION

For this research, I gave five groups, each of six to nine members, a special discussion theme which could enable me to measure the degree of intellectual productivity; then I had the groups hold group decision-making meetings. I videotaped the entire discussions for each group (about two hours each) for analysis. Participants in the meetings were all first-year students on the MBA programme at the Keio University Business School.

The groups were shown the first one-third of the film 'Twelve Angry Men'. Then each group was asked to forecast how the remaining two-thirds of the film would unfold, based on consensus among all members of the group. The film revolves around the discussions among twelve jurors who are required to determine whether a youth charged with murder is guilty or not guilty. At the beginning of the film, one of the twelve jurors insists on a not guilty verdict, while the other eleven believe the youth is guilty. As the film progresses, the eleven jurors who advocated a guilty verdict over time gradually changed their opinions to not guilty one after the other. The movie ends at the point when all twelve jurors have agreed on a not guilty verdict. The first one-third of the movie takes us up to the point just before the first of the eleven jurors who advocated a guilty verdict changes his opinion to not guilty. Before being shown the movie, participants were given sheets with the photograph and name of each of the twelve jurors.

Immediately after watching the first one-third of the movie, participants were asked to predict, from their individual points of view, the order in which the eleven jurors would change their opinion to not guilty. Following this, participants were asked to discuss their individual predictions within their respective groups for about two hours, and to reach a group decision on the order of change through consensus. The operation of this group decision making was the theme given to the participants.

Analysis 1: Degree of intellectual productivity

The difference between the order of the eleven jurors as disclosed during the remaining two-thirds of the movie (equivalent to the correct solution) and the forecasts based on group decision making (and individual decisions before that) can be measured as the forecast accuracy. A particularly important point to look at here is the extent to which the forecasts resulting from the two-hour group decision-making process improves over the individual forecasts made before the meetings. That is, if the accuracy of the group decision is higher than the average accuracy value of the individual decisions, we can say that the collaborative work of the meeting created and added new information that previously did not exist at the individual member level.

Of course, the aim of this research is not to explain what intellectual productivity is, so I shall regard intellectual productivity at these meetings as 'the increase in accuracy of the group forecast over the average accuracy value of the individual forecasts' in the context described above.

I used two methods of calculation: the sum of the absolute values and the square root of the average of the squares. That is, for both the individual decisions and group decisions, the first person in the order was the juror who advocated the not guilty verdict from the start of the movie, while the individual participants and later their groups were required to give each of the remaining eleven jurors a number from two to twelve representing the forecast order in which they would change their mind from guilty to not guilty. The sum of the absolute values (and the square root of the average of the squares) was then calculated as the difference between the number given to each of the twelve jurors by the participants, individually and as groups, and the correct solution as shown in the remaining two-thirds of the movie. This represents the accuracy of the individual decisions and the group decisions (the smaller the number, the more accurate the forecast). By subtracting the accuracy of the group decision from the average accuracy value of the individual decisions by the group members, I calculated how much the forecast accuracy improved as a result of the meeting. I then calculated this for each group, and set the result as the intellectual productivity for each of the group meetings.

The results are shown in Table 6.1. From this we can see that there were differences in the intellectual productivity level of the five groups; some groups were able to have a meeting which could improve the accuracy of their forecast, while others were not able. In both the sum of the absolute values and the square root of the average of the squares, the five groups could be divided into three levels – upper, middle, and lower – according to the degree of intellectual productivity. Two groups were in the upper level, two in the middle level, and one in the lower level.

Table 6.1 Analysis of five group decision-making meetings

	Upper G(1)	*Upper G(2)*	*Middle G(1)*	*Middle G(2)*	*Lower G*
Degree of intellectual productivity					
Sum of the absolute values	11.00	10.50	4.44	4.00	0.00
Square root of the average of the squares	3.70	3.75	1.35	1.63	0.57
Number of situation themes*	12.80	20.00	23.50	19.10	30.90
Number of context themes*	2.22	6.00	6.15	6.91	12.60
Percentage of time spent on context themes*	2.78	6.67	16.80	7.08	18.10
Number of inconclusive shifts from context themes*	0.00	0.00	1.11	2.86	4.00
Number of inconclusive shifts from context themes to content themes*	0.00	0.00	0.56	2.86	4.00

Note: * per hour

Analysis 2: Context-level theme and content-level theme

I then analysed how the degree of intellectual productivity of the groups is related to the quantity and quality of utterances during their respective meetings, especially the utterances related to rules on the meeting process. To examine this, I recorded in detail for each group the content and time of every utterance made by participants during the two-hour meetings, and then analysed the data. For my analysis, after each several utterance I grouped them together and looked at them as 'situation themes'. From this I could see that the flow of the meeting is the connection of situation themes. As an analyst in the position of the third party, I could understand clearly the situation theme of 'what participants were discussing' at a certain point of the meeting. I discovered that several groups of utterances as data were always made towards one situation theme.

I was able to classify all situation themes into either themes connected to the rules governing the conduct of the meeting (I have called these 'context themes') or themes connected with the substance of discussions carried out according to rules (I have called these 'content themes'). The result of this analysis is shown in Table 6.1. Looking at the number of context themes per hour of discussion and the percentage of time spent on context themes, we can see that a considerable part of meetings was allocated to this area. However, we cannot simply say that this decreased for meetings with a high degree of intellectual productivity. The result does not support the thesis that groups with higher intellectual productivity spent less time on discussing rules of discussion (context time) and others with lower intellectual productivity spent more time on discussing the subject in question (content time).

Analysis 3: Shift and drift of discussions

Next I analysed how discussions shifted from one subject theme to the next. This analysis showed that at times the theme shifted with an utterance that clearly indicated the beginning of the next theme, while at other times it changed with a vague utterance that only tacitly indicated the beginning of the next theme. There were also occasions when the theme shifted with an action that indicated the beginning of a new theme, such as the wave of a hand or a nod of the head, or because there was nothing more to say and the meeting became silent for a while.

When a subject theme (either context theme or content theme) shifted, the next theme was always either a context theme or content theme. I was able to discover the following points when I analysed the time series relationship between the two. A shift from one context theme to another context theme was a shift in the discussion about the meeting process. The relationship between the former theme and the next theme had a tiered nature with an inclusive relationship similar to a set and an element (or a parent and a child) as a logical structure of rules governing discusssions.

I discovered the following two cases in shifts from a context theme to a content theme. The first is one where the next content theme is discussed in a way that is in line with the meeting process discussed within the context theme immediately before. This kind of shift is one in which the logical nature is maintained. The second is one where the context theme shifts to a content theme without maintaining the discussed meeting process; this is a discussion on content theme which drifted away from the rules on the meeting process. This drift phenomenon has a significant relationship with the inconclusive shift that I shall mention later, so I shall touch on this point then.

Finally, when discussion shifted from one content theme to another content theme, the shift was parallel with no logical tiered nature as an inclusive relationship of the rules on the meeting process.

Another important point I discovered is that there were cases where the discussion shifted from one situation theme to another after discussion on the first theme had come to a conclusion (agreement, decision, completion), and cases where the discussion shifted from one situation theme to another without a conclusion being reached on the first theme. The latter case I have called an 'inconclusive shift'. The number of inconclusive shifts during the meetings is shown in the table. From this we can see that the higher the number of inconclusive shifts, the lower the intellectual productivity of the meeting.

The essential problem with the inconclusive shift is the discussion drift that I mentioned before. When there is an inconclusive shift from a context theme, there develops a low awareness or even confusion among participants about the rules that govern discussion on the subject theme. Discussion on the next situation theme moves away from the discussion method applied until then. As a result, the participants' awareness regarding the meeting process is no longer aligned, and discussion becomes confused and starts to drift. Needless to say, the drift is brought to an end when someone in the meeting opens a context theme in an attempt to bring the discussion back to the original meeting process.

Table 6.1 shows the number of inconclusive shifts from context themes, and the number of inconclusive shifts from context themes to content themes. It shows that there is a strong correlation between the intellectual productivity of the meeting and the number of inconclusive shifts.

CONCLUSION

Group decision-making meetings are extremely important to a business, and raising the intellectual productivity of meetings is essential. With latest information technologies, group decision support systems are promising to raise intellectual productivity. The observation studies I reported provide some useful knowledge for the design of the system. In summary this knowledge falls under three heads: the flow of a meeting is the connection of situation themes; themes are either context themes (the rules governing the conduct of the meeting) or content themes (the substance of discussions carried out according to the rules); and the intellectual productivity correlates highly with inconclusive shifts and discussion drifts.

As concluding remarks in the self-organization perspective, I can state two points. The first is that self-organization exists within rules on the meeting process, which stipulate the system acitivities in a group decision-making meeting. A meeting is a small social system. Participants in the meetings spent some of the meeting time discussing the meeting process, that is, the rules of the system (self-reference), and tried to amend them (self-examination). The second is that the intellectual productivity of the meeting bears no relationship to the quantity of self-organization (number of context themes or length of discussion time on them). What is related to is the quality of self-organization, that is the effective control of self-organization (avoiding inconclusive shifts from context themes).

REFERENCES

Bales, R.J. (1950) *Interaction Process Analysis*, Chicago: University of Chicago Press.

Bateson, G. (1972) *Steps to an Ecology of Mind: Collected Essays in Anthropology, Psychiatry, Evolution, and Epistemology*, New York: Ballantine Books.

—— (1979) *Mind and Nature: A Necessary Unity*, New York: John Brockman Associates.

Brightman, H.J. (1988) *Group Problem Solving: An Improved Managerial Approach*, Atlanta: Georgia State University Press.

Cartwright, D. and Zander, A. (1968) *Group Dynamics: Research and Theory*, New York: Harper & Row.

Hoffman, L. (1981) *Foundations of Family Therapy*, New York: Basic Books.

Homans, G.C. (1950) *The Human Group*, San Diego, CA: Harcourt Brace.

—— (1961) *Social Behavior: Its Elementary Forms*, San Diego, CA: Harcourt Brace.

Imada, T. (1986) *Jiko-Soshikisei – Shakai Riron no Fukkatsu* (Self-organization – Revival of the Social Theory), Tokyo: Sobunsha.

Imai, K. (1986) 'Nihon no Kigyo Network' (The Japanese Corporate Network), *Economics Today*, Autumn issue, pp. 181–203.

Janis, I.L. (1972) *Victims of Groupthink*, Boston: Houghton Mifflin.

—— (1982) *Groupthink: Psychological Studies of Policy Decisions and Fiascoes*, Boston: Houghton Mifflin.

Janis, I.L. and Mann, L. (1977) *Decision Making: A Psychological Analysis of Conflict, Choice, and Commitment*, New York: Free Press.

Lewin, K. (1951) *Field Theory in Social Science*, New York: Harper.

Nonaka, I. (1985) *Soshiki Shinkaron – Joho Sozo no Management* (Theory of Organizational Evolution – Management of Information Creation), Tokyo: Nihon Keizai Shinbunsha.

Schrage, M. (1990) *Shared Minds: The New Technology of Collaboration*, New York: Random.

Schweiger, D.M. and Sandberg, W. (1989) 'The Utilization of Individual Capabilities in Group Approaches to Strategic Decision Making', *Strategic Management Journal*, 10, pp. 31–47.

Schweiger, D.M., Sanberg, W.R. and Ragan, J.W. (1986) 'Group Approaches for Improving Strategic Decision Making: A Comparative Analysis of Dialectical Inquiry, Devil's Advocacy, and Consensus', *Academy of Management Journal*, 29(1), pp. 51–7.

Thibaut, J.W. and Kelley, H.H. (1959) *The Social Psychology of Groups*, New York: Wiley.

Van de Ven, A.H. and Delbecq, A.L. (1971) 'Nominal Versus Interacting Group Processes for Committee Decision Making Effectiveness', *Academy of Management Journal*, 14, pp. 203–12.

—— (1974) 'The Effectiveness of Nominal, Delphi, and Interacting Group Decision Making Process', *Academy of Management Journal*, 17(4), pp. 203–12.

Watzlawick, P., Bavelas, J.B. and Jackson, D.D. (1967) *Pragmatics of Human Communication: A Study of Interactional Patterns, Pathologies, and Paradoxes*, New York: Norton.

Watzlawick, P., Weakland, J.H. and Fish R. (1974) *Change: Principles of Problem Formation and Problem Resolution*, New York: Norton.

7 Progressive and degenerative problemshifts of organizations

Organizational evolutionism based on critical rationalism

Kenshu Kikuzawa

1 INTRODUCTION

A widely accepted view in Japan explains the development of organizational form in the following steps (Sakakibara 1989):

1 functional form emerged first;
2 then, multidivisional form was adopted;
3 thereafter, many companies moved to matrix form (including Strategic Business Unit); and
4 recently, the more decentralized form like *bunsha* form (a new form developed by Matsushita Electric Corporation) or *amoeba* form (a new form developed by Kyocera, a Japanese Ceramic manufacturer) has been quite popular.

The problem here is whether this development is a logical consequence of progressive process or only a historical stream of booms. It is often ignored that there is a difference between historical facts and logical things, and a historically newer form is often seen as a logically better form.

Nevertheless, a historically newer form is not necessarily better from a logical point of view. Even if a form is historically new, it might be logically ineffective. For example, according to our analysis, the change to a newer style like matrix organization is degenerative rather than progressive, contrary to the accepted view.

To prove this, we attempt to reconstruct the process of development of organizational form from a logical point of view. The basis of this reconstruction is the schema of the growth of knowledge developed by K.R. Popper. Through this reconstruction, we shall prove that a historically newer form is not always effective or useful.

Therefore, in this paper we proceed as follows:

1 We explain Popper's critical rationalism and his schema of the growth of knowledge via conjectures and refutations;

2 we will reconstruct progressive and degenerative problemshifts of organizational form on the basis of Popper's schema; and
3 in order to show the effectiveness of this rational reconstruction, we show some examples of its application to some Japanese companies.

Through this process, it is expected to shed light on the study of organizational form.

2 CRITICAL RATIONALISM AS A BASIC PRINCIPLE

2.1 Critical rationalism's view about science

First of all, we explain briefly the essence of Popper's philosophy of science, usually referred to as 'critical rationalism' (Popper 1959, 1963, 1976, 1986). Popper demonstrated that an infinite number of singular statements could be derived logically from a universal statement. Thus, if we try to verify the universal statement, we must verify those singular statements by means of an infinite number of observational data.

However, this procedure is clearly impossible. We cannot verify even the simplest statement such as 'all ravens are black'. For this reason we cannot argue that the universal statement is true. In contrast, we can falsify logically the universal statement by counter-evidence. For example, the universal statement 'all ravens are black' can be falsified by only one white raven.

Thus, we cannot verify the universal statement, but can falsify it; there is asymmetry between verification and falsification. We cannot decide on whether the universal theory is true or not. We must therefore admit that all human beings are ignorant. In this context, scientific method is seen as follows:

1 any theory that can be interpreted as experimentally falsifiable is 'scientific';
2 even if the theory is put to the test and survived it, this does not mean that the theory is proved, but it is only temporarily accepted, since we have found no reason to discard it;
3 but if the theory is falsified by an 'observation' which conflicts with it, we must try to search for a new theory that explains past events as well as newly found ones; and
4 if such a theory is discovered, this means an advance in scientific knowledge.

We say that there is progress in our knowledge if and only if a new theory has been proposed with the following characteristics:

1 a new theory (T_2) has excess empirical content over old theory (T_1): it successfully predicts new facts that (T_1) was unable to do;
2 (T_2) confirms the previous success of (T_1): all the unrefuted content of (T_1) is included in the content of (T_2); and
3 some of the excess contents of (T_2) are corroborated.

2.2 Schema of the growth of knowledge

Popper claims that the progressive process in scientific knowledge from the old theory (T_1) to new one (T_2) can be represented as a general tetradic schema (Popper 1986, p. 287, Sakakibara and Kikuzawa 1990, Lakatos 1970, p. 118).

$$\dots P_1 \rightarrow TT_1 \rightarrow EE \rightarrow P_2 \dots$$

Here (P), (TT), and (EE) stand for respectively, 'problem', 'tentative theory' and 'error-elimination'. The schema indicates the following:

1 if we can, we should propose a theory (TT_1) as an attempt to solve some given problem (P_1);
2 we should critically examine (EE) our tentative solution (TT_1); and
3 error-elimination (EE) necessarily implies the emergence of a new problem (P_2).

Here,

a if the new problem (P_2) turns out to be merely the old one (P_1) in disguise, then we say that the theory only manages to shift the problem a little; therefore it is taken as a decisive objection to our tentative theory (TT_1). In this case, we say that the problemshift is degenerative.
b If (P_2) is significantly different from (P_1), then we say that the problemshift is progressive. If this is the case, we learn a new thing (Popper 1986, p. 288).

2.3 Application of the schema

Popper insists that the schema is applicable not only to the emergence of new scientific problems but to the emergence of new forms of behaviour, and even to forms of living organisms (Popper 1986, p. 288). As he says, 'it can be interpreted as a description of biological evolution'. 'Animals, and even plants, are problem-solvers.' 'They solve their problems by the method of competitive tentative solutions and the elimination of errors' (Popper 1986, p. 145).

In this case, the schema is interpreted as follows:

1 human behaviour is a tentative solution (TT) of some given problem (P_1);
2 human behaviour as a tentative solution (TT) is tested to be whether it in fact solves the problem (P_1); and
3 the result of error-elimination (EE) is usually the emergence of a new problem (P_2).

In a similar way, we think that the schema can also be applied to the form of organization. In this case, this schema is interpreted as follows:

1 organizational form is a tentative solution (TT) of some given problem (P_1);
2 organizational form as a tentative solution (TT) is tested to see whether it in fact solves the problem (P_1); and
3 the result of error-elimination (EE) is usually the emergence of a new problem (P_2).

Using this, we can determine whether the change of organizational form is progressive or degenerative as follows:

a if the new problem (P_2) turns out to be merely the old problem (P_1) in disguise, then we say that the problemshift is degenerative; and
b if (P_2) is essentially different from (P_1), then we say that the problemshift is progressive.

3 RATIONAL RECONSTRUCTION OF ORGANIZATIONAL FORM

First, we explain the progressive problemshifts of organization according to the principle stated in the previous section. Then the degenerative problemshifts of organization are reviewed from the same viewpoint.

3.1 Progressive problemshifts to multidivisional form

(a) Line form

The simplest form of organization is the line form shown in Figure 7.1. The advantages are as follows:

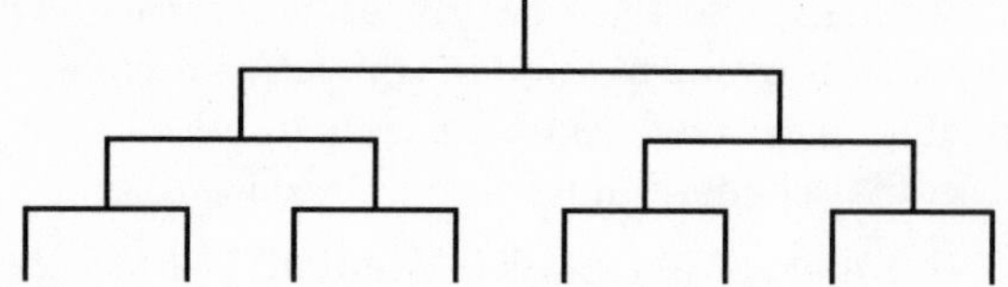

Figure 7.1 Line form

(T_L) since the channel of command is unified, neither inconsistency nor conflict results from the plurality of the channel of command; and

(T_L) for the same reason, where the responsibility lies is always clear.

However, along with the growth, the growth itself acts as a criticism of the prearranged organizational form. Generally, the following problem results from the line form:

(P_L) the limitation of managerial ability of a manager becomes prominent. Specifically, the limitation takes the following forms;

(P_{L-1}) the managers come to be unable to deal efficiently with the information ranging over the entire firm; and

(P_{L-2}) The managers can no longer make use of the managerial resources from the overall point of view.

Thus, if a firm continues to grow under the line form, it necessarily results in an ineffective organizational situation.

(b) Naive functional form

To solve these problems, the functional form was proposed by F.W. Taylor. This organizational form is characterized by the fact that it is functionally divided, and also that the authority is delegated to the divided units. This is represented in Figure 7.2.

The problem with the line form can be resolved by this organizational form, and the advantages are described as follows:

(T_F) the responsibility a manager assumes can be reduced by specialization and delegation of authority;

(T_F) efficiency results from specialization and delegation of authority; and

(T_F) managerial resources can be used efficiently under this organizational form.

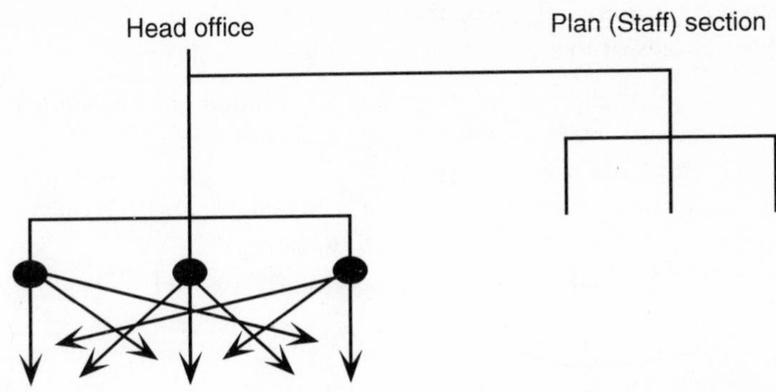

Figure 7.2 Naive functional form

However, since managers do their job mainly from a functional point of view, the following problems will eventually show up:

(P_F) conflict occurs between various functional commands and their authority. Specifically, this basic problem takes the following forms:

(P_{F-1}) since the channel of command is plural, the subordinates are puzzled with the inconsistency of the divergent and somewhat conflicting commands; and

(P_{F-2}) for the same reason, the bearer of the responsibility becomes unclear.

(c) Sophisticated functional organization (line and staff)

In order to solve the above problems, the line and staff form, which we call the 'sophisticated functional form', is developed. This is shown in Figure 7.3.

This form is proposed to take advantage of both line and naive functional forms of organization. In this form, the organization is functionally divided, authority is delegated to some extent and the channel of command is unified. Thus, the problems with the naive

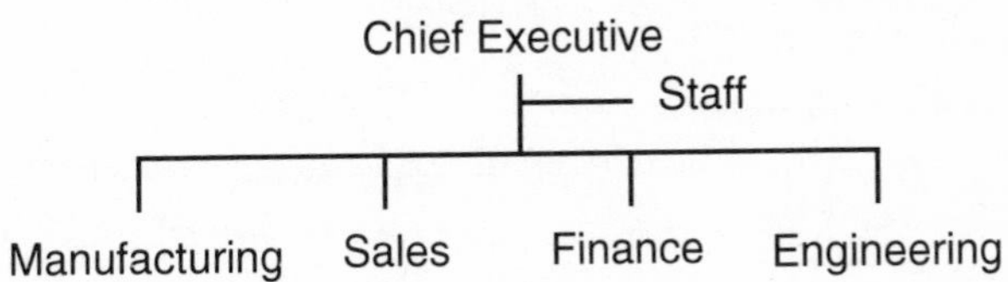

Figure 7.3 Sophisticated functional form

functional form are solved by this organizational form. In particular, the advantages of the latter can be described as follows:

(T_{SF}) since the channel of command is unified, inconsistency of commands from various sources does not occur;
(T_{SF}) for the same reason, who has the responsibility is always clear;
(T_{SF}) the burden of responsibility of a manager can be reduced by specialization and delegation of authority;
(T_{SF}) working is effective through specialization and delegation of authority; and
(T_{SF}) managerial resources are used effectively by specialization and delegation of authority.

However, if a firm continues to grow under this organizational form, the growth itself becomes a criticism against this form. The following problems, which are a mixture of the problems of both line and functional forms, result from the sophisticated functional form. These are:

(P_L) the limitation of managerial ability of management including the staff begins to appear; and
(P_F) conflict occurs between staff and worker or between each functional command and authority.

(d) Multidivisional form

In order to solve the problems with the line and staff organizational form, the multidivisional form is developed. This is shown in Figure 7.4 (Williamson 1975, p. 138).

Necessary and sufficient conditions for establishing this multidivisional form are explained as follows (Williamson 1975, p. 152):

(T_D) strategic decision making is clearly separated from operational decisions (decentralization); and
(T_D) the requisite internal control system has been established for evaluating the performance of each division (centralization).

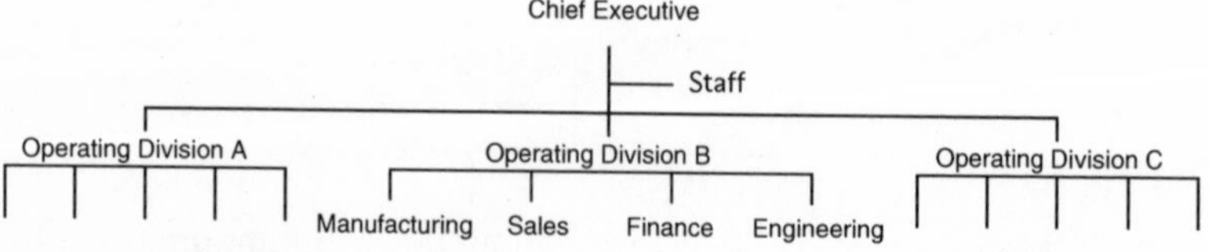

Figure 7.4 Multidivisional form

Under this form, the burden of the head office is clearly reduced by decentralization and delegation. Furthermore, since each division is given autonomy, there will be no conflict between each division. Also, since each divisional behaviour is evaluated by the head office, the allocation of managerial resources (labour, material, money) in the firm is effective and adapted to the environment.

The above problemshifts to multidivisional form clearly solve new problems. Thus we conclude that the problemshifts in this case are progressive. However, in fact, the problems of the sophisticated functional form are not always solved completely. For example, if the multidivisional form is not skilfully applied, it may not work well. It is logically deducible that there are two kinds of quasi-multidivisions as follows:

(T_{QD1}) multidivision where the controlling power of the head office is not strong: under such circumstances, each division is given autonomous standing to a high degree; and

(T_{QD2}) multidivision where the controlling power of the head office is very strong: in such a case, each division is given scarcely any autonomy.

The case of degenerative problemshift will be explained by analysing these quasi-multidivisions as in the next subsection.

3.2 Degenerative problemshift to matrix form

(e) Quasi-multidivisional form 1

First, assume that a firm under the functional form is suffering from the following problems:

(P_L) the limitation of managerial ability of management has emerged; and

(P_F) conflicts occur between staffs and workers or between various functional commands and their authority.

Assume further that in order to solve these problems, the firm shifts to the quasi-multidivisional form as follows:

(T_{QD1}) operational decision making is separated from strategic, and the authority of decision making is much delegated to the lower level divisions (decentralization); and

(T_{QD1}) internal control system for evaluating each division has not yet been established (non-centralization).

In this case, since the head office cannot control all the behaviour of each division, it cannot make effective use of the managerial resources in this company. In other words, the firm continues to suffer from the same old problem (P_L) as in the case of functional forms; so the quasi-multidivisional form cannot solve the problems with the sophisticated functional form. Thus this type of form scarcely shifts the problem at all.

(f) Matrix form

To solve the above problem, matrix form was developed as a possible solution in the United States of America. The matrix form is constructed on the basis of two axes. For example, as shown in Figure 7.5, organization is on the basis of the functional–business axes or on the operating division–strategic business unit axes.

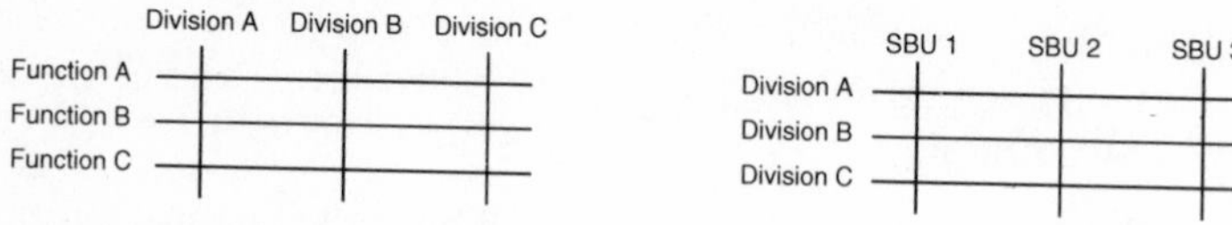

Figure 7.5 Matrix form

Nevertheless, if we analyse the structure of communication and authority in the matrix form, it is clear that it is essentially identical to the functional form. Since this matrix form cannot solve the problem stated in paragraph (b) of the section 3.1, it also suffers from the same old problem (P_F). Accordingly, the matrix form may partially solve the problems with the functional form, but at the same time, it may evoke the other problems. From a logical point of view, the problemshifts are circulating: this change of organizational form scarcely shifts the problem at all. Thus, contrary to the widely accepted view, we conclude that the problemshifts in this case are degenerative.

3.3 Degenerative problemshift by 'bunsha' form

(g) Quasi-multidivisional form 2

Assume that, in order to solve the problems associated with the sophisticated functional form, the firm shifts to the other quasi-multidivisional form characterized by the following:

(T_{QD2}) internal control system for evaluating each division has been established (centralization); and

(T_{QD2}) strategic decision making is not clearly distinguished from the operational one (non-decentralization).

In this case, since the head office in the firm is not powerful enough to direct all operating and strategic decision-making processes, the same problem (P_L) arises as stated in section 3.1(a).

(h) Bunsha form

To avoid the problem, the notion of *bunsha* (divided firm) form was proposed in Japan. This can be characterized as follows (Sakamoto and Shimotani 1989):

(T_B) in order to maintain the quasi-multidivisional form where the controlling power of the head office is strong, parts of the divisions are separated as *bunsha* from the head office's control, and each *bunsha* is given autonomy, while the rest of the divisions are still under direct control of the head office as shown in Figure 7.6.

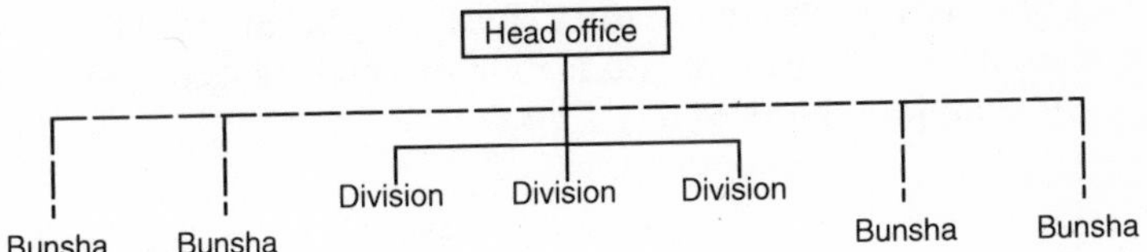

Figure 7.6 Bunsha form

In this way, the managerial control power of the head office is temporarily maintained.

However, this organizational form slightly shifts the problem because it does not completely solve the problem with the quasi-multidivisional form, that is, as stated in section 3.1(a), if the firm grows under the *bunsha* form, the head office will eventually suffer from the same problems (P_L). The problemshift is cyclical, too: this change from the quasi-multidivisional form to *bunsha* form scarcely shifts the problem. Again, contrary to the common view, we conclude that the problemshift is not progressive, but rather degenerative.

4 CASE STUDIES

In this section, we review several cases of Japanese companies from the viewpoint of progressive/degenerative problemshifts of organizations. Readers are referred to Okita (1990) for Mitsubishi, Kitano (1981) for Oki, Sakamoto and Shimotani (1989) for Matsushita and Nihon Keizai Shinbun Sha (1980), President Sha (1981) for Kyocera.

4.1 Mitsubishi Heavy Industries Corporation

Mitsubishi Heavy Industries Corporation was established in 1964 merging three independent companies within the Mitsubishi group. The product line of these three companies was much the same. Just after the merger, the organization of the new company was nothing but the union of three different companies. In other words, the established organizational form of Mitsubishi was not divided functionally: it was a kind of line form. Thus the typical problems of the line form came up along with the growth of the firm as stated in (P_l), (P_{L-1}), (P_{L-2}) of section 3.1(a).

To solve these problems, that is, to use resources more efficiently, Mitsubishi moved to the matrix form organization which was constructed on the axes of production-oriented division and sales division as indicated in Figure 7.7.

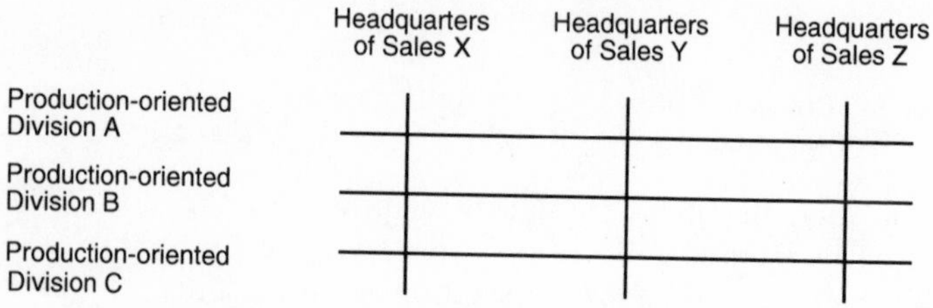

Headquarters of Sales X
Headquarters of Sales Y
Headquarters of Sales Z
Production-oriented Division A
Production-oriented Division B
Production-oriented Division C

Figure 7.7 Mitsubishi Heavy Industries

Analysing the structure of command and communication in the matrix form, we can safely say that the matrix form is equivalent, in its nature, to functional form. Thus, exactly the same problems (P_F), (P_{F-1}), (P_{F-2}) arose under the matrix form as they did under the functional organization.

However, to solve these problems, Mitsubishi further attempted to change its organizational form gradually from the matrix form to the multidivisional form as follows:

(T_D) the production divisions and the sales divisions were unified, with each unified unit negotiating with the head office and staff; and

(T_D) the system of financial control was established: under this system the headquarters finance each division when the latter needs capital, on condition that interest be paid for positive return and penalty for negative return.

In this way, Mitsubishi always tried to solve new problems by building up new organizational forms. The problemshift in this case is progressive from a logical point of view as well as from a historical point of view.

4.2 Oki Electric Industry Corporation

Oki Electric Industry Corporation began to review its organizational design with the Oil Shock in 1973 as a turning point. The design at that time was the functional form which was made up of several functionally divided departments. In those days, Oki was already aware of the general problems (P_F), (P_{F-1}), (P_{F-2}) associated with the functional organization. Thus, to solve them contemporary with the Oil Shock, Oki began to search for a new organizational design.

As a result, Oki moved to matrix form, which was very popular then. The new form was a sort of dual matrix; a matrix on company level and a matrix on division level. The matrix on company level was reconstructed on the basis of the axis of division and the axis of function in the head office as indicated in Figure 7.8. The matrix on division level was made up on the basis of the axis of SBU (Strategic Business Unit) and the axis of function in each division.

Here if we analyse the structure of command and communication in this matrix form, it is clear that the matrix form is nothing but the

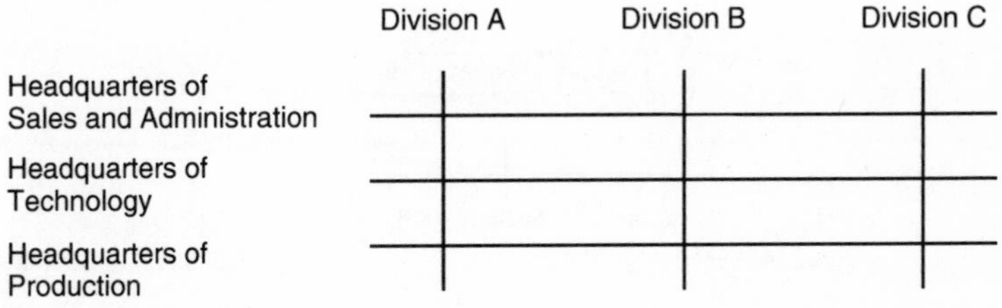

Figure 7.8 Oki

functional form. Thus, the general problems (P_F), (P_{F-1}), (P_{F-2}) with the functional organization eventually occurred.

Although Oki recognized these problems, they expected that this form might have built a new organizational culture which was ultimately profitable for the firm. For this reason, Oki remained in this form. This problemshift at Oki is cyclical from a logical point of view: Oki did not solve any problems with the organizational form, only managed to shift the problem a little. The problemshift at Oki is determined to be degenerative.

4.3 Matsushita Electrical Industrial Corporation and Kyocera Corporation

Matsushita had relatively earlier moved to the multidivisional form in Japan before World War II. Kyocera also earlier moved to the multi-divisional form. Nevertheless, in fact, all divisions of both companies were still under direct control of the chief executive; therefore, both of them were quasi-multidivisional forms. For this reason when both Matsushita and Kyocera grew larger and the number of divisions increased, they had inevitably come across the general problems (P_L), (P_{L-1}), (P_{L-2}) associated with the line form.

In order to solve these problems, Matsushita tried to reduce the number of divisions as much as possible. Nevertheless, as a result, it could not completely solve the problems. Thus, Matsushita moved to *bunsha* form on which Japanese theorists had set a high value. The characteristic feature of the *bunsha* form is as follows:

(T_B) in order to maintain the quasi-multidivisional form under the very strong control power of the head office, part of the divisions are separated from the head office's control and given autonomous position as the *bunsha*, while the rest of the divisions is still under direct control of the head office. This is shown in Figure 7.9.

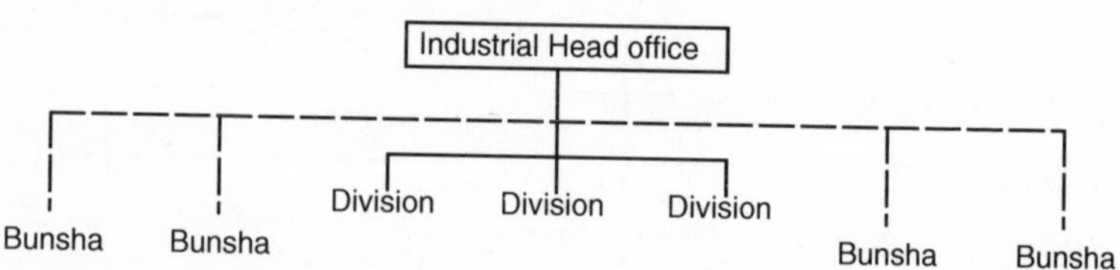

Figure 7.9 Matsushita

However, this is only a quasi-solution: it only slightly shifts the problem because the head office will experience again the same problem if the number of divisions under direct control increases. The problemshift at Matsushita is circular from a logical point of view: Matsushita managed to shift the problem only a little. We conclude that the problemshift in the case was degenerative.

In order to solve the same problems as Matsushita, Kyocera fractionalized each division as small as possible, except the accounting department and research department. Since the fractionalized unit is very small, pliable and flexible, the unit is called *amoeba*. The organization which is made of *amoeba* is called '*amoeba* organizational form' in Japan (see Figure 7.10). The manager of each *amoeba* has the responsibility of management of the unit. The manager is not the oldest person, but the most appropriate person for the *amoeba* unit. In this way, operational decision making was separated, and the burden of managerial responsibility of the chief executive in Kyocera was reduced.

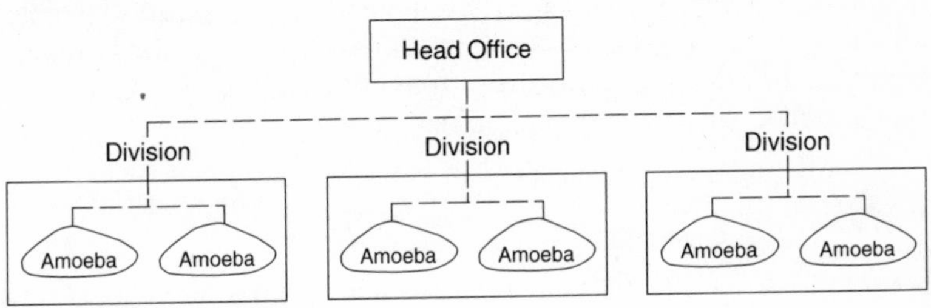

Figure 7.10 Kyocera

Furthermore, in Kyocera, when a unit gets positive return, its manager is valued. When a unit gets negative return, the reason is investigated. If the profits of the unit do not rise, a new manager will be substituted for the current manager. In order to make it clear whether or not a unit really gets positive return, all units must calculate and report the value/time ratio once a month. This system made it easy to evaluate each unit in all divisions: internal control system was establsihed at Kyocera.

$$\text{Value per unit time} = \frac{\text{Revenue} - \text{Cost}}{\text{All working time of members in a unit}}$$

In this way, on one hand, the burden of managerial responsibility of the chief executive could be reduced: Kyocera was decentralized. On the other hand, the internal control system was established: Kyocera was centralized and, by this procedure, the problemshift is made rather progressive.

5 CONCLUSION

In this chapter we explained Popper's critical rationalism and his schema of the growth of knowledge via conjectures and refutations. Then, we reconstructed progressive and degenerative problemshifts of organizational form on the basis of Popper's schema. Last, in order to show the effectiveness of this rational reconstruction, the application of the theory to some Japanese companies was made.

As we have seen in this analysis, the change to a new style like matrix organization or *bunsha* form is degenerative rather than progressive, contrary to the accepted view. Thus, we concluded that the historically newer form is not necessarily logically right. We think that this study sheds light to the study of organizational form. Besides, researchers as well as companies have tended to receive rather readily the newest organizational form developed in the United States, Germany and Japan without any serious critical discussion. Our study is expected to ring an alarm bell to this trend.

REFERENCES

Kikuzawa, K. (1990) 'The Organizational Theory and Reliability Engineering', *The Studies of Humanities and Social Sciences, Social Science Series* (The National Defense Academy, Japan), no. 60, pp. 1–34.

Kitano, T. (1981) *Matrix Soshiki no Hensei to Unei* (Construction and Operation of Matrix Organization), Tokyo: Daiyamondo Sha.

Kojima, S. (1986) *Gendai Kagaku Riron to Keiei Keizai Gaku* (Modern Philosophy of Science and Managerial Economics), Tokyo: Zeimu Keiri Kyokai.

Lakatos, I. (1970) 'Criticism and the Methodology of Scientific Research Programmes', in I. Lakatos and A. Musgrave (eds) *Criticism and the Growth of Knowledge*, Cambridge: Cambridge University Press.

Nihon Keizai Shinbun Sha (1980) *Nikkei Business 2–11*, Tokyo: Nihon Keizai Shinbun Sha.

Okita, K. (1990) 'Frontier Business and Firm Organization', *Organizational Science*, 24(1), pp. 82–92.

Popper, K.R. (1959) *The Logic of Scientific Discovery*, London: Hutchinson.

—— (1963) *Conjectures and Refutations. The Growth of Scientific Knowledge*, London: Routledge & Kegan Paul.

—— (1976) *Unended Quest: An Intellectual Autobiography*, Fontana: Collins.

—— (1986) *Objective Knowledge: An Evolutionary Approach*, Oxford: Clarendon Press.

President Sha (1981) *'Moeru Kigyo' no Karisuma – Inamori Kazuo* (Charisma of 'Dynamic Firm' – Kazuo Inamori), President 1, pp. 126–9.

Sakakibara, K. (1989) 'New Growth Strategy and Strategy-Emerging-Organization', *Organizational Science*, 23(2), pp. 71–9.

Sakakibara, K. and Kikuzawa, K. (1990) 'Rolle und Status des Rationalitätprinzips in Poppers kritischem Rationalismus', *Keio Business Review*, 27, pp. 53–64.

Sakamoto, K. and Shimotani, M. (1989) *Gendai Nihon no Kigyo Group* (Modern Japanese Firm's Group), Tokyo: Toyo Keizai Shinpo Sha.

Williamson, O.E. (1975) *Markets and Hierarchies: Analysis and Antitrust Implication*, New York: The Free Press.

—— (1986) *Economic Organization: Firms, Markets, and Policy Control*, New York: Wheatsheaf Books.

8 Neural network simulation of QC circle activities

Shigekazu Ishihara, Keiko Ishihara, Mitsuo Nagamachi and Alfredo Pinochet

INTRODUCTION

Japanese management style has been influencing other management cultures. Many organizational behaviour textbooks make reference to 'Theory Z' (Ouchi 1981) and other works about Japanese management style (e.g. Altman *et al.* 1985, Davis and Newstrom 1985, Dessler 1983, DuBrin 1984). Researchers have found some unique things about Japanese management in the relationships between each worker, and between managers and other groups. Examples of these are 'Individual Responsibility', 'Control systems that are less formal', and 'Consensus decision making'.

In recent studies of Japanese management style, Western researchers have taken more analytic approaches. Johnson (1988) investigated some Japanese-owned firms in the USA. He concluded that the success of Japanese firms was due to the introduction of particular management techniques and their development. He argues that Japanese firms introduced Quality Control circles in the 1950s, but American managers ignored them for a long time.

Lincoln (1989) and his colleagues surveyed 106 factories in the USA and Japan and 8,302 of their employees using questionnaires. They concluded from the results that Japanese employees were less satisfied with their work, but have a higher organizational commitment than American employees. He also pointed that Japanese are more active in informal work group socializing than Americans. Employees enmeshed in such networks of co-worker relationships, whether Japanese or American, had more positive attitudes towards the company and the job.

Whether Japanese management is really superior or not, is still a controversial problem. Nevertheless, Japanese management is distinctive on employees' participation in self-management, and QC circles are a typical form of participation. Nowadays, QC circles are regarded as an important contributor to the success of Japanese Industry (Ouchi 1981, DuBrin 1984).

QUALITY CONTROL CIRCLES

Quality Control circles are voluntary teams of workers, which also include supervisors. The circles are usually composed of people who work together. They meet regularly to produce ideas for solving production problems, such as quality, cost, efficiency and working conditions.

The circle activation provides opportunity for workers to uncover problems and to solve them by themselves. This activity is less formal than deliberately formed hierarchical groups such as one composed of a supervisor and subordinate employees. In a circle, all participants have an equal opportunity to make remarks. These spontaneous involvements are effective in raising members' and groups' productivity, motivation and satisfaction (Ouchi 1981).

Do QC circles produce a positive effect?

It is very difficult to measure the effectiveness of group participation on a company by doing an experiment. Neider (1980) has done a valuable comparative experiment. He investigated the influence of employee participation and its impact on productivity, in experimental conditions. 110 employees of four department stores from a family-owned chain of retail stores of New York participated in the experiment. Each store was assigned to different experimental conditions.

1 In participation-only condition, all employees in one store (store P) were divided into six groups. In the first 4 weeks of experiment period, these groups were made to discuss ideas and suggestions regarding how to approach customers, and members reached a consensus on a new form of preferred approach. Afterwards, the store manager called all employees and let them know that he had reviewed their ideas and that they could put them into effect for 4 weeks.
2 Incentive-only condition was done at another store (store I). Employees were told that individuals were able to choose from a variety of incentives (movie tickets, a day off with pay, etc.), corresponding to average hourly sales over a 4-week period.
3 In a combined condition (store PI), both the incentive scheme and discussion groups were initiated and the experimental period lasted for 4 weeks.

4 In a control condition (store C), no experimental changes were undergone during the 4 weeks.

Performances of employees for each store were measured as average sales per hour. During the test, only store PI had a statistically significant increase in sales. Other stores had no significant increase. A self-assessment questionnaire about degree of participation was used for measuring the participation in decision making, before and after the experiment

Stores P and PI showed significantly higher participation scores than the other two stores. Neider's experiment gave very important factors for motivating work organizations. Group discussion alone could not motivate, and the reward incentive alone could not motivate employees. Until now, the effect of reward on motivation has been mainly discussed in the context of management. Nevertheless, participation is indispensable to motivate performance. The contribution of the QC circle activity to productivity was proved by this experimental organizational study.

In another study, Nagamachi (1987) emphasized the need for voluntary participation for the activation of QC circles. Many instances appearing in his book follow a typical interesting path. An idea that strikes one member can be shared with all the participants through discussion in the circle, then the meeting gets more activated. As a result, all the members get more ability for problem solving. Afterwards, good ideas get more opportunities to occur, the ideas are shared with group members, the members get more ability, and so on.

An example is shown in Nagamachi (1987). A QC circle activity was introduced in a golf club. The employees are called together to a 'casual meeting for uncovering any problems' instead of 'training', because most of them would become tense and do not feel like attending. One of the problems that many members pointed out was that some golfers smoke on the golfcourse while playing. They talked about how to make golfers quit smoking on the course. If the circle had not organized, the solution might have been putting up many warning posters saying 'Don't smoke on the course'. Actually, the circle members patiently discussed the problem then someone in the group suggested that they had to try to find a solution which the customers would be willing to accept. The final solution through the meetings was that each caddie took a little ashtray on the round and handed it to the golfers with a smile when they started to smoke. When all the caddies carried out their idea the golfers were surprised at the new service, and then they thanked the caddies and were ashamed at breaking the rules. Two months after introducing the idea, no player smoked on the course; thus the problem was successfully solved. Since then, all the members are getting skills to find solutions while keeping customers' satisfaction in mind, and they succeeded in solving many kinds of problems by themselves, without direction of any supervisors.

Self-controlled QC circle activity can be regarded as a type of self-organizing behaviour. In the next section, self-organizing ideas will be applied to QC circle behaviours.

SELF-ORGANIZING BEHAVIOUR

Self-organization consists of building a distinctive structure spontaneously from chaotic uniformness. Amari explained self-organizing in the following terms (Amari 1986).

In a factory, processing materials into products by following blueprints is not called self-organizing, even if that entails a complicated structure. On the other hand, life does decode its DNA and organize itself. Life contains its own blueprint, but at the same time, it builds mechanisms that decode, control and decide the ongoing processes. This is a self-organizing process. A nervous system, which builds optimal mechanisms for information processing by learning from the external information structure, is also a good example of self-organization. Differing from a factory, the external world only presents its information, and does not teach the concrete neuron connections needed for information processing.

Self-organizing phenomena

Originally, self-organization phenomena were discussed in relation to physics and chemistry phenomena. Haken (1981) explained the self-organization process of a laser. Prigogine and Stengers (1984) showed self-organization in chemical processes and chaotic processes.

In computational neuroscience, Amari and his colleagues have been developing a mathematical model of the self-organizing process of neurons. Their studies can explain how the columnar neuron structure, found in the visual cortex, is formed (Amari 1986).

Haken (1981) applied his ideas on self-organization to explain processes ranging from the neuronal process of visual cognition to the emergence of economical order. His proposals to social and brain science are not based on his own empirical experiments or research, but are very suggestive for a systematical view of the problems found in these sciences.

Self-organization in organization behaviour

Nonaka (1988) developed a theory about 'Creating Organizational Order out of Chaos' in company management. He stated that the self-renewal of an organization is done by the creation of meaningful information from chaos. He used the term 'chaos' to mean the creation of different kinds of information, and he argued that to keep creating chaos is necessary for organization renewal. A new order in the organization is formed through making chaos and resolving contradictions.

He pointed out that the QC circle is an example of information creation. Different kinds of information created by their members compete and complement each other, then the new collective information leads the organization to change. Nonaka stressed that the top manager's role is to create chaos, and he gives examples of companies that have succeeded by using this method. His theory illustrates change processes of entire companies initiated by top management.

The term 'self-organization' has not been widely used in social psychology. However, psychology has accumulated scientific knowledge based on an experimental approach to group dynamics. Group dynamics research includes group cohesiveness, group norms, motivation, leadership, communication structure, and so on. Recently, organizational psychology researchers have begun to pay attention not only to the intra-group environment (which has specific cognitive and behavioural traits as factors of mutual influence between members), but also to considering groups as organisms that adapt to their external environment (Starbuck 1983).

We hypothesize that self-organization of a QC circle is established through interaction between members such as communication and leadership, individual learning of each member, and adaptation or processing of information from the external environment.

A SELF-ORGANIZING MODEL

This chapter will consider the self-organization of small work groups. The approach presented here to modelling self-organization takes into account organizational psychology theory. We define self-organization as a formation process of informal networks or work groups. We consider the formation of informal groups such as QC circles or task force groups for new projects.

Our aim is to build an organizational behaviour model that can incorporate parameters concerning different group dynamics factors. In this study, we attempt to incorporate factors of a QC circle that represent the interaction between members such as communication and leadership, individual learning of each member, and adaptation or processing ability of information from the external environment. In order to model such dynamic behaviour, we utilize a self-organizing neural network.

Modelling and organization using a Kohonen-type neural network

We have used a neural network model based on a Kohonen type of self-organizing mapping which learns without the aid of a teacher (Kohonen 1982). We modified the architecture of the Kohonen model to enable the modelling of human groups. Kohonen's model of the self-organizing process was done by changing the weights of synapses for each neuron unit to represent signals coming from the external environment.

In the visual and auditory area of the brain cortex, neurons are arranged anatomically in the direction that elicits the greatest response from each neuron. These organizations are called a column structure, and are considered to be created during a learning stage by a self-organization process. Kohonen and his collaborators present one such algorithm which produces what they call a self-organizing feature map similar to those that occur in the brain. They showed the usefulness of their model for the generation of a colour mapping similar to the visual cortex (Saarinen and Kohonen 1985). Other applications were done by Kohonen and other researchers for audio signal recognition. These applications aim at the micro and biological structure of cognition. In our research, we apply such a network structure to model human groups, the macro-structure of cognition done by more than one person.

Kohonen's network architecture consists of one layer of mutually connected neurons that each have several input synapses. Each synapse has a synapse weight. When the network receives an input signal, the neuron that has the most similar synapse weights to the input signal is selected. This selection is called the winner-take-all process. The winner neuron and its neighbouring neurons change their synapse weights and approximate to the input signal. After many iterations of this process, the neurons of the network finally represent the characteristics of the input signals.

The distinctive character of Kohonen's network is building internal representation of information from outside, by adaptation through local interaction among neurons. We suggest the idea of adaptation through local interaction can be applied to the adaptation process of human organization.

The improving process of QC circles can be reproduced on the Kohonen network. The neuron that has the most similar synapse weights to an input signal is activated. We can regard that neuron as a member who has a good idea. Then, the neuron and its neighbour neurons change their synapse weights, so that they bring their weights close to the input signal. These processes are similar to human groups, in that neighbouring members communicate each other and share the idea for the current problem, and then they improve themselves toward that problem. Based on the consideration described above, we can draw an analogy between the neural process and organizational problem solving.

Modelling the group formation process

In modelling the group formation process for problem solving, we represented the factors of group formation for variables in the neural network. Neurons each represent a potential member of a group. Synapse weights correspond to the information processing ability of information coming from the external environment.

The signals inputted to the neural net correspond to information from the external environment which needs to be processed by the organization. The information processing is then done by members of the organization who have some ability in processing given information, and do it spontaneously. Through repetition of the input processing cycle, the organization gradually enters into a specialized state.

Usually, information from the external environment does not consist of a single factor, but has multiple factors in it. To process complex information, different abilities are needed. In our simulation, we assumed that the input signals have three values, and each component corresponds to one of the three factors of information. Each information set has a different combination of these three factors.

We developed a simulation program for this specialized neural network. The simulator is called NOBES (a Neural network Organizational Behavior Simulator).

QC CIRCLE ACTIVITY MODELLED BY NOBES

Modelling QC circle by NOBES

In the simulation of QC activity done by NOBES, each unit represents a member of a QC circle, and problems that arise in the organization are solved by capable members. A time aspect of organizational change is as follows: before starting a QC circle, members' problem solving capability is small, and the difficulties of solving problems are relatively large. By putting a QC circle in action, and as members exchange their knowledge, their problem solving capability begins to rise. After the activation of a circle, the problem solution mechanisms are self-organized by group(s) of specialized members.

Setting parameters from a case study based on an actual organization

Parameters were taken for this article from a case about a QC circle. In that case, a best practice company in the quality control field was selected. The company was commended by a QC committee. Problems related to the company and the activation of members were surveyed when (1) the QC circle was first established, and (2) when the company regarded the QC circle as firmly set up. For a comparison of the change in competence in problem solving, members who engaged in the same problems at time (a) and (b) were selected as participants in the survey (Nagamachi, Kaneda and Matsubara 1993).

Questionnaires for problem discovery and assessment

A problem discovering questionnaire was used to assess the problems existing before the starting of QC circles, and problem estimation questionnaires were used to measure degrees of difficulties. Three questionnaires were completed by division managers who knew the problems well. The problem discovering questionnaire was of a free answer type. The estimation questionnaire was adapted from the problems found through the results of the discovering questionnaire and difficulties of problems were estimated on a 10-point scale.

A questionnaire for each member's ability in problem solving: all members of circles received a questionnaire that had questions related to problem solving capability for the problems found in the problem discovering questionnaire. Each question was answered by indicating the most relevant alternative on a 10-point scale, with 1 representing a very low solving ability and 10 indicating a very high solving ability.

This questionnaire was presented in a double fashion: first, questions were asked in relation to the time before QC circles were established and second in relation to the present state.

Table 8.1 shows the averaged value (between subjects) of self-estimated problem solving ability, on three of the problems encountered: 'Business efficiency'; 'Expanding the business'; and 'Willingness to change'. A comparison of time (a) with (b), reveals that the problem solving capability has raised in time (b). Members' capability was improved, and the organization was activated.

Table 8.1 Averaged value of circle members' self-estimated problem solving ability

	Business efficiency	*Expanding business*	*Willingness to change*
(a) Before QC circle set up	1.4	2.2	1.5
(b) Some considerable time after QC circle set up	6.8	7.6	7.2

Simulation of self-organization through a QC circle

We implemented empirical organization data into QC circle self-organization simulation using NOBES. The problem solving ability of each member at the starting time of the QC circle, was set as initial value of synapse weights of each neuron. Parameters for the adaptation rate to information coming from the outside were set as 0.5, and the influence rate to neighbours was set as 0.2.

We found that a combination of three types of problems that related to Business efficiency, Expanding the business and Willingness To Change, are present at a given moment and that members of the organization are expected to improve their ability to process those problems. We found further that, through the adaptation and influence processes, members raised their capability. Output obtained from the simulation model and questionnaires are shown in Table 8.2. Empirical data was successfully mapped on our model.

The simulation result is very similar to the questionnaire data at the time the circle was firmly set up. In our simulation using NOBES, the hypothesis of self-organization process based on influence or information exchange and members' adaptation was tested. The test showed that QC circle activity changes each member's awareness of problems and problem solving ability. Simulating the QC circle's

Table 8.2 Comparison of the simulation result with questionnaire data at time (b)

	Business efficiency	*Expanding business*	*Willingness to change*
Questionnaire	6.8	7.6	7.2
Simulation	8.0	7.9	7.7

self-organization activity shows as well as the validity of NOBES, the influence and adaptation model.

To complete our simulation, in the next section, we consider the leadership process in group formation. Leadership has large influence on forming and stimulating QC circle activity.

MODELLING LEADER INFLUENCE ON GROUP FORMATION

Social-psychological view of groups and leaders

Regarding the adaptation process of a group to the external environment, it has been noted that an organization is made up of subsystems which relate to each other, and that this adaptation to the external environment will be better achieved by providing the grounds for a harmonic relationship between subsystems.

To adjust an organization to the complex and changeable environment using a decentralized organization design with many autonomous, small and specialized groups (e.g. QC circles, taskforce) is more advantageous than with an organizational design of groups that are highly dependent on a central authority. The formation of decentralized groups is usually not arranged directly from outside the group, but is rather achieved by a self-organizing process. Groups are autonomously formed when members of an organization who have various abilities in getting and processing information from the external environment and share common interests or goals, interact with each other on a regular basis. Thus, the characteristics of the individual members of an organization will make each of them join groups where other members show the same traits.

In situations where groups self-organize, the specialization of the leader has an important influence on group members. This specialization can be thought of as the field where the leader has distinctive abilities which he wants to use to the benefit of the group. Leadership can be measured by the amount of influence that a member of the group exerts on other members. The group formation process done by members of an organization has been simulated in this research for three cases: (1) the existence of appointed leaders; (2) the existence of emergent leaders; and (3) a peer situation where nobody is capable of becoming the leader.

To model the self-organizing group process including leadership, NOBES was used again, this time with test data. In our model, each possible member of a group is represented as one neuron, with a different synapse weight, which allows for representing the different information processing ability or alertness to a given type of information of each individual. The interaction between members of a group is represented as the change of synapse weights of the neurons, i.e., a gradual specialization. NOBES allows the formation of groups around leaders who influence group members with their ideas and suggestions. The aim of this simulation is to clarify the way leaders use outside information to influence other individuals who choose to become members of the group they lead.

Characteristics of leader behaviour

There have been many studies of leadership, but the traits found in leaders are highly task specific. Academics have cited various traits, such as personality characteristics, authority, maintenance of groups, and so on (Pfeffer 1984). In an article by Carter *et al.* (1951), only two distinctive leader behaviours were found out of 165 types of behavioural categories. Categories like 'diagnoses the situation – makes interpretations' and 'gives information on how to carry out an action' are statistically significant at different levels of activity throughout all types of leadership and situations. Thus, interpreting the external environment, and giving information to other members on how to carry out tasks are regarded as typical leader behaviour.

In this chapter we regard leaders as being more able to process information that comes from the external environment and to have more influence over other members when interpreting information. Thus, we built our model based on those two factors as distinguishing features of leaders.

The appointed and the emergent leader

Carter *et al.* (1951) proposed two types of leaders according to their experimental group studies. They made an experiment on three types of tasks: reasoning; mechanical assembly; and discussion. Forty subjects were assigned to five groups of eight subjects each. Each group was arranged as equal as possible in relation to the leadership potential and mutual friendship of subjects based on the observers' ratings. The five groups were all presented with the three types of tasks. After these tasks were completed, each group was divided in halves, taking care that all new groups would have an equal distribution of leadership abilities, according to observers' ratings during the first tasks. Then, the ten groups were again presented with the three types of tasks as above, under the following two situations:

1 Emergent leader situation
In this situation, one of the four subjects in the group got the highest leadership rating during the tasks by the group observers. That person was regarded as an 'emergent leader'.
2 Appointed leader situation
Before re-running the experiment with four member teams, each group had one member removed and replaced with a subject from another group who had a similar leadership rating. This newly entered subject was appointed by the observer as a leader in the presence of the other three group members. The subject who was appointed performed adequately as a leader, although he/she was not necessarily regarded as the emergent leader in the previous experiment.

Appointed leaders regarded themselves as the group coordinator. Emergent leaders took over the leadership position with energetic action and by trying to get the other members' acceptance for their leadership. In the discussion task, the difference between the two types of leaders was most significant. In their study, Carter *et al.* (1951) considered that the difference in behaviour between the emergent and the appointed leader seems to be dependent on the kinds of tasks assigned to the group, thus, it was difficult for them to conclude a general theory.

In a recent meta-analysis research from many past studies in task-oriented groups, group members who engage in task-oriented behaviour are likely to emerge as leaders. In groups where members' attention is devoted to maintaining a social relationship, members who engage in an interpersonal oriented behaviour emerge as leaders (Eagly and Karau 1991).

For this chapter, we have made a simulation of an organization which includes members with different traits, and which shows the appearance of emergent leaders. The task assigned was a problem solving situation that required novel solutions. Problem solving is the task that is most frequently used in leadership studies. Problem solving tasks in a wide sense are used in 69 per cent of group studies among the 75 listed studies in the meta-analysis done by Eagly and Karau (1991). We consider that problem solving is one the most important tasks in an organization today.

Our simulation allows for the study of the dynamics of group formation, and not only the effects on the company and its members, of already established groups. This is possible through the use of neural network models which simulate the individual behaviour of the persons that belong to a company and are trying to form a group. At the same time, our model allows us to visualize the effect of different styles of leadership on group formation.

SIMULATIONS OF DIFFERENT TYPES OF LEADERSHIP

Incorporating leadership into the model

When social influence plays a role in the outcome, it is important to take into account the amount of influence each leader exerts on other members of the organization. To include different degrees of influence in our model we have had to enhance Kohonen's model. In Kohonen's model there is an assumption that all neurons have the same interaction area at a given moment (i.e., the same influence area) and also the same Nc and a.

Our enhancement consists in introducing special neurons with a large communication area Nc, large W and an a with a different value. This change allows us to model a leader who has a large communication area and influence.

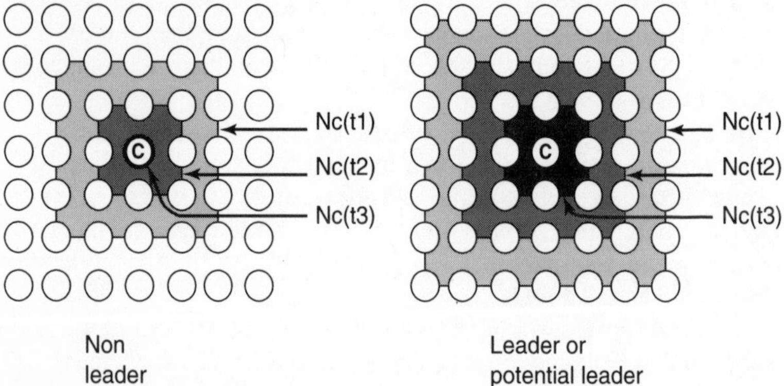

Figure 8.1 Difference of influence area

This simulation reveals how leaders influence the group formation process. In this leadership influence simulation, we use hypothesized organization and problems, different from the previous simulation. Information from the external environment includes three types of factors (A, B and C), which are expressed as the distribution of the values of each of the three dimensions, and in relation to which each member has processing abilities of various degrees. In a simulation model members of the organization have been distributed according to their weight (i.e., their ability to process information).

In the simulations we assumed three types of situations, each one with a different type of leader, and thus three types of group formation processes: (1) peer situation where nobody is capable of becoming the leader; (2) existence of appointed leaders with a specialization; and (3) two persons have the potential to become an emergent leader, but have no specialization. In this last case, an emergent leader will appear, and hopefully end up specializing in the processing of one factor. In the three situations, the organization was composed of 100 members, and the simulation was run through 2,000 state changes (i.e., the arrival, 2,000 times, of new information).

Three different types of information are present at a given moment and members of the organization are expected to improve their ability to process one type of information. These three types of situations are modelled by varying the change rate of synapse weights. In situation (1) members have the same ability to adapt to the changes from the external environment and the same power to influence neighbours. In situation (2) three leaders are appointed. Appointed leaders already have enough ability and larger influence power than other members. These leaders are specialized from the beginning, so they are located at a suitable position throughout the simulation. In situation (3) there are two members who have the potential to become an emergent leader, but their ability is not specialized at the initial state. They have a larger influence power than other members, but their ability is not fixed, and they gradually specialize their ability as well as other members. They are expected to promote group formation as they specialize.

Results and discussion

In situation (1) the members do not end up specializing, and show a fuzzy distribution. In situation (2) organization members formed specialized groups around the points A, B and C. Appointed leaders promoted group formation using their larger influence. In situation (3), one influential member is located at point B, and the other is halfway between the points A and C.

Organization in the first situation (i.e., no leaders), ends up without specialized groups. The second situation shows that after 2,000 cycles specialized groups were formed by the appointed leaders. In the third case one of the influential members succeeded in reaching the point B, along with other group members. This member is regarded as an emergent leader who promoted group formation. But the other influential member has not yet reached a desirable specialization (i.e., either A or C). This member did not show convincing leadership, so no group formed around him/her. This result can be interpreted as follows. This member has the potential to become an emergent leader, that is, has bigger Nc than other members. The organization, however, received from the external environment little information at which this member was skilled in processing, thus, this member could not show his/her capability. Thus, although this member has a larger influence, he/she could not become specialized, and was not successful in promoting the self-organization of a new group.

Leaders promote group specialization, usually in the direction of their own experience or education. When they are deficient in these, or their abilities are not suitable for processing the information that comes from the external environment, they may end up in an inefficient middle point. As the simulation points out, leaders have an important role in group formation.

CONCLUSION

In this chapter we introduced NOBES, a neural network based simulator of self-organizational behaviour. Simulations of several organizational behaviours, such as QC circle activity and the influence of different styles of leadership were done. These simulation results show NOBES has the ability to model self-organization behaviours which include personal traits such as personality, problem solving ability and influence with other members.

The establishment of electronic communication networks today is changing our work style. We can communicate with each other even if we are not in the same place nor the same time. The new style of communication will bring up different influences to our organizing behaviour from the face-to-face comunication style. Computational models of dynamic organizational processes will be powerful tools for probing new organizational problems.

REFERENCES

Altman, S., Valenzi, E. and Hodgetts, R.M. (1985) *Organizational Behavior: Theory and Practice*, Orlando, FL: Academic Press.

Amari, S. (1986) 'On self-organization', *Mathematical Science*, 277, pp. 5–7.

Carter, L., Haythorn, W., Shriver, B. and Lanzetta, J. (1951) 'The Behavior of Leaders and Other Group Members', *Journal of Abnormal and Social Psychology*, 46, pp. 589–95.

Davis, K. and Newstrom, J.W. (1985) *Human Behavior at Work: Organizational Behavior*, 7th edn, New York: McGraw-Hill.

Dessler, G. (1983) *Applied Human Relations*, Virginia: Reston Publishing.

DuBrin, A.J. (1984) *Foundations of Organizational Behavior: An Applied Perspective*, Englewood Cliffs, NJ: Prentice Hall.

Eagly, A.H. and Karau, S.J. (1991) 'Gender and the Emergence of Leaders: A Meta-Analysis', *Journal of Personality and Social Psychology*, 60(5), pp. 685–710.

Haken, H. (1981) *Erfolgsgeheimnisse der Natur: Synergetik, die Lehre vom Zusammenwirken*, Stuttgart: Deutsche Verlags-Anstalt.

Johnson, C. (1988) 'Japanese-Style Management in America', *California Management Review*, 30, pp. 34–45.

Kohonen, T. (1982) 'Self-Organized Formation of Topologically Correct Feature Maps', *Biological Cybernetics*, 43, pp. 59–69.

Lincoln, J.R. (1989) 'Employee Work Attitudes and Management Practice in the U.S. and Japan: Evidence from a Large Comparative Survey', *California Management Review*, 32, pp. 89–106.

Lippmann, R.P. (1987) 'An Introduction to Computing with Neural Nets', *IEEE ASSP Magazine*, 4, pp. 4–22.

Nagamachi, M. (1987) *Psychology of QC Circles*, Tokyo: Kaibundo.

Nagamachi, M., Kaneda, K. and Matsubara, Y. (1993) 'A Study of Extended Garbage Can Model on Self-Organization', *Journal of Japan Industrial Management Association*, 44(3), pp. 191–9.

Neider, L.L. (1980) 'An Experimental Field Investigation Utilizing an Expectancy Theory View of Participation', *Organization Behavior and Human Performance*, 26, pp. 425–42.

Nonaka, I. (1988) 'Creating Organizational Order Out of Chaos', *California Management Review*, 30, pp. 57–73.

Ouchi, W.G. (1981) *Theory Z: How American Business Can Meet the Japanese Challenge*, Reading, MA: Addison-Wesley.

Pfeffer, J. (1984) 'The Ambiguity of Leadership', in W.E. Rosenbach and R.L. Taylor (eds) *Contemporary Issues in Leadership*, New York: Westview Press, pp. 4–17.

Prigogine, Y. and Stengers, I. (1984) *Order Out of Chaos: Man's New Dialogue with Nature*, New York: Bantam Books.

Saarinen, J. and Kohonen, T. (1985) 'Self-Organized Formation of Colour Maps in a Model Cortex', *Perception*, 14, pp. 711–19.

Starbuck, W.H. (1983) 'Organizations and their Environments', in M.D. Dunette (ed.) *Handbook of Industrial and Organizational Psychology*, New York: John Wiley and Sons, pp. 1069–123.

[illegible] operations [illegible] capabilities [illegible] evolution [illegible] environment [illegible] proposals to formulate strategies based [illegible] knowledge.

> Recognizing that corporations as individuals are members of [illegible] communities they should take active roles in social contribution [illegible] corporations should not hesitate to share the burden [illegible] community problems. Corporations should fully recognize the importance of environment protection and energy saving [illegible] environment, resources, energy are common [illegible] human beings.
>
> Morita 1992, p. [illegible]

[illegible] very [illegible] among Japanese corporations [illegible] those which have a history of international orientation from their foundations. For example, Sony is considered to be a typical example of [illegible] oriented corporations.

In summary, [illegible] as open systems in academia as well as business communities, the focus of study should shift from [illegible] to the interaction process with the environment. The next section [illegible] organizations' relations [illegible] environment [illegible]

ORGANIZATION AND EXTERNAL ENVIRONMENT

According to Ewing-Mensah

> [illegible] take an active interaction [illegible] [which] occurs when an organization, using its resources and creative capabilities, [illegible] conditions in the environment.
>
> Ewing-Mensah 1981, p. [illegible]

Through the [illegible] interactive interaction, organizations seek to [illegible] that is [illegible] their own interests [illegible] play a major role in [illegible] interaction with [illegible] interaction with the environment [illegible] the public, [illegible] agencies, public relations [illegible] in order to [illegible] the public [illegible] and Bleev[illegible]

Part III

Symbiotic interaction with the environment

9 Population ecology versus network dynamics

From evolution to co-evolution

Frank-Jürgen Richter and Yoshiya Teramoto

INTRODUCTION

Organizations are one of the most characteristic signs of our times and scholars of organizational science made different proposals to describe the economic reality of organizations. Organizations are complex phenomena and can be understood in many different ways. Thus, the analysis of organizations always rests in applying some kind of theory to the situations being considered.

Most of the available literature on organizations focuses on static analyses of organizational behaviour and do not grasp any perspectives of organizational change. The mainstream of organizational analysis is embraced by the so called transaction cost theory (Williamson 1975), which provides static tools to select the less costly and therefore optimizing organizational forms. It is assumed that organizations usually approximate an efficient equilibrium.

Because the economic environments of the 1990s become increasingly uncertain and unpredictable, static concerns of organizational theory are no longer satisfactory and sufficient. Viewing organizations by theories which consider their time path, on the other hand, could prove fruitful to the extent that equilibrium assumptions are unrealistic (Richter 1995).

One particular alternative to perceive organizational change is the population ecology approach, which has its origin in biology and which has been adapted for the purpose of organizational analysis.

> Recent work in population ecology has specified how social changes affect forms of organization as well as how competition shapes the diversity of forms.
>
> Hannan and Freeman 1989, p. 11

The term population ecology was chosen to recognize the focus on the evolution of whole sets of organizations rather than on single ones. The work of Hannan and Freeman (1977, 1989) especially has had a strong influence on the establishment of an evolutionary approach to organizational reality and will be discussed in some depth in order to illustrate how it extends our knowledge about evolutionary change processes of organizations. The population ecology approach will further be critized in order to develop a new understanding of evolution encompassing interfirm cooperation within corporate networks.

POPULATION ECOLOGY AND ECONOMIC REALITY

The population ecology view of organizations uses Darwin's theory of evolution for organizational analysis. The main emphasis is the evolution of organizations as their replacement by new ones which occurs as processes of variation, selection, and retention. The transfer of Darwin's theory on social systems has a long tradition and influenced essentially the ideas of social change and progress. Campbell for example understands by socio-cultural evolution

> a selective accumulation of skills, technologies, recipes, belief, customs and organizational structures.
>
> Campbell 1975, p. 1104

Nelson and Winter whose theory of social evolution is bound to economic progress more directly argue in a similar way:

> It [the theory] contemplates both the inheritance of acquired characteristics and the timely appearance of variation under the stimulus of adversity.
>
> Nelson and Winter 1982, p. 11

These approaches have in common that the social variation with advantageous features will survive and that Darwin's principle of natural selection is widely accepted. Most schools of evolutionary theory take Darwin's selection model for granted and Adams even argues that

> Darwinist concepts seem to have entered the common vocabulary and require no exegesis. It apparently does not occur to anyone discussing 'selection' or 'reproduction' to give Darwin the kind of political obeisance that often was de rigueur for Marx.
>
> Adams 1991, p. 230

The population ecology approach, in particular, puts out the idea of survival in clear terms: when the competitive relations change, positive selection of the fittest organizations take place. Since there is usually a resource scarcity in the organization's environment, only the most robust organizations have a chance for survival. Large organizations normally have superior capacities of adaptation because they have broader access to resources than smaller ones. The business environment is therefore the critical factor for the organization's evolution.

Hannan and Freeman's approach has been appropriate in an economic world characterized by steady growth and increasing competitiveness. Companies needed to grow in size to support their expansion in new markets and the realization of technological innovations. Large companies continued to outperform smaller companies and they desired to drive for larger size through mergers and acquisitions. Those companies which accumulated the most resources were likely to survive. Both economic reality and theory presumed that organizations and environments are separate phenomena.

Since the mid 1980s, this scenario has changed. Several companies have been partly abandoning their competitive behaviour and entered close cooperative relationships with suppliers, customers and even competitors (Teramoto 1990). This behaviour is guided by the insight that cooperation can lead to better profits and to strategic advantages than if they were to continue competing in antagonistic ways. Due to the numerous cooperative linkages between companies, whole interfirm networks have emerged.

In particular, Japanese companies are operating new kinds of cooperative networks, where there is no clear boundary between the companies and their environments (Teramoto 1990). The following trends of economic transitions in Japan can be seen:

1 Japanese companies are often collaborating within temporally limited projects to perform joint product developments. They are not just exchanging technological knowledge, but are rather generating totally new knowledge. The cooperative agreements help the firms to learn from each other and to mobilize new knowledge resources.
2 Japanese companies are often voluntarily limiting their corporate growth. They externalize a majority of their business operations with *keiretsu* companies and subcontractors are performing much of the work. Mergers and acquisitions are quite rare. Japanese companies sometimes even devolve in order to become a set of only loosely connected agents.

3 Japanese business leaders as well as bureaucracy representatives appeal for a new age of symbiosis. They argue that if Japanese companies want to conserve their reputations, they have to contribute actively for worldwide economic welfare and have to reduce, by a certain degree, their own ambitions. A way to realize symbiosis is to enter strategic alliances with Western firms.

These trends show that organizational evolution is always a pattern of relations between single organizational units and their environments. This idea was already developed by some newer system approaches in which it was stated that organizations do not live in isolation but are elements of a complex ecosystem (von Foerster 1960, Holling 1978, Varela 1984). In our view, organizations do not evolve by adapting to environmental changes but rather by their cooperative relations with the surrounding environments. Organizations are actors operating with others in the construction of their environments rather than depending upon external forces. Thus, one could talk about the co-evolution of organizations rather than about the evolution of individual organizations, as seen by traditional approaches.

It is the aim of this chapter to develop a theoretical approach describing the cooperative interaction between organizations and their environments. The approach will be named 'network dynamics' to express the time path of organizational evolution as well as the interwoven interplay of organizations. The connotation 'network' says that organizations have shared futures and that they are not absolutely discrete entities. In recent years there has been an explosion of literature on corporate networks (e.g. Håkansson 1987, Gilroy 1992). The approaches describe, however, how single firms can take the largest possible amount of profit by cooperating within networks. In this sense, cooperation means a zero-sum game situation and remains almost wholly confined within the Darwinian mould. The network dynamics approach, on the other hand, describes positive-sum situations and will be developed in the following sections by comparison with the population ecology approach.

BASIC EVOLUTIONARY MECHANISMS

In this section the question concerning the mechanism which acts as the driving force for organizational evolution will be answered. As argued by most scholars working with the metaphor of evolution, the growth of a given system is directed forward and occurs as long as elementary forces impact on or within the system (Campbell 1975,

Holling 1976). Social laws comprehend propositions about organizational change that hold over time and space. The basic evolutionary mechanisms within populations as well as networks of organizations can be seen in Table 9.1.

Table 9.1 Basic evolutionary mechanisms

Population ecology approach	*Network dynamics approach*
Adaptation	Learning
Reaction on economic context	Creation of economic context
Contextual determination	Collective interaction

As already mentioned, the population ecology approach analyses the genesis of organizations as a process of variation, selection and retention. Organizations react to changing environmental conditions by the variation of existing organizational structures and strategies. The new structures and strategies are then exposed to environmental tests. After a certain time it will be clear which organizations are the better adapted to the environmental conditions and which organizations can survive. Such a perspective assumes that organizations react to changed environmental conditions and adapt to them. Hence

> the organizational variability reflects designed changes in the strategy and structure of individual organizations in response to environmental changes, threats and opportunities.
>
> Hannan and Freeman 1989, pp. 12

This corresponds with Darwin's argument that adaptation is the basic mechanism for evolution. Adaptation is the process by which biological forms come to be attuned to their environment. A butterfly, for example, which has a better camouflage has a better chance of survival than less well camouflaged individuals of the same species. Hence, adaptation is a reactive process. The hostile environment has to be adapted to if an organism is not to become the victim of the negative selection of its environment.

By the transfer of the Darwinist principle of adaptation, organizations are seen as phenomena which change due to environmental influences. Similarly, in the contingency view of organizations (Burns and Stalker 1961), organizations are perceived to be in continual change in response to their environments. This exchange is crucial for sustaining the life and the form of organizations.

The mechanism of adaptation occurs, because the resources which are present in a particular 'ecological niche' are limited. There is usually a resource scarcity and only the best adapted survive. The nature of organizations is dependent on resource availability and on competition between different organizations. Thus, the importance of resource limitations shapes the growth, development and decline of organizations. This idea has been developed in the 'resource dependency' theory (Pfeffer and Salancik 1978). Organizations are competing for the resources in the same environment because they are scarce.

Hence, Hannan and Freeman's approach focuses on the nature and distribution of resources between organizations as the central force of change. Adaptation is not a creative learning process, but rather the passive response to environmental factors. Organizations' forces of self-renewal, like the ability to make strategic choice, are merely taken for granted.

The network dynamics approach takes a different point of view. The basic evolutionary mechanism is not seen as adaptation, but as learning. The companies within a network do not reactively adapt to environmental influences but become actively responsible for their evolution by initiating learning procedures within the boundaries of their organizations as well as within the whole network.

Intra-organizational learning procedures have been well known for a long time. Argyris and Schön argued that organizational learning is a necessary mechanism for the evolutionary potential of firms (Argyris and Schön 1978). They further found that organizational learning occurs on different levels. Through single-loop learning organizations are guided towards a desired outcome within their given structures. Influences from the outside trigger such learning mechanisms so that one could also talk about adaptive learning. On a higher level of abstraction, double-loop learning occurs. Here, the given structures of organizations are questioned and newly formed. Double-loop learning is creative and does not occur as passive responses forced by outside stimuli.

Concering the network dynamics approach, double-loop learning has an evolutionary mechanism effect. The creation of corporate internal structures and values is the driving force for the evolution of organizations. Due to internal forces, organizations do not merely react to environmental influences, but create their environments actively on their own. By the integration into networks, they have increased the chance to perform inter-organizational learning processes. These are learning processes which are jointly made with other network members (Richter 1995). Instead of struggling for resources, firms are exchanging resources. These resources consist usually of product or market knowledge. When markets change and competition increases, only those firms which steadily generate new knowledge can be successful. Instead of hoarding knowledge resources and struggling for the limited resources currently available, exchange of knowledge leads them to a rapid increase of the potentially available resources.

The exchange of resources is followed by the joint creation of knowledge. Companies often link up to perform product development and innovation jointly. Due to the externalization of resources, the probability of generating new knowledge increases. The firms are evolving together and become co-learners in a jointly perceived environment. Such common learning processes are evolutionary mechanisms of a higher level, because new opportunities rather than justifications of old ones occur.

The evolutionary mechanism of learning breaks the Darwinist mould of pure adaptations to a hostile environment. On the contrary, learning as a mechanism for the evolution of organizations comes rather close to the biological theory of Kenichi Imanishi, the famous Japanese biologist, whose ideas paved the way for a new understanding of evolution. Imanishi argued that organisms evolve by a conscious force to live rather than by adaptation for survival (Imanishi, Shibatani and Yonemoto 1984). In his study of monkey populations he found that organisms communicate and share knowledge about their common destiny. One of his experiments, in particular, clarifies the collective learning behaviour: monkeys living in an observation station near the Japanese sea were fed with potatoes daily. One of the monkeys began, before the meal, washing the potatoes in the sea. Soon the other monkeys learned its behaviour and all members of the population began washing potatoes before eating them. There is no stringent necessity to wash potatoes and the monkeys did not adapt to environmental threats. On this view, the unique force of nature is not struggle, but rather co-evolution.

PERCEPTION OF THE SYSTEM BOUNDARIES

There is a long tradition of describing organizations as systems (Burns and Stalker 1961). A system is defined as a set of entities and their relations among each other as well as with the system's environment (von Bertalanffy 1968). Living systems are often taken as a model to understand complex economic organizations. There are different ways, however, of comparing organizations with living systems in general and to define the system boundaries in particular. The boundary perceptions on the micro-level of organizational systems for the population ecology and the network dynamics approaches are set out in Table 9.2.

Table 9.2 Organizations on the micro-level

Populations ecology approach	*Network dynamics approach*
Open systems	Operationally closed systems
Cycles of input and reaction	Environmental perturbations
Organizational inertia	Internal coherences

Hannan and Freeman perceive organizations as open systems which are adapting to their environments. In order to survive, they rely on resource imports from their environments which they transform into an input. This view is borrowed from the systems approach as developed by von Bertalanffy, who argued that organizations are 'open' to their environment (Bertalanffy 1968). The exchange of resources with the environment is crucial for sustaining a system's life. Environment and system are in continual interaction whereby the organization is shaped by the environment. It is therefore the dependent variable. While maintaining a continual exchange with the environment, local equilibria can be achieved. Organizations as open systems evolve from one steady state to the next and the evolutionary process is perceived to be a succession of local equilibria.

The reaction on environmental inputs does not occur directly, but starts after a delay. Hannan and Freeman argue that

> the most important issues about the applicability of evolutionary–ecological theories to organizations concern the timing of changes.
>
> Hannan and Freeman, p. 70

and talk further about the 'relative inertia' of organizations. Changes are infrequent and cannot be predicted. Organizations respond relatively slowly to the occurrence of threats and opportunities in their environments due to internal hindrances and to the environment itself. The politics of resource allocation in organizations and the external legitimation of organizational activity prevent them from responding too quickly to pressures to alter organizational practices or to initiate new kinds of action.

The network dynamics approach takes a different stance. Systems are no longer perceived to be open. This decision in theory design has far reaching consequences: systems cannot be voluntarily directed into a certain direction by environmental influences, but have specific eigenvalues which mark them against their environment. They are operationally closed. The notion of 'operational closeness' has been introduced by Varela:

> For such . . . systems, the main guideline for their characterization is not a set of inputs, but the nature of their internal coherences which arise out of their interconnectedness. Hence the term operational closeness.
>
> Varela 1984, p. 25

This does not mean that the existence of the environment is neglected, as was done in the case of the traditional management theories which devoted little attention to the environment (e.g. Taylor 1911, Fayol 1949). Operationally closed systems are rather linked to their environments and receive from them the conditions which are necessary for evolution. No system, which is part of a more comprehending system, can be totally autonomous. But the important difference between open and operationally closed systems is that organizations are no longer arbitrary influenceable units, but active agents operating with others to achieve a construction of their business environment.

The organizations within networks are not passively reacting to environmental influences, but are coupling with each other in order to evolve jointly. They develop an independent existence and are breaking away from the rigid environmental dependency. Thanks to their independent existence organizations are not inert constructs. Fluctuations within the organizations spontaneously change their structures, strategies and cultures. Such an emancipated perception of economic reality is in stark contrast to the idea of an organizational inertia by which organizational forms are conserved and exposed to the environment for which then selects those which are to survive.

Concerning the definition of organizations on the macro-level, too, there are essential differences between the population ecology and the network dynamics models. These are shown in Table 9.3.

Table 9.3 Organizations on the macro-level

Population ecology approach	*Network dynamics approach*
Closed systems	Operationally closed systems
Environmental isolation	Environmental perturbations
Internal power balances	Internal connections

The population ecology model assumes that populations of organizations are perfectly identifiable and demarcable.

> The main idea is to locate the boundaries and the processes that sustain them as a first step in identifying the structure and dynamics of the niche.
>
> Hannan and Freeman 1989, p. 54

Organizations gather in niches, because they depend on the same economic limitations and struggle for the same resources within a niche. The best adapted organizations can survive within a niche whereas the unfit members have to exit. Economic niches and therefore also the populations within the niches are relatively closed systems and the transition of an organization from one niche to another is rare and not probable. Thus, the influence of the external environments on the population's growth is widely neglected. The concept of stable niches is evident in most approaches to strategic management. Porter for example assumes that the competing firms of an industrial sector are clearly identifiable and that the efficiency of their competitive strategies decides their success within that sector. The internal balances within niches decide an organization's power position and its long-term competitiveness (Porter 1980).

In terms of the network dynamics approach, distinctive system boundaries of populations of organizations with their environment are not perceivable. The economic reality of the last few years showed that more and more companies diversify into bordering industries and nest into new niches. One possibility of diversification is the entering of partnership relationships with companies of bordering sectors (Teramoto 1990). By opening up new activity fields through joint innovation projects, companies are not just entering already existing sectors, but creating totally new niches. It is not only that the boundaries of an industry are changing but also that the boundary cannot be clearly defined for the industries created by network activities.

As a matter of fact, the boundaries of a network are not closed against such companies which do not yet take part in the network. Networks are always in the midst of change. Whereas some companies decide to exit the network, others join the network. The boundaries are blurring. During the affiliation to the network, however, the companies are shielding themselves against their external environments beyond the network and become a relatively autonomous unit. The objectives of the firms are coordinated and the firms have a common perception of reality. Hence, corporate networks are operationally closed systems. Networks are disturbed by their external environments and the organizations' inter-connectedness guides the network's growth.

EVOLUTIONARY PROCESSES

The population ecology approach sees corporate evolution as a process of variation, selection, and retention. Evolution occurs as a gradual development of the fittest organizations within a population of organizations.

During the variation phase a stock of possibilities is created from which the best adapted can be selected later on. According to Hannan and Freeman an organization

> with greater organizational diversity has a higher probability of having in hand some form that does a reasonable satisfactory job with the changed environmental conditions.
>
> Hannan and Freeman 1989, p. 9

Organizations are responding to changing environmental conditions by the development of new organizational forms. Similar to biological processes of mutation, random variations occur quite often and are not necessarily the result of consciously adopted ideas. Variation need not to be a planned strategy and may be a result of imperfect attempts to imitate other organizations. Random variations are sufficient to keep the evolutionary process going.

Organizations enclosed within a population which best fit the environmental conditions are selected over a longer time span.

> Natural selection . . . serves as an optimizing process.
>
> Hannan and Freeman 1989, p. 19

Selection is an optimizing principle which leads to the survival of only the most robust organizations. The unfit organizations are weeded out by the environment and have to exit the population, whereas the others survive under the same conditions.

In the last step, retention, the fittest organizations are conserved. They passed the selection test at the expense of the less robust organizations and won the struggle for the scarce resources positioned in the environment. Retention comprehends the historical perception of organizational evolution that

> permits analysts to work either forward or backward in time.
>
> Hannan and Freeman 1989, p. 19

The retained characteristics of the successful organizations are subjected to random variation again, creating the potential that allows the process to continue. In this way, the successful organizations evolve from variations which survived the environmental test of selection.

A major limitation of this wholly Darwinist view is that the environmental selection view gives the organizations little influence over their struggle for survival. It could be a quite different matter when organizations consider the possibility of cooperating in pursuit of plural interests to shape a desired environment. Based on the basic evolutionary mechanism of learning which takes place within the organizations as well as between them, co-evolution of organizations can be seen as a series of steps.

In the first step, organizations create redundancy. Due to entering cooperative relationships, certain activities of the firms overlap. Companies link in order to perform joint product developments or to jointly enter markets. Thus, networks are a redundant form of organizational structure, because the boundaries of the single organizations begin to blur and to be integrated in a whole. Not all activities, however, are externalized in networks. Certain core competences remain within the boundaries of the firms. This tension between redundancy and internalization is important for the evolution of individual organizations in line with other organizations. The generation of redundancy occurs intentionally and not as a random process. Hence, the overlapping of corporate activities is the source of corporate co-evolution. If each firm was determined to conserve its knowledge resources, co-evolution could not be triggered. Firms are jointly generating more variety than each organization could do on its own.

In the next step, the activities of the companies become recursivley linked. The increase of complexity which is caused by the overlapping of the corporate activities, is not selected by selection mechanisms, but accepted, conserved and promoted. The activities of the network members react upon the members themselves and become the starting point for further actions. The activities of the firms are the result of internal coherences rather than simple reactions to the environment. The recursive linkages provide the companies with joint advantages against their environment and shield them against influences from outside. Inter-organizational learning processes improve the fitting of the firms with each other.

In a last step, the jointly learned knowledge is conserved and is made recallable for further learning activities. Co-evolution of organizations is an historic process. The knowledge generated in networks as well as the knowledge of how to create knowledge becomes memorized. Hence, recallability is not a simple retention mechanism but bases rather on the firm's organizational memory. With the recallability of jointly generated knowledge, redundancy occurs again, this time by enlarging existing partnerships or entering new partnerships. Recallability is the interface for new circles of evolution.

The evolutionary mechanism within the network dynamics approach relies on organizational learning and occurs in the steps of redundancy, recursivity, and recallability. The steps are not linearly bounded like the Darwinist course of evolution, but are mutually correlated and overlapped. Hence, the co-evolution of organizations does not occur in a linear development, but rather in the form of a helix. The helix model seeks for a synthesis between the Darwinist cause–effect argumentation and the logic of cybernetic circles. Cybernetic circle models perceive the interconnectedness of single processes (von Foerster 1960), but do not embrace a system's higher development, because the circles cannot be broken through. Such circle models of evolution have been proposed by the German philosopher Friedrich Nietzsche, who postulated the eternal recurrence of the same in a world without direction. History is always repeating (Nietzsche 1974). The helix model of co-evolution, however, links circular with linear developments and leads to a long-term progress for all parties acting in a network.

There are delaying circles within the helix model. After reaching the state of memorizing newly acquired knowledge (recallability), there is a huge push on a higher evolutionary level. But, by creating redundancy again, the organizations lose some of their evolutionary speed. After being recursively linked again, evolution accelerates until the next memorization triggers further evolutionary pushes. Organizations which co-evolve sometimes sacrifice evolutionary speed in the short run but receive indirect long-run rewards that compensate for the immediate sacrifice. Simon calls such an organizational strategy 'weak altruism' (Simon 1983, p. 83). Weakly altruistic organizations are finally exposed to more benevolent environments than are non-altruistic ones.

The general trend of organizations' co-evolution is much less predictable than it is in the case of linear (adaptive) evolution of individual organizations. The population ecology perspective rejects saltational views of biological evolution and earns, by doing so, the advantage of becoming able to formalize organizational evolution. Regularities which have been found in processes that shape the vital rate of organizational populations have even been expressed by formal mathematical equations (Hannan and Freeman 1989, Part II).

The tendency towards evolutionary gradualism was first emphasized by Darwin himself and became deeply embedded in the core of evolutionary theory.

The overlapping of different evolutionary tracks consisting each in redundancy, recursivity, and recallability, leads to fluctuations and erratic swings. There is no predictable goal, only a process of mutual searching and ameliorating.

CONCLUSION

This chapter has tried to show that the population ecology approach is no longer appropriate to explain economic reality. We sought to develop a theory which emancipates us from the wholly Darwinist confined principle of environmental selection. Firms are not absolutely demarcating themselves against their environments and do not perceive them to be restraining or hostile. They are not passively reacting and adapting to environmental threats, but use their environments as opportunity for further growth. They are entering cooperative partnerships with other firms and achieve corporate growth through interaction with these firms.

The firms in a corporate network obtain similar advantages in regard to their business environments. Their growth process is linked to each other. Through the expansion of each company's activity space, the activity space of all companies included in a network becomes enlarged. In this sense, cooperation is a positive sum-game, all partners may ameliorate their competitive positions. Players in networks elicit behaviour from their counterparts, which allows all to do well. The players evolve at the same speed and intensity due to their inter-organizational learning activities.

Cooperation within networks requires a deep rethinking of managerial practice. It is not the point to compare the advantages of cooperation with those of competition. Such a consideration would be close to the static comparison of the transaction costs of two alternatives. The cooperation within networks leads rather to a new understanding of reality. In the words of Kuhn's science theory (Kuhn 1962), one could talk about paradigms which imply a way of thinking and acting that pervade our understanding of the world. Paradigms offer alternative views of social reality and are often contradictory. By the new paradigm of cooperation within networks, firms are no longer adapting to their environments, but create their environments by themselves.

By perceiving economic reality with the paradigm of networking, the role of managers in guiding their organizations will substantively change. Their deterministic orientation to reaction to environmental influences will be superseded by a voluntaristic orientation to social interaction. Network dynamics provide the opportunity for organizational emancipation.

Paradigms which originated in different times could coexist, even if one paradigm dominates another at a given time. Hence, probably not all firms are conscious, to the same extent, about the new paradigm. One could even say that the survival of those firms is in danger which struggle for survival by competing. The survival of cooperating firms, on the other hand, is more probable.

REFERENCES

Adams, R.N. (1991) 'Concluding Observations: The Evolution of Evolutionary Theory and Mechanisms', *Cultural Dynamics*, IV, 2, pp. 229–38.

Aldrich, H.E. (1979) *Organizations and Environments*, Englewood Cliffs, NJ: Prentice Hall.

Argyris, C. and Schön, D.A. (1987) *Organizational Learning: a Theory of Action Perspective*, Reading, MA: Addison Wesley.

Bertalanffy, L. von (1968) *General Systems Theory*, New York: Braziller.

Burns, T. and Stalker, G.M. (1961) *The Management of Innovation*, London: Tavistock.

Campbell, D.T. (1975) 'On the Conflict between Biological and Social Evolution and between Psychology and Moral Tradition', *American Psychologist*, December, pp. 1103–26.

Fayol, H. (1949) *General Industrial Management*, New York: Pitman.

Foerster, H. von (1960) 'On Self-organizing Systems and their Environments', in M.C. Yovitis and S. Cameron (eds) *Self-organizing Systems*, New York: Pergamon.

Gilroy, B.M. (1992) *Networking in Multinational Enterprises*, Columbia, SC: University of South Columbia Press.

Håkansson, H. (1987) *Industrial Technological Development: A Network Approach*, London: Croom Helm.

Hannan, M.T. and Freeman, J. (1977) 'The Population Ecology of Organizations', *American Journal of Sociology*, 82, pp. 929–64.

Hannan, M.T. and Freeman, J. (1989) *Organizational Ecology*, London: Harvard Business Press.

Holling, C.S. (1976) 'Resilience and Stability of Ecosystems', in E. Jantsch and C.H. Waddington (eds) *Evolution and Consciousness: Human Systems and Transition*, Reading, MA: Addison Wesley.

Imanishi, K., Shibatani, A. and Yonemoto S. (1984) *Shinkaron mo Shinka Suru*, Tokyo: Libro Talk.

Kuhn, T.S. (1962) *The Structure of Scientific Revolutions*, Chicago: University of Chicago Press.

Nelson, R.R. and Winter, S.G. (1982) *An Evolutionary Theory of Economic Change*, Cambridge, MA.: Harvard University Press.

Nietzsche, F. (1974) *The Gay Science*, New York: Vintage.
Pfeffer, J. and Salancik, G.R. (1978) *The External Control of Organizations: A Resource Dependency Approach*, New York: Harper & Row.
Porter, M.E. (1980) *Competitive Strategy*, New York: The Free Press.
Richter, F.J. (1995) *Die Selbstorganisation von Unternehmen in strategischen Netzwerken: Bausteine zu einer Theorie des evolutionären Managements*, Frankfurt: Peter Lang.
Simon, H.A. (1983) *Reason in Human Affairs*, Stanford, CA: Stanford University Press.
Taylor, F. (1911) *The Principles of Scientific Management*, New York: Harper & Row.
Teramoto, Y. (1990) *Network Power*, Tokyo: NTT Press.
Varela, F.J. (1984) 'Two Principles of Self-organization', in H. Ulrich and G.J.B. Probst (eds) *Self-organization and Management of Social Systems. Insights, Promises, Doubts and Questions*, Berlin: Springer.
Williamson, O.E. (1975) *Markets and Hierarchies: Analysis and Antitrust Implications*, New York: Free Press.

10 Comparative management systems

Trade-offs-free concept

Milan Zeleny

INTRODUCTION

Comparison of American and Japanese management systems is often focused on relatively unimportant manifestations of corporate culture, work ethics, decision-making process, group behaviour, intensity of work, quality ethics, etc.

The underlying management system has been rarely identified and unravelled. The notions of total quality management and continuous improvement, although sound and admirable, come to a full fruition *only* if they are an integral part of a sound management system.

There is no point in 'continually improving' the horse carriage when the automobile represents the new competitive alternative. There is little to be gained from focusing on quality in a system which does not allow quality maximization by its very design and structure.

Sound management systems must be designed to allow continuous improvement not in terms of self-preservation and refinement, but in terms of its own re-organization and re-engineering. Sound systems must be *designed* for quality and profit maximization or cost minimization – they cannot be just any, haphazardly assembled systems.

In this chapter we introduce a management system concept which is based on optimal design of a corporate portfolio of resources. While most US companies are far from operating an optimal portfolio, many Japanese companies are very close to it: they are capable of achieving lower costs, higher quality and increasing profits – all at the same time. Portfolio of resources, its composition and its flexibility, is at the core of their corporate performance. All other characteristics are either derived or incidental.

Working very hard with a badly designed system is being close to pathetic; continually improving a system which should be scrapped or replaced could be outright foolish.

THE ISSUE OF TRADE-OFFS

A new, somewhat discomforting, possibly radical and certainly challenging idea has started making the rounds in some business management literature: '*Are trade-offs really necessary?*' ask Robert H. Hayes and Gary P. Pisano (Hayes and Pisano 1994).

The answer is no, *trade-offs are not necessary*. Pursuing and achieving lower cost, higher quality (and improved flexibility), all at the same time, is not only possible but clearly desirable and – within a new management paradigm – also necessary.

Trade-offs can be postulated among different, conflicting objectives or criteria. Conventional wisdom recommends dealing with such conflicts via tough choices and a careful analysis of the trade-offs. Yet, according to Hayes and Pisano, many Japanese factories have achieved lower cost, higher quality, faster product introductions, and greater flexibility, all at the same time:

> Lean manufacturing has apparently eliminated the trade-offs among productivity, investment, and variety.
>
> Hayes and Pisano 1994, p. 77

Similarly, Pine *et al.*, in their article 'Making Mass Customization Work' (Pine *et al.* 1993), recall that [in the old paradigm]: 'Quality and low cost and customization and low cost were assumed to be trade-offs.' Their analysis also concludes that: '. . . companies can overcome the traditional trade-offs'. In other words, companies can have it all if they embrace the trade-offs-free thinking and trade-offs-free methodology of optimal systems design.

How can traditional trade-offs be 'eliminated' or 'overcome'? Are not trade-offs generic to multiple-criteria conflicts? Can we have it both ways? Can one decrease cost and increase quality at the same time – and continue doing so? The answer is yes: trade-offs are properties of improperly designed systems and thus can be eliminated by designing better, preferably optimal, systems.

In this chapter we present practical and theoretical arguments for suggested trade-offs elimination, show how profitability and productivity can be improved through optimal system design, and provide a simple numerical example demonstrating basic trade-offs-free (TOF) process and its competitive benefits.

The key to trade-off free management (or production) system is not necessarily strategic focus or strategic flexibility of executives and managers, but optimal portfolio of corporate resources.

In other words, it does matter how the levels of individual resources are determined with respect to each other, as a totality of a system. As long as this requirement is not recognized and resources are treated separately, one-by-one, and in the *ceteris paribus* fashion, the resulting system must be by definition suboptimal, i.e. characterized by trade-offs. Suboptimal systems are the remains of the old paradigm and are becoming increasingly non-competitive.

MULTIPLE OBJECTIVES AND TRADE-OFFS

There are no conflicting objectives per se. No human objectives are in conflict by definition, that is, inherently conflicting. Everything depends on the given situation, the historical state of affairs, the reigning paradigm, or the lack of imagination.

We often hear that one cannot minimize unemployment and inflation at the same time. We are used to the notion that maximizing quality precludes minimizing costs, that safety conflicts with profits, Arabs with Jews, and industry with the environment. Although these generalizations may be true, they are only conditionally true. Usually inadequate means or technology, insufficient exploration of new alternatives, lack of innovation – not the objectives or criteria themselves – are the causes of apparent conflict.

Trade-offs among multiple objectives (there can be no trade-offs when only a single objective is considered) are *not* properties of the objectives themselves, but of the set of alternatives or options they are engaged to measure. This simple truth is often lost in the self-assured whirlwind of conventional economics.

For example, trade-offs between cost and quality have little if anything to do with criteria of cost and quality themselves: rather, they are implied by the limits and constraints on the characteristics of available automobiles they measure. Measuring sticks are neutral and any apparent relations (like trade-offs) are only induced *by the measured*.

Realizing and acknowledging this fundamental truth provides sufficient proof that a shift from the trade-offs-based to trade-offs-free thinking does not constitute continuous improvement or a refinement but must be of paradigmatic nature.

GRAPHICAL EXAMPLE

Suppose that objectives f_1 = Profit and f_2 = Quality. Both of these objectives are to be maximized with respect to given resource constraints (feasible options).

In Figure 10.1, the polyhedron of system-feasible options is well defined, System I. Maximizing functions f_1 and f_2 separately, leads to two different optimal solutions and levels of criteria performance (designated as *max*). If System I remains fixed, observe that the maximal, separately attainable levels of both objectives lead to an *infeasible* 'ideal' option. The trade-offs between quality and profits are explicit and must be dealt with (selecting from the heavy boundary, i.e., non-dominated solutions, of System I).

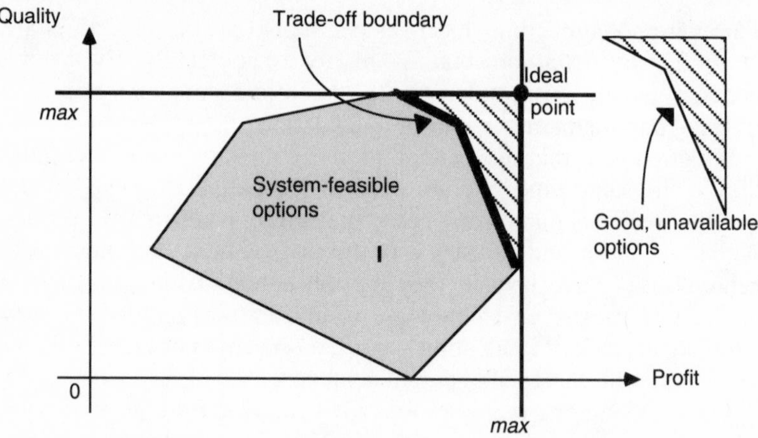

Figure 10.1 System I: given design with natural quality-profit trade-offs

In Figure 10.1, observe that the System I is poorly designed because there exists a set of good, currently unavailable options which would make the 'ideal' point feasible and thus allow the maxima of f_1 and f_2 (Profits and Quality) be attained both at the same time.

Any manager's lifetime of work in System I will unfailingly lead to the following wisdom: There is always a trade-off between profits (or costs) and quality, one cannot have it both ways, one has to pay for quality. As more and more managers derive (from their own experience) the same wisdom, textbook writers and instructors accept the wisdom as conventional, incorporate it in their own educational efforts and teach it to multitudes who had no such prior experience. Trade-off-based systems and culture are thus perpetuated.

In other words, reshaping the feasible set (reconfiguring resource constraints) in order to include the 'missing' alternatives, if realizable at the same or comparable costs, would lead to a superior system design with higher levels of criteria performance.

Such desirable 'reshaping' of the feasible set is represented in

Figure 10.2, where System II of system-feasible options is sketched. Given System II, both objectives are maximized at the same point (or option): System II is superior in design to System I.

From all such possible 'reshapings' of system configurations, given some cost or effort constraint, the best possible *optimal design* or configuration of resources can be chosen. Such a system (like System II below) will be superior with respect to both profit and quality and no trade-offs between them are possible. Trade-offs have been eliminated through optimal system design.

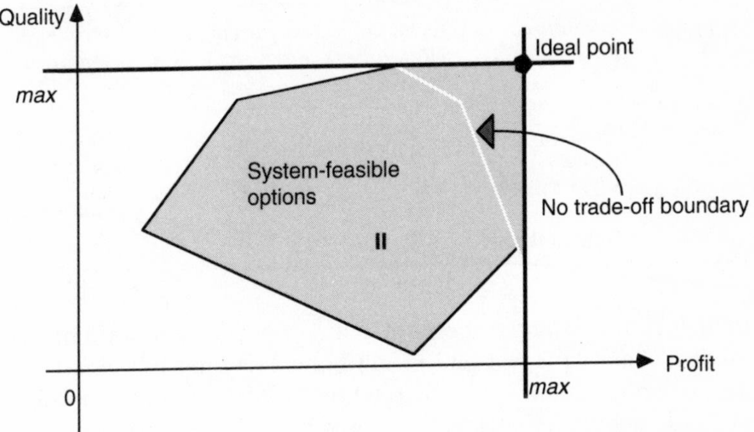

Figure 10.2 System II: optimal design with no apparent quality-profit trade-offs

In Figure 10.2, a system with no quality–profit trade-offs is presented. Observe that the maximal separately attainable levels of both criteria now form a feasible ideal option. Consequently, the trade-offs between quality and profit ceased to exist (heavy trade-off boundary of System I has disappeared in System II).

Any manager's lifetime of work in System II will unfailingly lead to the following wisdom: There is never a trade-off between profits (or costs) and quality, one cannot have one without the other, quality pays for itself. As more and more managers derive (from their own experience) the same wisdom, textbook writers and instructors accept the wisdom as conventional, embed it in their own educational efforts and teach it to multitudes who had no such prior experience. Trade-off-free systems and culture are thus perpetuated.

NUMERICAL EXAMPLE

Let us consider a simple production problem involving two different products, say suits (S) and dresses (D), in quantities x and y, each of them consuming five different resources (nylon through golden thread) according to technologically determined requirements (technological coefficients). Unit market prices of resources are also given, as are the levels (no. of units) of resources currently available (portfolio of resources). The data are summarized in Table 10.1.

Table 10.1 Original data for production example

Unit price $	*Resource (Raw material)*	*Technological coefficients (Resource requirements)* $x = 1$	$y = 1$	*Number of units (Resource portfolio)*
30	Nylon	4	0	20
40	Velvet	2	6	24
9.5	Silver thread	12	4	60
20	Silk	0	3	10.5
10	Golden thread	4	4	26

In the above example, observe that producing one unit of each product S and D ($x = 1$ and $y = 1$) requires 4 units of nylon (4×1 + 0×1), 8 units of velvet (2×1 + 6×1), etc. Total number of available units of each material (given resource portfolio) is given in the last column of Table 10.1.

Current market prices of resources (first column) allow us to calculate the costs of the given resource portfolio:

$$(30\times20) + (40\times24) + (9.5\times60) + (20\times10.5) + (10\times26) = \$2{,}600$$

The same prices can be used to compute unit costs of producing one unit of each of the two products:

$$S = 1:\ (30\times4) + (40\times2) + (9.5\times12) + (20\times0) + (10\times4) = \$354$$
$$D = 1:\ (30\times0) + (40\times6) + (9.5\times4) + (20\times3) + (10\times4) = \$378$$

In other words, it costs $354 to produce one suit and $378 to produce one dress. Suppose that we can sell all we produce at current market prices of $754/unit of S and $678/unit of D.

Expected profit margins (price-cost) are:

$$S: 754–354 = \$400/\text{unit}; \qquad D: 678–378 = \$300/\text{unit}$$

As profit maximizers, we are interested in maximizing total value of function $f_1 = 400x + 300y$.

As a second criterion let us consider some quality index: say 6 points per S and 8 points per D (scale from 0 to 10), so that we can maximize the total quality index or function $f_2 = 6x + 8y$.

We are now in a position to analyse the above outlined production system with respect to profits and quality. Maximizing levels of x and y together (best product mix) can be easily calculated by techniques of mathematical programming (here we need only the results).

1 Function f_1 is maximized at $x = 4.25$ and $y = 2.25$, thus achieving maximum of $(400 \times 4.25) + (300 \times 2.25) = \$2,375$ in profits.
2 Function f_2 is maximized at $x = 3.75$ and $y = 2.75$, achieving maximum of $(6 \times 3.75) + (8 \times 2.75) = 44.5$ in total quality index.

This situation corresponds to the situation in Figure 10.1. The two maximizing points are the endpoints of trade-off boundary. One can trade off quality for profits by moving from $x = 3.75$, $y = 2.75$ to $x = 4.25$, $y = 2.25$ and back again, trading profits for quality. Because we can produce only one product mix at a time, we can choose to either maximize profits ($x = 4.25$, $y = 2.25$) or maximize quality ($x = 3.75$, $y = 2.75$), but *not both*. The choice is difficult because of the trade-offs between profits and quality. Their importance is difficult to evaluate.

Let us heed productivity consultant's advice and purchase a portfolio of resources different from that in Table 10.1, other things being equal. We keep this new production system comparable and compatible in all respects, except the last column of Table 10.1. The new portfolio of resources in Table 10.2 has been proposed by the consultant.

Table 10.2 New data for production example

Unit price $	*Resource* (*Raw material*)	*Technological coefficients* (*Resource requirements*) $x = 1$	$y = 1$	*Number of units* (*Resource portfolio*)
30	Nylon	4	0	16.12
40	Velvet	2	6	23.3
9.5	Silver thread	12	4	58.52
20	Silk	0	3	7.62
10	Golden thread	4	4	26.28

We are now in a position to analyse the newly proposed production system under the same conditions.

1 Function f_1 is now maximized at $x = 4.03$ and $y = 2.54$, achieving maximum of $(400 \times 4.03) + (300 \times 2.54) = \$2,375$ in profits.

2 Function f_2 is maximized also at $x = 4.03$ and $y = 2.54$, achieving maximum of (6×4.03) + (8×2.54) = 44.5 in total quality index.

Both previously achieved maximum values of f_1 and f_2 have been matched. More importantly, *both* maximum profits ($2,375) and maximum quality index (44.5) are achieved through a single product mix: $x= 4.03$ and $y = 2.54$. This particular product mix, or ideal point in Figures 10.1 and 10.2, was infeasible in the previous system. By allowing its feasibility now, we have eliminated all and any trade-offs between the criteria of profits and quality.

The previous trade-offs-based system (Table 10.1) was operated at the cost of $2,600. The newly designed trade-offs-free system (Table 10.2) is realizable at the following cost:

(30×16.12)+(40×23.3)+(9.5×58.52)+(20×7.62)+(10×26.28) = $2,386.74

The superior performance of the newly designed system comes at $213.26 cheaper than the suboptimal performance of the original system.

OPTIMAL PORTFOLIO OF RESOURCES

The above example demonstrates that the chosen portfolio of resources is crucial for assessing maximum achievable levels of profits, costs, quality, flexibility, etc., at which corresponding production systems can be operated, other things being equal.

In our example, should any company choose to operate *any* other resource portfolio (at cost ≤ $2,600) than that of Table 10.2, other things being equal, then its performance with respect to f_1 and f_2 would be necessarily inferior. Simple rearrangement of resource levels (comparing Table 10.1 with Table 10.2) 'reshapes' the management system (of feasible opportunities) and from Figure 10.1 and Figure 10.2 provides superior performance at the same or even lower costs. None of this can be achieved through traditional optimization methodology (like, e. g., linear programming) which assumes the levels of resources to be given and fixed a priori. In such 'optimization', market prices of resources are not even considered.

The explanation is simple. Productive resources should not be engaged individually and separately because they do not contribute one by one according to their marginal productivities. Productive resources perform best as a whole system: they should be determined and engaged jointly as a portfolio and in an optimal fashion.

Consequently, any company running any other than optimal

portfolio of resources cannot outperform a company running the optimal portfolio, *ceteris paribus*. A company of Figure 10.1 has, under these conditions, no chance of successfully competing with the company of Figure 10.2. Regardless of its product-mix positioning along its trade-off boundary, the trade-offs-free company is bound to *always* do better. Of course, the 'other things' are not always equal and the *ceteris paribus* conditions never hold in business reality. But one could never argue the superiority of one management system over another without invoking such conditions in theory. All other things being equal, the trade-offs-free company is bound to do better than any trade-offs-based company.

We have identified the portfolio of resources to be the key to a system's potential performance and maximum productivity. The issues of technology, education, skills, work intensity, innovation, flexibility, quality, etc., are all very important in business. But they could only come to their full fruition if applied to optimally designed, trade-offs-free systems.

It is difficult (if not surreal) to argue for a high-tech re-engineering of one's bicycle, for pedalling harder, practising vigorously, developing muscles, using protective gear and improving the road surface – all very expensive and demanding pursuits – if the other guy is driving a motorcycle in the race.

PROFIT MAXIMIZATION

Free market systems are rooted in the assumption of profit maximization by individuals and their corporations.

This time-honoured premise is usually not further specified or elaborated, as if there was only a single form of profit maximization.

Yet, rational economic agents can maximize profits in *at least two* fundamentally different – often mutually exclusive – ways:

1 Manage (operate) a *given* system so that a profit function is maximized.
2 *Design* a system so that its management (operation) would result in maximum profits.

These two forms of profit maximization are not the same. In the first case, one is doing his managing best and squeezing maximum profits from a *given* system. This is known as profit maximization.

In the second case, one designs (re-engineers) a profit-maximizing system: doing one's managing best leads to maximum profits. This is, undoubtedly, also profit maximization.

The two modes are mutually exclusive because one cannot follow the second without first dismantling the first. It is not sufficient to (continually) improve the given system: because there is only one optimally designed system, then all other systems must be suboptimal by definition.

One mode of profit maximization leads to consistently lower profits than the other, other things being equal.

Because the second case is, *ceteris paribus*, always superior to the first case, we are facing two strategically different concepts of profit maximization. It does matter – in business, economics and management – which particular mode of profit maximization the individuals, corporations or cultures mostly adhere to: free markets are committed to reward those who consistently adhere to the second mode of operation.

CONCLUSIONS

The race is on towards transforming production and management systems from trade-offs-based to trade-offs-free. This race moves well beyond the assorted World-class, TQM, Lean production or Mass customization labels. In a global competition, no company will be able to afford not joining the race. Corporate (and national) portfolios of resources will have to be optimized before all other relevant efforts could become effective.

The US business and management is well posed to succeed in the race towards the trade-offs-free management paradigm. Its free markets and profit-maximizing institutions, habits and intuitions are the most reliable in the world. They continue being applied, rather wastefully, to suboptimal portfolios of resources. As soon as our systems turn into resources-optimal systems, as soon as we provide the right 'substrate' for our already correct instincts and behaviours, our businesses will flourish.

Due to US-specific and successful historical developments (command hierarchies, mass production, 'given' systems, advanced specialization, division of labour, etc.), most of the good free-market and profit-maximizing instincts and efforts are being increasingly misapplied to systems that are less-than-competitive.

There are two fundamental dimensions to management: *what* is your system and *how* do you operate it. One can operate quite well a bad system or a good system quite badly. The main competitive challenge, yet to be recognized and achieved in the USA, is to operate good systems very well. US managers operate well, often performing virtual miracles with quite inadequate and often outdated systems.

Running optimally designed, high-performance trade-offs-free systems would undoubtedly return joy, pride and self-confidence into business and management endeavours.

REFERENCES

Hayes, R.H. and Pisano, G.P. (1994) 'Beyond World-Class: The New Manufacturing Strategy', *Harvard Business Review*, January–February, p. 77.

Pine II, B.J., Bart V. and Boynton, A.C. (1993) 'Making Mass Customization Work', *Harvard Business Review*, September–October, p. 108.

Zeleny, M. (1982) *Multiple Criteria Decision Making*, New York: McGraw-Hill.

—— (1986) 'Optimal System Design with Multiple Criteria: De Novo Programming Approach', *Engineering Costs and Production Economics*, 10, pp. 89–94.

11 Communicating through on-line database systems

A strategy for monitoring corporate environments

Nobuyuki Chikudate

INTRODUCTION

The development of information technologies has had a significant beneficial impact on business communities. As a result, the adoption of information technologies in organizations has had a focus of attention and has also become an academic domain, namely Management Information System (MIS). The researchers in the field of communication, library, and information sciences also have conducted studies in this topic. Ewusi-Mensah (1981) reviewed the studies in the association between information technologies and organizations and concluded that most of the studies in MIS have implicitly dealt with information technologies from internal organizational perspectives.

This study is, however, based on the external perspectives; it suggests the application of information technologies to deal with external environments for organizations. As a theoretical foundation, the models and approaches derived from General Systems Theory are re-examined and applied for the purpose of this study. Then, on-line database systems are chosen as the examples of the application of information technologies to deal with external environments.

ORGANIZATION AND ENVIRONMENT

Before discussing the application of information technologies to organizations, it is necessary to re-examine the relationship between organizations and information. Organizations are considered *open* systems that grow or evolve by a process of being in constant interaction with environments (e.g. von Bertalanffy 1956, Katz and Kahn 1966). In this view, organizations are considered to be inescapably bound up with the conditions of environments (Pfeffer and Salancik 1978).

When organizations formulate the strategies derived from this view, they adopt transactive strategies. Fiol and Lyles (1985) explain that the essence of the transactive strategies is based on interaction and learning rather than the execution of a predetermined plan. Transactive strategies are crafted based upon ongoing dialogue with key stakeholders – employees, shareholders, suppliers, customers, governments, and regulators (Hart 1992). This strategy usually necessitates the creation of cross-functional communication channels and new mechanisms for involving employees, customers, and other key stakeholders in planning and decision making. Thus, transactive strategy derived from an open system perspective considers both external and internal mechanisms for organizations.

There has been, however, some criticism about focusing on only one-sided (either internal or external) mechanisms of organizations. From the point of view of management or organizational theorists, the criticism about being blind to external mechanisms was raised. Pfeffer and Salancik (1978), for example, criticize that:

> Although the idea of open systems theory, organization and environment, and social constraint are not new, such ideas really have had much impact on research and training in management and organizational behaviour. After some pro forma acknowledgement of social constraints, the environment, and open systems, most authors spend much of their time, space and research documentation dealing with the same old concepts out of which organizational behaviour grew – leadership, motivation, task design, communication, and context.
>
> Pfeffer and Salancik 1978, p. 14

Ewusi-Mensah says that management and organizational theorists tend to only consider *reactive* interaction, which occurs

> when the organization takes the environmental constraints as given and seeks to improve the organization's measure of performance by restructuring its resources to accommodate those constraints.
>
> Ewusi-Mensah 1981, p. 303

This tendency to focus more on the external process than on the internal mechanism has recently been echoed by the Japanese multinational business communities. Akio Morita (1992), the president of Sony, for example, asserted that the survival of Japanese corporations in international communities depends on whether they could successfully adopt *kyosei* (symbiotic relations with environment) ideology. He further argues that the success of Japanese corporations in international operations was based on their capabilities for adapting to the environments by changing internal mechanisms, mostly production processes up to 1980s, but they no longer could operate their business without considering the relationship itself with the environment. Morita showed proposals to formulate strategies based on *kyosei* ideology:

> Recognising that corporations or individuals are members of societies or communities, they should take active roles in social contribution . . . corporations should not hesitate to share the burden of community problems. Corporations should fully recognize the importance of environment protection and energy saving; it should be stressed that environment, recources, energy are common properties of human beings.
>
> Morita 1992, p. 102

This *kyosei* ideology seems not to be a very common approach among Japanese corporations; it rather seems to be taken by those which have a history of international orientation from their foundations. For example, Sony is considered to be a typical example of *kyosei* oriented corporations.

In summary, to best consider organizations as open systems in academia as well as business communities, the focus of study should shift from the internal mechanisms to the interaction process with the environment. The next section discusses the organizations' relations to external environments.

ORGANIZATION AND EXTERNAL ENVIRONMENT

According to Ewusi-Mensah

> organizations may take an active interaction . . . [which] occurs when an organization, using its resources and creative capabilities, aggressively seeks to alter conditions in the environment.
>
> Ewusi-Mensah 1981, p. 303

Through the process of an active interaction, organizations seek to cultivate an environment that is favourable to their own interests. Public relations used to play a major role in active interaction with environments. When corporations take active interaction with the environments, especially the public, they engage advertising agencies, public relations firms, and their own publicity specialists in order to favourably influence what the public knows (Kripendorff and Eleey 1986).

However, this view of interacting with environments, especially the public, received criticism from public relations researchers. In their influential paper 'Public relations: functional or functionary?' Bell and Bell argued that public relations practitioners in business are only concerned with supplying information to the environment and not supplying information to the organization about environment (Bell and Bell 1976). They call this approach to environments functionary which only considers the one-way communication from organizations to environments. Several public relations researchers and practitioners argue that public relations should go beyond this one-way communication approach to interacting with environments (e.g. Bell and Bell 1976, Grunig and Hunt 1984, Cutlip *et al.* 1985). Thus organizations' external relations with their environments need some reconsideration.

Terryberry (1968) suggests that the adaptability of organizations to the environment depends on their abilities to learn and to perform in changing contingencies of the evironment. In other words, organizations need adequate feedback mechanisms from their environments (Bell and Bell 1976, Krippendorff and Eleey 1986). The autogenetic model views that all organizations are governed by the sets of rules, and these are considered as a set of input/output statements linking positional information to action (Drazin and Sandelands 1992). In other words, a focal organization might gather information about the states of environments, and on that basis decide to preserve or change its state (Drazin and Sandelands 1992).

This view of interacting with the environment is similar to what Thompson (1967) calls opportunistic surveillance. Opportunistic surveillance is the approach by which organizations may actively interact with their environments. They do not wait to be activated by a problem and therefore do not have to stop when a problem arises because (hopefully) the solution has already been found. The organization continuously monitors the environment for opportunities to cultivate an ever more supportive and favourable environment.

There are crucial differences between Ewusi-Mansah's active interaction and Thompson's opportunistic surveillance. While active interaction stresses aggressive alteration of environments, opportunistic surveillance does not stress. Furthermore, opportunistic surveillance takes an additional step in the process of interacting with environments; it takes full consideration of the state of environment through monitoring environments. This step does not exist in active interaction. Thompson's approach stresses this monitoring process for interacting corporate environment.

Boundary units are subsystems of organizations which are considered as including this monitoring function (Aldrich and Herker 1977). They are designed to collect and transact the information from the environments. As a result, the efficiency of boundary units influences the adaptability of organizations to the environments (Child 1969).

Bell and Bell (1976) imply that public relations can take a role of boundary units in organizations:

> Public relations can influence the organization's ability to change and grow through observation and analysis of environmental conditions.... If observations of external ... environments indicate that a policy or practice is detrimental to the best interests of the organization (and, increasingly, society) management can be encouraged to adjust.
>
> Bell and Bell 1976, p. 53

The organizations that utilize such public relations functions may be able to respond appropriately to changes in environments (Krippendorff and Eleey 1986). In this view, public relations managers have the combined roles of expert prescriber, communication process facilitator, and problem-solving process facilitator (Cutlip *et al.* 1985). This perspective is what Grunig and Hunt (1984) call the two-way symmetric model, meaning that communication is two-way and that the information exchange causes change on both sides. This study no longer uses the term public relations hereafter. Instead, the term corporate communication (CC) is used. The reason is that public relations traditionally have ignored the functional communication process but they shift their function from publicizing to communicating for corporations.

The efficiency of CC as a boundary unit is examined by focusing on the process of collecting and filtering the information through them (Aldrich and Herker 1977). Through the interaction with environments, boundary units are usually exposed to large amounts of potentially relevant information in their information collecting activities. Consequently, the purposeful sensing of the environment to anticipate and detect changes that affect the organization's relationships with its environments is required (Cutlip *et al.* 1985, Krippendorff and Eleey 1986).

Cutlip *et al.* (1985) suggest that public relations must be selectively sensitive to those environments that are involved with the organization's policies, procedures, and actions. They further argue that this not only requires specifically defined organizations, but also the research skills to monitor environments. The selective sensing is also necessary to prevent information overload (Cyert and March 1963). To filter information, interpretation and summary of information are indispensable functions (Aldrich and Herker 1977). Additionally, boundary units may store information for future use.

When public relations do the jobs of boundary units, they are likely to be exposed to the enormous amounts of information need to be transacted in this process. Cutlip *et al.* (1985) describe eleven methods that include informal and formal techniques to handle this situation. The eleven methods include: (1) personal contacts; (2) key informants; (3) community forums and focus groups; (4) advisory committees and boards; (5) ombudsmen; (6) call-in telephone lines; (7) mail analysis; (8) field reports; (9) media content analysis; (10) secondary analysis; and (11) surveys. The selection of a specific method depends on the purpose of research. Krippendorff and Eleey (1986) suggest that the combination of several methods among these may yield more accurate results that the single usage of these methods depending on the types of environments to be monitored. This study, however, only focuses on media content analysis, because the development of information technologies essentially may be able to provide media content analysis with much more powerful monitoring techniques than other methods or combination of methods.

ENVIRONMENT MONITORING AND CONTENT ANALYSIS

Content analysts have long used press clippings and broadcast monitor reports, all available from commercial services as resources. These resources used to be considered as indicators of only what is being printed or broadcast, not what is read or heard, and if so, whether or not the audiences learned or believed the message content. However, Krippendorff and Eleey (1986) propose a different usage of content analysis. They explain that

> content analysis can provide surveillance of the environment. . . . Surveillance is accomplished by measures that provide an accurate picture of the current state of and changes in the image, attitudes and knowledge of selected features of the environment. For example, content analysis can spotlight the attitudes and prejudices of journalists and editors regarding the organization as a whole.
>
> Krippendorff and Eleey 1986, p. 17

Krippendorff and Eleey demonstrated content analytic procedures to monitor the symbolic environment which defines an organization's identity in public image from various dimensions of environments. Their procedures also include other types of research methods, such as public opinion surveys, to present an accurate picture of public image. Furthermore, they are developed for detailed analysis which require sophisticated social scientific skills.

Cutlip *et al.* (1985) imply the hint for developing other utilities of content analysis. They say that

> the media are better at telling us what to think about than they are telling us what to think.
>
> Cutlip *et al.* 1985, p. 215

Naisbitt (1984) demonstrated if all the available resources about media reporting can be systematically content analysed, it is possible to forecast social/economic conditions long before they are apparent to most observers. Today many corporations and governments subscribe to *Trend Report*, a quarterly newsletter of early warning systems. This type of newsletter would be beneficial for monitoring potential environment changes in general over a long period of time. However, it is expected that each corporation has different needs for monitoring different domains of environments. They also may need trend reports as much up to date as possible. As a result, so called customized trend reports would be in high demand. The following section discusses the idea of designing a customized trend report.

CUSTOMIZED TREND REPORT

Customized trend report refers to the reports that are designed for each corporation's needs to monitor specific sectors in its environments over a certain period of time. Krippendorff and Eleey (1986) suggest that content analysis can be utilized for monitoring specific sectors in corporate environments. As indicated in the previous section, press clippings and broadcast monitor reports have been used as the bases for content analysis. If corporate communication researchers wanted to achieve a high degree of accuracy and extendibility in creating the customized trend report, they would need a large pool of media resources and have to spend a tremendous amount of money, labour, and time on content analysis.

Therefore, it may be impossible to require a high degree of accuracy, extendibility, and being timely in previous content analysis procedure in the past. In their content analytic procedures, Krippendorff and Eleey (1986) took a sample of 900 news clipping from over 450 publications around the USA, covering 45 episodes of some 17 PBS (public broadcasting channel in the USA) television series to monitor the symbolic environment of the PBS. Since the priority of their content analysis is to present as accurate a public image of

PBS as possible, it is reasonable to conduct such a detailed content analysis manually. However, if corporations need a trend report which presents less analytical but more updated and more extensive information it is reasonable to consider the different approach to content analysis. The development of information technologies has made it possible to provide corporate communication researchers with a high level of satisfaction in designing the customized trend report for their own corporation.

An on-line database system is one of the information technologies which can give corporate communication researchers a great advantage to create customized trend reports. It refers to a collection of records and information stored and retrieved electronically in computer-readable forms. The system of on-line databases allows simultaneous interaction between the user and computer and is accessible via communication facilities such as conventional telephone, microwave, and fibre optics and satellite networks. On-line database can provide information from the environment in a variety of forms that include bibliographic references, citation indices, numerical data such as time series or company financial reports, abstracts of articles, and full-text articles (Reggazzi *et al.* 1980).

NEXIS, currently available in the USA, for example, contains the library of more than 145 files of updated information from US and overseas newspapers, wire services and broadcast transcripts. During the presidential campaign of 1993, NEXIS was fully utilized to monitor media reporting activities and analyse the personal history of opponents. Beside NEXIS, there are various kinds of on-line database systems all over the world. The following section discusses one of the potential applications of on-line databases to corporate communication activities.

ON-LINE DATABASE AND CRISIS MANAGEMENT

Although Krippendorff and Eleey (1986) demonstrated that content analysis can be a powerful research technique to survey the symbolic environment, their procedures seem to be developed under the assumption of static conditions. However, corporations are likely to be exposed to dynamic changes of their environments. Unexpected crises or problematic situations are major sources of dynamic changes of environments. In this study, monitoring symbolic sectors of environments is discussed as an example of crisis management.

Crisis can seriously affect the public image of corporations. Truitt and Kelly point out that

> a crisis can get out of hand quickly . . . and the media descend on the company.
>
> Truitt and Kelly 1989, p. 7

The media may report problems of the company before they are reported to the management. Arnold mentions that managements are faced with the constant struggle to be informed about bad news before it becomes a matter of crisis. The reason is that regardless of the reporting structure and safeguards in place to assure bad news will move from bottom to top, employees are reluctant to push negative information through the system (Arnold 1988). As a result, management may discover the problems of their own company through the media. Such a nightmare is always likely to be actualized in business operations.

It may be possible to avoid such a nightmare for corporations. Crises or problems can be anticipated or dedected depending on the amount of intelligence and sensitivity that go into structuring the monitoring apparatus (Truitt and Kelly 1989). The research techniques employing on-line database systems could be equipped with huge amount of intelligence and sensitivity. In this study, NEXIS is chosen as an example from various sources of on-line databases.

There are basically two ways of utilizing on-line database systems for handling crises or problems depending on the purpose – anticipation or detection. The first efficient use is for the situation where potential crises or problems can be anticipated. This is similar to Naisbitt's (1984) early warning system, but it is differentiated in terms of the specificity of searching for risk. The search is customized for the purposes of individual corporations.

NEXIS contains the library of more than 145 files of information from US and overseas newspapers, wire services and broadcast transcripts. In other words, it can be used for studying many world wide incidents in the past. The important point in studying similar crises or problems is that the researchers need to focus on four major aspects of crisis. They are: (1) nature of crisis or problems; (2) editorial styles of media; (3) how focal corporations interacted with media; and (4) feedback from the public. To conduct such a crisis analysis using NEXIS, the researchers need to combine several possible words describing the crisis in selecting search terms.

The second efficient use of the system is for the purpose of detection. In the nightmare described above, it may be possible to protect the corporation before the media descend if it can detect the media reporting about it at an early stage. Media are not always reporting accurate pictures of a corporation. Grunig and Hunt (1984) showed the case of Illinois Power Company which was unfairly reported by CBS's 60-minute programme. In this case, the corporation could successfully battle with CBS to protect its public image. It was possible to detect the media reporting activities in this case because the TV station which mistakenly reported the corporation was one of the national networks in the USA. However, if various kinds of media report them, it may not be possible to detect all the media reporting in the past. The advance of information technologies has made it possible to conduct this practice.

NEXIS, for example, contains updated information including wire services and broadcast transcripts besides various kinds of locally printed media. Systematic update services using pre-selected search terms, in this case, the name of the corporation, would deliver the media reporting about it with a high level of extendibility. The corporate communication practitioners may be able to formulate the appropriate strategies. Media can be the watchdogs of corporations, but corporations can be watchdogs of the media today.

CONCLUSION

On-line database systems have been applied to financial and economic analysis, marketing, assessing securities and commodities, and so on. This study suggests a different application of on-line database systems: for corporate communication. The application is based on transactive strategy, autogenetic model of organizations, functional approach to public relations, and two-way symmetric model of public relations. These emphazise the significance of monitoring external environments.

Japanese multinational corporations, such as Sony and Honda seem to have already applied these communication models to operate successfully in international communities. They have put an emphasis on corporate communication activities and created so called Divisions of Corporate Communication. On-line database systems would be powerful tools for their activities. Although this study selects only symbolic environments to show how on-line database systems would function, their potential applications may be unlimited.

REFERENCES

Aldrich, H. and Herker, D. (1977) 'Boundary Spanning Roles and Organizational Structure', *Academy of Management Review*, 2, pp. 217–30.

Arnold, J.E. (1988) 'Communications and Strategy: The CEO gets (and gives) the Message', *Public Relations Quarterly*, 33, pp. 5–13.

Bell, S.H. and Bell, E.C. (1976) 'Public Relations: Functional or Functionary?', *Public Relations Review*, 2, pp. 47–57.

Bertalanffy, L. von (1956) 'General Systems Theory', in *Yearbook of the Society of the Advancement of General Systems Theory*, 1, pp. 1–10.

Cutlip, S.M., Center, A.H. and Broom, G.M. (1985) *Effective Public Relations*, 6th edn, Englewood Cliffs, NJ: Prentice Hall.

Child, J. (1969) *The Business Enterprise in Modern Industrial Society*, London: Collier Macmillan.

Cyert, R.M. and March, J.A. (1963) *A Behavioural Theory of the Firm*, Englewood Cliffs, NJ: Prentice Hall.

Drazin, R. and Sandelands, L. (1992) 'Autogenesis: A Perspective on the Process of Organizing', *Organization Science*, 4, pp. 230–49.

Ewusi-Mensah, K. (1981) 'The External Organizational Environment and its Impact on Management Information Systems', *Accounting, Organizations and Society*, 6, pp. 301–16.

Fiol, M. and Lyles, M. (1985) 'Organizational Learning', *Academy of Management Review*, 10, pp. 803–13.

Grunig, J.E. and Hunt, T. (1984) *Managing Public Relations*, Orlando, FL: Holt.

Hart, S.L. (1992) 'An Integrative Framework for Strategy-Making Process', *Academy of Management Review*, 17, pp. 327–51.

Katz, D. and Kahn, R.L. (1966) *The Social Psychology of Organizations*, New York: John Wiley and Sons.

Krippendorff, K. and Eleey, M.F. (1986) 'Monitoring a Group's Symbolic Environment', *Public Relations Review*, 12, pp. 13–36.

Morita, A. (1992) 'Japanese Style Management in Danger', *Bungei-shunjyu*, 70, pp. 94–103.

Naisbitt, J. (1984) *Megatrends*, New York: Warner Books.

Pfeffer, J. and Salancik, G.R. (1978) *The External Control of Organizations*, New York: Harper & Row.

Reggazzi, J.J., Bennion, B. and Roberts, S. (1980) 'On-line Systems of Disciplines and Speciality Areas in Science and Technology', *Journal of the American Society for Information Science*, pp. 161–70.

Terryberry, S. (1968) 'The Evolution of the Organizational Environments', *Administrative Science Quarterly*, 7, pp. 590–614.

Thompson, J.D. (1967) *Organizations in Action*, New York: McGraw-Hill.

Truitt, R.H. and Kelly, S.S. (1989) 'Battling a Crisis in Advance', *Public Relations Quarterly*, 34, pp. 6–8.

12 Autonomous anticipative management and its evolutionary process

Kenji Tanaka

INTRODUCTION

Practical management systems in a changing environment need to provide adaptive management as well as dynamic management. To provide the dynamic management, an anticipative management system which is a kind of feedforward control based on an internal model, has been proposed by Kijima *et al.* (1986). This anticipative management system is a technological implementation of the biological anticipatory system that Rosen (1985) introduced as a system allowing future states to determine present changes of state.

The internal model in the anticipative management system represents the information about the dynamics of the environment and can therefore make effective prediction possible. If the management system remains in a fixed internal model that does not incorporate the information about the changes of the dynamics of the environment, the management system may lose the expected function in a changed environment. In this chapter we call those undesired situations *management failures* and, to prevent them, we focus on an anticipative management system that has a mechanism for improving an internal model by itself. We will call this kind of management system, an *autonomous* one. Our aim here is to show that the autonomous anticipative management system evolves through alternative repetitions of anticipative and autonomous processes, and that this evolution prevents fatal management failures.

ANTICIPATIVE MANAGEMENT SYSTEM

Model representation

To introduce an anticipative management system, we consider a simple framework consisting of a management system (*MS*), and the object system (*OS*) managed by the *MS*. A management system incorporates two processes: one observing the various states of the object, and the other acting on the object (see Figure 12.1). The observation process grasps the current states of the real world and the action process pushes states in the desired directions. We assume that the management system cannot observe any real state $w \in W$ (where W is a set of states that belongs to the object) directly, but can only measure the value of $f_o(w)$ through an observation function f_o (Rosen 1978a). For example, when a manager in a bank concerns the service time for customer at service window, he has some methods to observe it. Those are measures such as each service time, average service time, and maximum service time in a period. In this case, f_o is a function of real states to certain measure. The function f_o, thus, specifies some characteristics. In other words, it determines the level at which the state of the object is recognized.

A management system has to choose desired actions from a set A of actions for the states observed through the observation function. The choice is based on the management system's evaluation system, which includes a decision principle and a decision function. A decision principle is one that determines how to select an action, such as optimally or satisfactorily. We will call the evaluation system the *internal evaluation system*, and denote it by G. And in this paper we assume that the decision principle is an optimal one.

Thus, we express the management system by $MS(f_o, A, G)$, in which the main task is to decide the optimal control rule d^* as a function of observed states to actions.

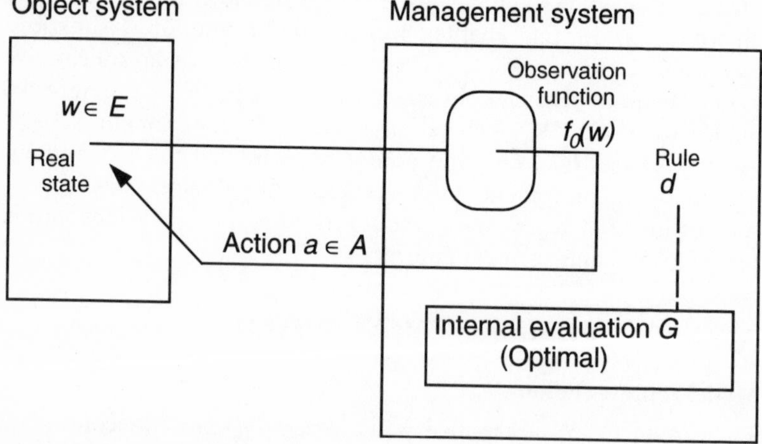

Figure 12.1 Management system $MS(f_o, A, G)$ and object

Anticipative management based on an internal model

A management system is expected to anticipatively select actions that satisfy the internal evaluation. Kijima *et al.* (1986) introduced an internal model that generates a sequence of such actions, and they called the system that has an internal model the *anticipative management system*. The internal model provides information about the state dynamics of the object with respect to the internal evaluation. Hence, if a management system has an internal model, its choice of a current desired action could be based on the future states predicted by the internal model.

Necessary and sufficient conditions for the existence of an internal model have already been given mathematically; here we show these conditions conceptually.

Proposition 1 (Kijima 1986)

When a management system $MS(f_o, A, G)$ is *consistent* with an object, the system can have an internal model if and only if the (f_o, d^*) in the management system is a *solution* for the object.

A *consistency* between the management system and the object means that the state transition does not change so rapidly with respect to the internal evaluation. A *solution* (f_o,d) for the object means that every action selected by the rule d for the observed state $f_0(w)$ satisfies the management system's internal evaluation. This is a static property and does not include any dynamic nor anticipative property.

Proposition 1 reveals that if the management system has a solution, a management system is able to anticipatively manage the object by considering only the internal model.

LIMITS OF ANTICIPATIVE MANAGEMENT SYSTEM

One of the most important issues concerning management processes is systems failures. This section therefore discusses the relationship between limits of anticipative management systems and systems failures.

Management failures

It is not easy for a management system to obtain an adequate internal model and manage anticipatively. In fact, as Rosen (1978b) indicates, unless a management system resets the states of the internal model, the model may become useless for making predictions about states of the object. Also, even if the states of the object can be predicted, the management system should be considered a failed system when users do not satisfy the management. As an example, let us consider a bank that offers different kinds of service by means of an automatic terminal machine (ATM). If the ATMs are not easy to use, customers will leave the bank. In this case, the bank company should consider that its management has failed even if the ATM performs without mechanical difficulty. This example reveals that the internal model is not necessarily adequate for customers, or that the model cannot predict a sequence of customers' requirements. In our model, we call the customers users. Other examples of systems failures can be found in Bignel and Fortune (1984). We should remark that the condition for the existence of an internal model is independent of its users (see Proposition 1).

The failures we refer to here are not physical failures but failures in the management process. These kinds of failures are results from discrepancies between the users and the management system. In fact, most practical systems failures are considered to be due to conflicts between the feelings of the users and a policy adopted by the management system. In this chapter we call these systems failures *management failures*. So far, there are only a few approaches to understanding management failures. Bignell and Fortune (1984) defined systems failures as subjective concepts and proposed a systems approach to them, and Gigch (1986) tried to classify them from the viewpoint of metasystem modelling. Although these approaches are effective, they provide methodologies and do not give a model for analysing the management process in detail. We therefore extend our model in order to define the term management failures formally.

Doubled structure of evaluation

To analyse management failures, we need to consider another evaluation system distinguished from internal evaluation: it is an evaluation system in the user's mind, and we call it an *external evaluation system*.

The internal evaluation system G was a criterion that a management system can use in deciding how to control the object, whereas an external evaluation system is a criterion by which users evaluate both the management system and the object. Users are usually not concerned with the functions of the object but with whether or not the management system operates the object properly. That is to say, whether or not users have a complaint about the operation of the management system, depends on the external evaluation system. This also means that the user's criterion is not optimal, but satisfactory.

We represent users by *U(Ge)*, where *Ge* denotes the external evaluation system, and we assume that a decision principle in the external evaluation is satisfactory rather than optimal.

Now in our extended system model – the triplet ($MS(f_0, A, G)$, *OS*, *U(Ge)*) – we can formally define management failures as management that does not satisfy the external evaluation of users. If we call both evaluation systems a *doubled structure of evaluation*, we can say that management failures are due to discrepancies in the doubled structure.

Usually, every management system determines its internal evaluation in consideration of the external one. However, as in the above example of bank service, management based on the internal evaluation *G* does not always satisfy the user's external evaluation *Ge*. Figure 12.2 shows that management failures occur in the interaction between a management system and the object and that they are distinguished from physical failures occurring in the object. This concept of management failures includes the concept of systems failures proposed by Bignell and Fortune (1984).

External model

To prevent management failures, most practical management systems require that a sequence of the optimal actions always satisfies the external evaluation of the users. This depends on whether or not the

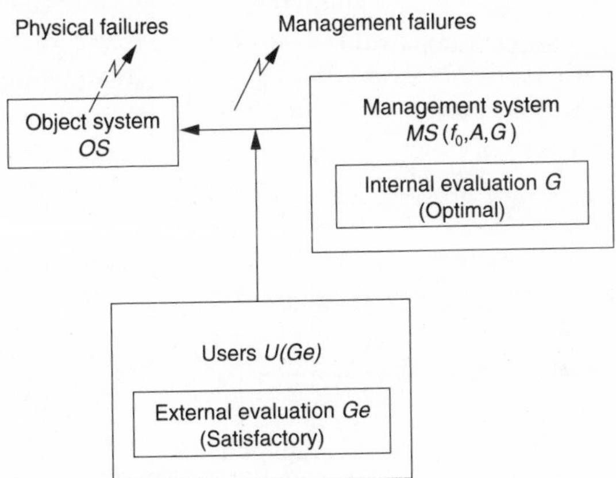

Figure 12.2 Management failures

management system's internal model generates a sequence of actions that satisfies the external evaluation. If the model does that it provides the information for the state dynamics with respect to the external evaluation. We call such a model an *external model*, and we note here that an external model is not uniquely defined under satisfactory decision principle in *Ge*, since there is more than one satisfactory action for any one state.

Tanaka and Kijima (1992) showed the following conditions guaranteeing the existence of the external model.

Proposition 2 (Tanaka and Kijima 1992)

When a management system is consistent with the object and the users, it can have an external model if and only if (f_o,d) is an *admissible solution* for the object and the users.

When the solution (f_o,d) for the object and the users is an *admissible solution*, any action selected by the rule d for the observed state $f_o(w)$ satisfies the external evaluation. And a management system consistent with both the object and the users is one for which a state transition does not change so rapidly with respect to the external evaluation *Ge*.

The condition that the internal model is also an external one is sufficient for a management system to prevent management failures. This condition is often presupposed implicitly in theoretical models or analyses. It is easy to obtain such a model empirically in simple systems, but not in complex systems. In complex systems, implying the condition is more important than choosing the optimal rule d^* under a given internal evaluation G and observation function f_o. Propositions 1 and 2 reveal that a management system needs to decide G and f_o carefully. Proposition 2, for example, says that a pair, consisting of function f_o and rule d, is expected to be not only a solution for the object but also an admissible solution for both users and the object.

In the next section, we consider how a management system obtains an admissible pair (f_o,d) or G adaptively.

AUTONOMOUS SYSTEM BY METAMANAGEMENT

Requirement for autonomous management

As described in the preceeding section, when the internal model is also an external model, a management system can prevent systems failures. This condition does not hold in most systems, however, because obtaining an admissible solution is difficult.

One reason is that a management system cannot directly confirm whether or not an admissible property holds in advance, since a management system usually cannot recognize how users evaluate it until its actions are actually implemented. Only when management failures occur can the management system get the information about admissibility. Moreover, what it obtains from management failures is only negative information: the fact that its current pair is not admissible. It is another reason for the difficulty. Since management failures are caused by discrepancies between the management system and the expectations of its users, the occurrences of management failures reveal that the current solution pair is not admissible for the object and the users. Clearly, even if no management failure occurs for a long time, the current pair might not be admissible.

The final reason for the difficulty of obtaining an admissible solution is that an admissible solution is not uniquely determined, since the satisfactory principle is adopted in the external evaluation.

A management system is thus unable to have enough knowledge about the admissible solutions it requires. The management system, therefore, has to provide a mechanism for improving itself adaptively. The second reason above implies that this improvement must be based only on negative information. In our extended system model – $(MS(f_o, A, G), OS, U(Ge))$ –, the management system must have a mechanism for improving f_o, A, or G by itself because $U(Ge)$ are uncontrollable. The optimal rule d is uniquely determined for f_o, and improving f_o is the easiest because this means changing the observing level; we therefore focus on this improvement.

The improvement process is a repeated and goal-generating process. In fact, the process must be repeated until an admissible pair is obtained. One method of improvement is to change the observed level by refining or coarsening the observation function f_o (Figure 12.3). The finer the refined partition is, the closer to real states the model is. On the other hand, we may miss emergent properties if we divide states excessively. Adequate levels will be obtained only after repeated improvements, and Proposition 2 says that the desired internal model cannot be obtained until these adequate levels are attained.

These repeated processes make the management system appear to look for a goal by trial and error rather than by seeking a goal. Since a management system cannot know an admissible pair as a goal and user's external evaluation, the process is not a goal-seeking but a goal-generating one.

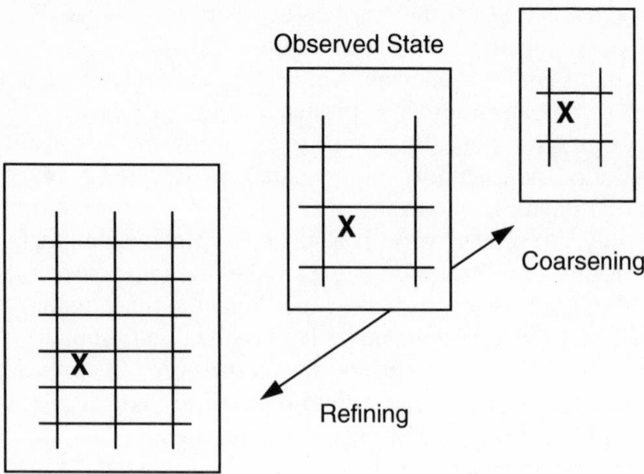

Figure 12.3 Refining and coarsening the observation function

A management system that can improve itself through such a repeated goal-generating process is called an autonomous management system. And an anticipative management system implementing autonomous processes is called an *autonomous anticipative management system.*

Metamanagement system

A simple management system controls an object, whereas the above improvements are activities controlling the management system itself. The improvement processes are thus an upper level of management activities. Upper management activities correspond to decision making about decision making (Gigch 1987), or these are metacontrol activities. In this paper we call those upper management activities a *metamanagement system* (*MetaMS*). The management system and *MetaMS* constitute a total management system. If we express a $MS(f_0, A, G)$ by $MS(\gamma) = MS(f_0(\gamma), A(\gamma), G(\gamma))$, where γ is a parameter, we can say that *MetaMS* controls the *MS* in $\{MS(\gamma) | \gamma \in \Gamma\}$ (where Γ denotes a super set of γ) by selecting γ.

Ashby (1991) suggested that a system *S* can be self-organized only by the extended mechanism '*S+a*.' The *MetaMS* clearly corresponds to this '*a*.' That is to say, a total management system, '*MS* + *MetaMS*,' is a kind of self-organization system.

The potential power of the *MetaMS* enables management failures

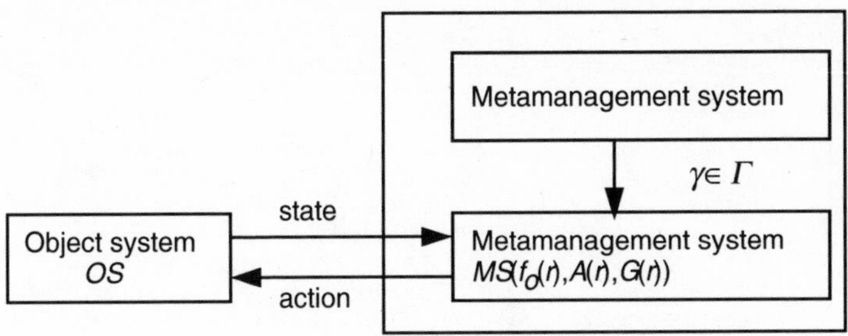

Figure 12.4 Total management system

to be divided into two kinds. Assume that a management failure occurs in $MS(\gamma)$. If the external evaluation cannot be satisfied by any $\gamma \in \Gamma$, the total management system comes down and we call this a *fatal failure*. If, on the other hand, the external evaluation can be satisfied by some $\gamma \in \Gamma$, we call it a *failure for progress*. A failure for progress means that improvement of the *MS* can be based on the management failures, and that '*MS* + *MetaMS*' does not fail but evolves.

Thus, we obtain the seemingly paradoxical result that the attainment of adequate observed levels requires several management failures – failures, however, that are not fatal failures. Moreover, the management system can autonomously evolve by learning from those.

Evolutionary process by autonomous anticipative management

The autonomous anticipative management system process consists of a stationary anticipative process and an autonomous improvement process. The stationary process performs actions based on the admissible solution: whereas, the autonomous process obtains new admissible solutions. These two processes are performed alternately.

Figure 12.5 illustrates a cycle of these alternating processes. Assume that anticipative management is performed. If the anticipative property is lost when the management system fails because of environmental changes, the *MetaMS* has to obtain a new admissible solution. A new pair of (f_0,d) introduced autonomously by *MetaMS*, however, is not always admissible. If the new pair is not admissible, management failures will occur again. By using the information obtained from each management failure, the *MetaMS* can improve the current pair. If after some repeated improvements a new admissible pair is created, the management system becomes anticipative again.

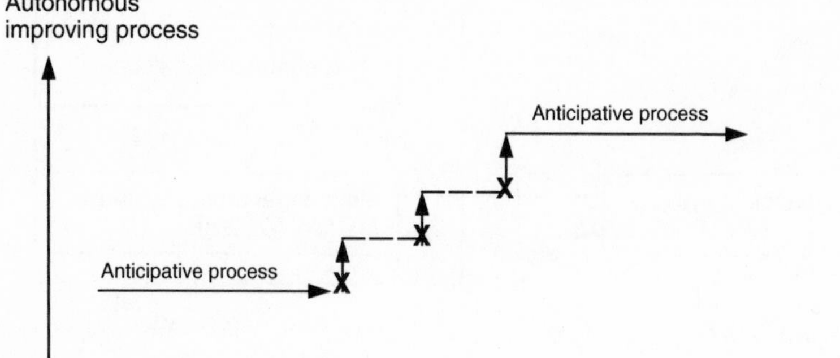

Figure 12.5 Cycle of the two processes in an autonomous anticipative management system

Repetition of the autonomous improvement process generates, and accumulates, new observation functions and new decision rules for new environments.

Such cyclical repetitions of anticipative and autonomous processes are similar to those of self-stabilization and self-organization processes (Laszlo 1971). That is, the stationary anticipative process corresponds to a self-stabilization process, and the autonomous process correspondents to a self-organization process. When this cycle operates smoothly, the system continues to learn new situations adaptively and to evolve by self-improvement; that is, to be a self-organization system.

Autonomous decentralized system

Autonomous decentralized systems (ADS) have received attention recently (ISADS 1993). These systems have characteristics of living things composed of largely autonomous and decentralized units. Each unit is directed towards its own individual goal, while the system as a whole achieves its goal. Such a system has many desirable characteristics, such as adaptability, high reliability, and expandability.

Our models can be applied to ADS by substituting other units for users. Since an interaction with other units is considered as a restriction from them, it can be expressed as an external evaluation in the users. We can also consider management failures to correspond to inconsistency between one unit and the others.

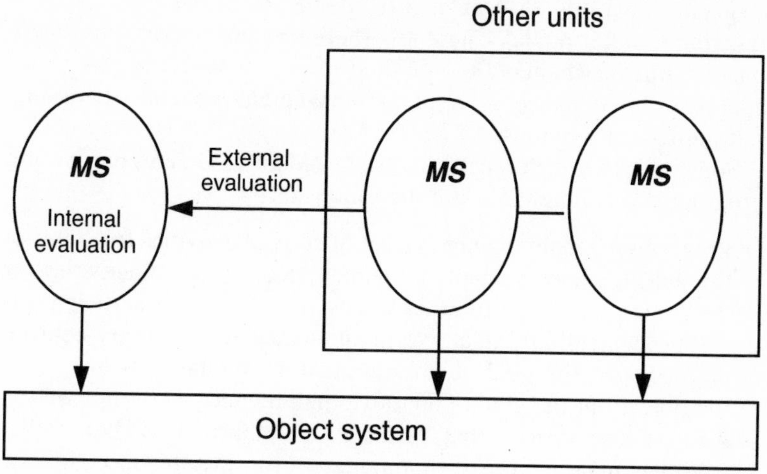

Other units

MS

Internal evaluation

External evaluation

MS

MS

Object system

Figure 12.6 Autonomous decentralized system

Our model can thus be expected to provide a basic model for analysing the structure of ADS.

APPLICATION TO MAINTENANCE MANAGEMENT SYSTEM

The purpose of a maintenance management system is to maintain the reliability and performance of the managed object. The maintenance system is usually designed before the object system starts to operate, and some maintenance methods or rules are programmed in advance. The maintenance system, however, often encounters unpredictable situations and is required to ensure quality by changing its methods or adding new actions.

A maintenance system is also expected to satisfy the user's changeable requirements. Requirements for computer software are especially changeable in progress and unpredictable in advance. Free or discounted upgrading of software versions is therefore considered to be a maintenance activity. Unfortunately, most programmed maintenance management systems cannot do this, so Tanaka (1990c) proposed a new kind of maintenance that can. This new maintenance is called adaptive maintenance to distinguish it from current programmed maintenance.

The activities of adaptive maintenance include adding new actions, changing inspection periods, and changing inspection items. Deciding inspection periods or items corresponds to serving observation function f_o in our model. These are, therefore, not activities for maintenance but for changing the method of maintenance. In this sense, adaptive maintenance is a metamanagement system performing self-improving activities.

Some of the differences between adaptive maintenance and programmed maintenance are the following:

1 Programmed maintenance is a set of control activities for states of the object, whereas adaptive maintenance is a set of activities for the control activities. In other words, programmed maintenance is a state control, and adaptive maintenance is an activity control. Accordingly, the goal of programmed maintenance is to restore the object but the goal of adaptive maintenance is to improve the maintenance system that restores the object. This means that adaptive maintenance is maintenance for maintenance, by the maintenance system itself; that is, autonomous metamaintenance.

   Condition monitoring maintenance is a very effective method and is used in many complex systems. In programmed maintenance, it is based on the monitored states of the object, whereas in adaptive maintenance it monitors the maintenance process.

2 Programmed maintenance is a simple goal seeking system whose goal is a good state or a good condition of the object. Adaptive maintenance, on the other hand, is a sequential goal-generating process dedicated to the creation of admissible pairs, which is an adaptive learning process.

   Programmed maintenance is a stationary anticipative process and adaptive maintenance is an autonomous improving process. Every maintenance system can therefore evolve only by modifying both kinds of maintenance activities.

Large scale systems, especially, will require autonomous metamaintenance management systems in addition to high reliability design and fault tolerance design. Tanaka (1990b) has also proposed a soft type of methodology for performing autonomous metamaintenance, a methodology based on the Soft Systems Methodology proposed by Checkland (1981).

SUMMARY

The internal model that serves as the basis for anticipative management should be improved according to changes of users' requirements. We have shown here that an autonomous anticipative system having a mechanism for self-improvement of the internal model is implemented by metamanagement, and that it evolves by the repeating cycles of a stationary anticipative process followed by an autonomous improvement process. We have also shown that these evolutionary processes utilizing the information obtained from management failures maintain high reliability and quality.

REFERENCES

Ashby, W.R. (1991) 'Principles of the Self-Organizing System', in G.J. Klir (ed.) *Facets of Systems Science*, New York: Plenum Press.

Bignel, V. and Fortune, J. (1984) *Understanding Systems Failures*, Manchester: Manchester University Press.

Checkland, P. (1981) *Systems Thinking, Systems Practice*, Chichester: John Wiley and Sons.

Gigch, J.P. (1986) 'Modeling, Metamodeling, and Taxonomy of System Failures', *IEEE Trans. on Reliability*, 35(2), pp. 131–6.

—— (1987) *Decision Making about Decision Making*, Cambridge, MA: Abacus Press.

ISADS (1993) *Proceedings of the International Symposium of Autonomous Decentralized Systems (ISADS)*, Tokyo: IEEE Press.

Kickert, W.J.M. and Gigch, J.P. (1979) 'A Metasystem Approach to Organizational Decision-making', *Management Science*, 25, pp. 1217–31.

Kijima, K., Takahara, Y. and Nakano B. (1986) 'Algebraic Formulation of Relationship between a Goal Seeking System and its Environment', *International Journal of General Systems*, 12(4), pp. 341–58.

Kijima, K. and Tanaka K. (1992) 'Universal Maps for Binary Preference Structure Generating Decision Principles', *International Journal of Systems Science*, 23(7), pp. 1083–99.

Laszlo, E. (1971) *Introduction to Systems Philosophy*, New York: Gordon and Breach.

Rosen, R. (1978a) *Fundamentals of Measurement and Representation of Natural Systems*, New York: North-Holland.

—— (1978b) 'Feedforwards and Global System Failure', *Journal of Theoretical Biology*, 74, pp. 579–90.

—— (1985) *Anticipatory Systems*, Oxford: Pergamon Press.

Tanaka, K. (1990a) 'A Metasystem Approach To Learning From Systems Failures', *Proceedings of 34th Annual Meetings of ISSS*, Portland, pp. 604–10.

—— (1990b) 'A "Soft" Systems Methodology Utilizing Information Obtained from Systems Failures' (in Japanese), *Trans. on SICE*, 26(8), pp. 908–15.

—— (1990c) 'On a New Concept of Adaptive Maintenance for Systems Failures', *Proceedings of International Symposium on Reliability and Maintainability*, Tokyo, JUSE, pp. 580–5.

Tanaka, K. and Kijima, K. (1992) 'A Metamodeling of Autonomous Anticipative Management for Preventing Systems Failures', *Proceedings of CEMIT92/CECOIA3*, Tokyo, pp. 479–82.

Index